A Life of Giving

Narayan Shrestha

01-08-23

First Edition
Published by the Sreejana Foundation

ISBN: 978-0-9990157-6-6 (Paperback Edition)

Cover Design: Jessica Bell

The Sreejana Foundation partners with Helping Hands Health Education to provide health and education services in Nepal and around the world.

Visit helpinghandsusa.org

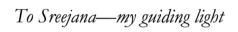

To Sreejana—my guiding light

Contents

Foreword by Jean Watson

Narayan Shrestha is a living legend, a larger-than-life benefactor to humankind through his life of giving. His life history and exceptional accomplishments, from his humble and impoverished beginnings to global achievements, make him a living legend in service to humanity. *A Life of Giving* is a portrait of his life of giving; a testimony to human inspiration, inner motivation, divine spirit, and a sense of a destiny guiding his life dreams.

I have had the privilege of witnessing firsthand his birthplace in Nepal and Narayan's gifts of service to better human health and consciousness.

This book will touch your heart and mind with many personal stories showing how Narayan's life of limitation transformed to one of prosperity and translated into dedication and global generosity. Once Narayan established his life in America and eventually in Boulder, Colorado, he more than excelled in global nonprofit work with humility and a generous spirit. You will discover that his story unfolds in a divine order. All his miraculous successes are lovingly inspired and energized by, and attributed to his radiant and enlightened wife, Sreejana, a mystical wonder.

Narayan's compassionate and heart-stirring human experiences are informed and motivated by his childhood dreams and destiny. His passion, intellect, and moral inspiration to serve humanity have led to multiple global nonprofit services. You will be mesmerized by Narayan's unbelievable adventures and accomplishments.

His dedicated service to humankind has rewarded him with reciprocal karmic-like gifts of prosperity. He, in turn, has used his blessings to spread goodwill in countries needing education and healthcare. This book explores one man's spirit, miracles, motivations, and mysteries—all unfolding and flowing from grace and guidance to be of service to others in need.

Narayan Shrestha's book, *A Life of Giving,* is a gift to anyone who wishes to trust life's destiny. It's an inner guide to a life of giving and therefore receiving. This book is a personal history that informs, inspires, and inspirits others to pursue a life of human service, making the world a better place.

Narayan's life story is a loving message—how the presence and power of one person with a generous human spirit of giving, against all odds, offers hope and trust in a world filled with despair.

Jean Watson, PhD, RN, AHN-BC, FAAN, LL (AAN) – American nurse, theorist, and nursing professor is best known for her theory of human caring. She is the author of *Nursing: The Philosophy and Science of Caring.* Her research on caring has been incorporated into education and patient care at hundreds of nursing schools and healthcare facilities worldwide.

Foreword by Douglas Brown

As the Twin Otter began a rapidly descending turn more than a mile deep in the mountainous river valley, I spotted the airport on top of a long plateau. The pilot rolled out onto a steep final approach, and—as he put in more flaps—we could now see over the nose through the open cockpit door that the airstrip was grass and dirt with a footpath cutting across the middle. Everything seemed lush green, and in the distance, way above scattered clouds, rose the massive, spectacular, snow-covered Himalayan peaks of Chamlang and Makalu, nearly five miles above our flight path.

I was a 23-year-old Peace Corps Volunteer serving in the remote, exotic kingdom of Nepal. After completing my undergraduate degree in physics with a double major in Oriental philosophy, I had spent most of a year with the Peace Corps in Borneo until political instability caused me to transfer to Nepal. I was now excited to be en route to Chainpur Bazaar, the village where I would spend my next two years teaching math and science to high school students in their own language. In those days, there was no motor road or rail into the region, leaving only two practical means from the capital city of Kathmandu. One was an all-day bus ride to the southern town of Dhankuta, then trekking 85 miles for several days over the mountains or up the river valley by foot. The faster way was a 19-seat Pilatus Twin Otter STOL (Short Take Off and Landing) turboprop aircraft to the small airstrip at Tumlingtar. But this was possible only when the weather was good because the airport had no instrument approaches.

Being the dry season, the flight was operating, and two classmates from our three-month-long intensive language training program joined me on the way to their new posts. The scene which greeted us when we disembarked in Tumlingtar was one of intense activity because another plane was due to arrive in a few minutes, so the ground crew needed to offload our flight's inbound passengers and luggage, then load the outbound ones as quickly as possible, all while sorting out last-minute passenger substitutions and handling nonstandard luggage like baskets of live chickens and bundles of produce, performing weight and balance calculations, and chasing people and animals off the dirt runway so the next plane would be able to land. At first, it all seemed terribly confused, but soon it became clear that at the center of everything was a handsome, smiling, energetic airport manager—Narayan Shrestha—who efficiently and diplomatically dealt with all the issues. It was late in the day, and we each had a four-hour trek ahead of us, so we only had a chance to meet Narayan briefly. My initial impression of the very outgoing, intelligent, English-fluent, 20-year-old was to prove true—except in one respect. Despite his apparent maturity, he was only my age, yet very effectively performing a job of great responsibility in a manner well beyond it.

The process of acclimatizing to life in Chainpur held many interesting surprises, but in one regard, things were as expected. We had been told that a big benefit of our location was the excellent mail service. This certainly did NOT mean the Nepal Government postal service, which was agonizingly slow and usually lost our letters and packages, but rather the informal, free mail service which Narayan efficiently ran for the PCVs in the region. To those readers living in the West, efficiency and reliability may seem unremarkable, but it was the Nepal government's service level that represented the cultural norm. It was quite unusual to find someone whose word was their bond and made the effort to promptly overcome obstacles, unless perhaps they were family or friends.

Despite being separated by a half-day trek, Narayan and I became very good friends. We confided in each other our challenges, aspirations, and fears, and he served as a guide in understanding the more subtle aspects of Nepali culture, such as dating. With his help, I enjoyed my life and the work I was doing in Chainpur and signed up to extend my two-year Peace Corps teaching commitment for a third year.

But then, just as the last school term of my second year was ending, a telegram arrived. My dad was gravely ill, and my family urged an immediate return home. As I said my hurried goodbyes, many Nepali acquaintances pled with me to sponsor their immigration to the US. At that time, sponsorship was a prerequisite for immigration, and it meant a written guarantee to the US government that if the immigrant ran out of money or were deported, the sponsor would shoulder their debts and pay for a ticket back to Nepal.

I could understand their desire to immigrate. Most Nepalis "knew" that all Americans had large houses, a car, and an airplane. So, the logic was simple; if you moved to America, you would be rich. Since most spoke little to no English and had few marketable skills, and since I had meager resources to promise as a guarantee, it seemed a risky proposition, so—sadly—I had to tell them no. But Narayan was unique; he had the skills, language, and work ethic required for success. He was not expecting instant wealth; he wanted a level playing field where he could reap what he sowed. So, once I returned home, I began the process.

At the time, I had no idea how consequential an act this would be. Beyond the idea of immigrating to the US, Narayan's dreams were not yet fully formed; how could I possibly foresee that by helping one person, I would indirectly help thousands of people to receive much-needed healthcare, expand their horizons with the benefits of a sound education, or gain a foothold in the land of opportunity? But I knew in my heart that Narayan, who was my friend, had great potential and sound values. For such a consequential decision, it was an amazingly easy one.

And so, Narayan was set to embark on an amazing journey. The first step was flying from Nepal to meet me at the University of Chicago, where I was doing graduate studies—the first step in my own career as an executive in high tech. He had his first immersion in a strange new culture At O'Hare airport and the first of many entertaining stories that would follow.

The challenges, insights, and rewards of realizing his mission and finding the life partner without whom he could not have achieved it were many. But I will leave the telling of those chapters to my very good friend, Narayan.

Douglas Brown — Executive with a broad range of experience in leadership at Applied Materials and FMC in the areas of M&A integration, technology programs, operations, and product management for high-technology capital equipment.

Foreword by Igor Gamow

I first met Narayan in 1987 through Judge Bud Holmes, one of Narayan's dear friends and a Nepali trekker. Bud Holmes had just returned from a trip to Nepal with Narayan's Gateway to Nepal and suggested I meet Narayan to discuss my invention which eventually became known as the Gamow Bag. It is a lightweight, synthetic fabric chamber used to treat mountain climbers with altitude sickness. The patient is placed inside the bag, which is sealed and inflated. Within minutes, the ambient altitude can be decreased by about 3,300 to 9,800 feet, depending on the elevation.

The next day, I went to Narayan's store, Old Tibet in Boulder, Colorado, to discuss my invention. With a twinkle in his eye, Narayan said, "Getting you to the basecamp of Everest is a piece of cake for me. I'll help you if you help me!" Narayan went on to explain that he was launching a semester in Nepal program, and the professors he had asked had turned him down. Being an avid outdoorsman who loved the mountains, I said, "Yes!" when he asked me. Little did I know that this opportunity would change the trajectory of my life and introduce me to one of my greatest passions—the incredible country of Nepal.

At the time, I was on the faculty of the University of Colorado (CU) departments of Aerospace Engineering and Chemical and Biological Engineering. I taught chemical engineering at the university by day and rode my Arabian stallion, Pegasus, by night. I was well-known at the university for my work and because of my father, George Gamow, the celebrated cosmologist and physicist, who was a prime developer of the Big Bang Theory of the origin of the universe. Father hated the term "Big Bang" because the initial universe was not big and certainly did not go "bang." The Gamow Tower on campus is the namesake of my father.

On my first of over twenty trips to Nepal, I led seven CU students on the greatest adventure of their lives. The sheltered students were wide-eyed the minute they got off the plane in Kathmandu. They had traded sterile, windowless classrooms on campus for a world where everything was new, unpredictable, and exciting. Sometimes we saw an elephant roaming the streets of Kathmandu. Over the years, the study abroad program became a huge success with more demand than we could accommodate. On a scale of 1-10, the program was an 11! I led many trips, including jaunts to Namibia and Australia, but none worked as well as Nepal.

The two- to four-week treks in the Himalayas were remote, but that turned out to be a good thing. We had nothing to do but talk, think, learn, and walk. In the evening, we'd sit by the fire and converse well into the night. Students sometimes woke me up in the middle of the night in my sleeping bag to ask for my help with a perplexing question. We had such freedom with one another. The small group learning experience was wonderful. It was much easier to inspire students when the classroom was as fascinating as Nepal, where you could never predict what would happen next. It kept us on our toes. It kept us awake and alive and receptive to learning.

On our fifth trip in Nepal, traversing rugged landscape, we came upon rivulets of water six feet wide streaming down the mountainside and blocking our passage. *How the heck are we going to cross?* The next thing I knew, Narayan squatted down Indian-style next to a boulder and leaped like a frog straight up in the air and over the streaming water! Not being leap-froggers, the students and I got soaked.

Another time on a trek, our group approached a wide, roaring river in a deserted area. Narayan had reassured me beforehand, "Don't worry. I'll arrange for a boat." But when we got to the river, no Narayan, no boat. Nothing. I panicked. *Now what?* Then I heard some commotion. I knelt on the ground and peered over the edge of the cliff. Sure enough. Two boats were waiting for us. *Son of a gun! He did it again!* That's Narayan for you. I never worried too much that things wouldn't work out. I just never knew how. One way or another, Narayan always figured things out.

Every day for him is an exciting day. He's an eternal optimist. His enthusiasm is contagious. He loves what he does and is unstoppable. When I met people in Nepal, Nepalis and tourists alike, all I had to do was say "Narayan." His name is known everywhere in Nepal—from the remote mountain villages to Kathmandu and beyond.

A quality I admire most in Narayan is his willingness to do the craziest things. He tapped me, a classroom professor, to teach in Nepal while trekking, something I had never done before. Things could have gone terribly wrong. But, instead, we offered a refreshingly unstructured program that allowed for unexpected and memorable learning experiences. When I met my students years later, they always talked about Nepal; it was a highlight of their Boulder experience.

Narayan took the risk of hiring me as his study abroad professor. And while everyone else dismissed the Gamow Bag, Narayan was game for giving it a try—for making the Himalayas a testing ground. At 15,000 feet, trekkers and climbers huffed and puffed as they traversed lofty peaks. But then they slipped into the bag and slept like babies. Our motto was climb high, sleep low! The bag worked beautifully, and over the years, has saved the lives of countless mountain climbers suffering from high altitude pulmonary and cerebral edema.

Narayan can see things before they happen—the sign of a true visionary. Sometimes it takes someone who dares to dream the craziest things. That is my friend, Narayan Shrestha. Crazy enough to change the world.

Igor Gamow – Inventor and former microbiology professor at the University of Colorado. His best-known inventions include the Gamow bag and the Shallow Underwater Breathing Apparatus (SUBA

Foreword by Alan Imai Sensei

I first met Mr. Narayan Shrestha in 2010, when my colleagues and I were invited to his home in Superior, Colorado. Narayan and his wife, Sreejana, provided a warm welcome and her tasty Nepalese food awaited us.

In the summer of that year, Mr. and Mrs. Shrestha had visited our Shumei International Institute in Crestone, Colorado. On a tour of our grounds, they plucked a robust daikon radish from the ground. It seems our daikon radish inspired and motivated him to bring Shumei's Natural Agriculture method to the school he founded in Khandbari, Nepal. I learned of his passion and commitment to bring Shumei's Natural Agriculture to the school curriculum. Since Nepali people know the climate, soil, and foods of Nepal, I suggested that Narayan bring two of his teachers to Crestone for training.

In January of the following year, I traveled to Nepal for the first time to interview teachers and help choose two people to come to Crestone. At Surya Boarding School, elementary school children studied English. I was so touched by the scene of kids learning numbers with their cute, loud voices in such a humble classroom in a remote mountain region of Nepal.

Narayan spoke to students who were about to graduate. He said, "You were very privileged students with an opportunity to study in this school. After graduating, most of you will go on to higher education, and some of you will study abroad. I want you to use what you have learned for the development of our country, not just for your own success."

Narayan's passion for education moved me very deeply. We also visited a hospital, a nursing school, and a college in Kathmandu, also founded by Narayan in Kathmandu.

Two teachers were selected and stayed in Crestone for a year. They learned the Shumei Natural Agriculture method and the Shumei philosophy and its spiritual practices. Narayan was surprised and impressed by significant positive changes in the teachers' character, personalities, and their spiritual growth. Because of what he witnessed in the teachers Narayan became personally interested in Shumei's philosophy. He became a member and decided to include Shumei's philosophy as a core principle of Surya Boarding School's education.

He has visited Shumei's International Headquarters in Japan many times, as well as Shumei's local centers in Japan, US, Taiwan, and UK, sharing his thoughts and commitment on what Shumei philosophy can do for the world. I have frequently visited his home and his shop in Boulder, Colorado, and our friendship has grown and deepened. I have also taken groups of young people to his home, where they learn about and are inspired by Narayan's life.

Narayan began by setting up medical camps in remote areas of Nepal where there were no clinics. He went on to establish a hospital, clinics, a nursing school, and a college. By connecting people in the United States and Nepal, one man—Mr. Narayan Shrestha—has achieved great things. When an opportunity arises, he has the courage to seize it, and he spares no effort to help people improve their lives. He shows deep gratitude for what he has received and, as such, has devoted his life to development in his home country of Nepal. I have learned so much from him. He has given me courage and encouragement in Shumei's and my own work in Africa. I am very grateful to Narayan.

Alan Imai – Alan Imai Sensei currently serves as Executive Director of the Shumei International Institute in Crestone, Colorado. He also serves as director of Shumei International's Natural Agriculture global programs.

Foreword by Jeff Pinkerton

This afterword has no poetry, no music, and no literary offerings. And seeing as I have no in-service sea stories to tell, none of those either. Instead, this is a story of inspiration, dedication, immigration, and giving back.

Narayan Shrestha came to the US from Nepal when he was in his early 20s. He had $300 in his pocket, landed in Dallas, and went to the University of Texas—but first, he had to gain command of the English language. (The story is told, perhaps apocryphal, that he understood "elevator" and "alligator" to be the same—and was afraid he'd have to ride one.) He lived in an instructor's attic, traded manual labor for rent, slept on a rug that he brought with him from Nepal, and washed dishes in the college cafeteria to earn tuition money.

A few years later, he stumbled into Boulder and decided he wanted to buy a Nepalese gift shop for $25,000—money he didn't have. He borrowed money from another countryman, opened the store, and eight years later, paid off the loan. Following that, he also opened a restaurant, then another, then another. Sooner or later, he had 11 restaurants, five gift shops, five gas stations, and a mountain bike shop. As a sideline, he started a travel company that specialized in treks to Nepal.

But this isn't only a story about an immigrant made good. It's also a story about what one man can do and about giving back. On one of those treks in Nepal, there happened to be a doctor and a nurse, and they encountered a Nepali who needed medical care. That gave Narayan the idea to repeat that encounter. So, he started Helping Hands Health Education—an organization that brings medical professionals to Nepal (and subsequently Nicaragua and Namibia) to provide care to the locals.

This became Narayan's passion and mission.

Since its founding, Helping Hands has sent 6,000 doctors, nurses, physician assistants, medical students, and non-medical volunteers from the

Western world to provide health care and health education to Nepal. More than 2,000,000 Nepalis have been seen since he started this endeavor (neither number is a typo).

He also started a school in his village, Khandbari. Initially, it had two teachers and 35 students in a rented house. Now the school is in 13 buildings on 150 acres, with 40 teachers and 850 students! By way of reference, for $650, a student can go to school for a year.

Oh—and he also provides housing. For $1,750, he can build a three-bedroom home for a family.

To date, he has raised/spent $36,000,000; all to help others. Along the way, he has attracted a notable following. Igor Gamow (of Gamow Bag fame), several members of Congress, prominent businessmen, and Colorado Governor Jared Polis are regulars at his home.

In a normal year, he is out of the country 2/3 of the time, either in Nepal initiating/managing projects or on fundraising trips here and there.

In 1996, Kathleen and I wanted to do a trek in Nepal. As it happens, our dates coincided with a medical mission, and we became hooked. Neither of us is qualified to provide medical care, but we were awestruck by the dedication of the volunteers—and with Narayan himself and his mission. He and I stayed in touch over the years.

In 2015, Narayan arranged one of those medical missions to Bhutan—my favorite place (This was the second of six trips I've made there). I recruited my cousin, Jennifer, who is a nurse and biking buddy—Tom, a pediatrician—to come along. There were eight medical professionals (plus me as a gofer) providing care for whoever walked in the door.

Given the paucity of medical availability in the countryside, parents would bring their kids from miles and miles away—most of them hitchhiked. Some would sleep nearby (who knows where). Each day for a week, the crew would do medical exams on 70+ kids, plus OB-GYN checkups on the women. Thus, 350+ kids were helped by Narayan's organization that week.

Note, the medical professionals who helped flew halfway around the world (literally—Bhutan is 12 hours offset from Denver) at their own expense, paid to be there, and (some) took time off work to be there. This is not unique—the 6,000 doctors, nurses, physician assistants, medical students, and non-medical volunteers he has recruited have done so under the same spirit of volunteerism. Narayan has great powers of persuasion.

I have lunch with him every other month or so (when he is in-country), where he is almost always successful in picking my pocket. We joke that he is better off with me dead than alive (his organization is a key beneficiary of my will).

This story is one of inspiration, of what one person can do, of the importance of helping those less fortunate (and one more argument for a rational immigration policy). His impact on those less fortunate is a powerful lesson for us all who are able to give back.

I'll end with a quote from him:

"All the wealth we make, when we die, we're not going to take it with us. This is the way we enjoy life. This is the way to make the world a better place. When we go to bed, we smile."

I'm pleased and proud to call him a friend.

Jeff Pinkerton – Retired real estate investor who previously spent decades managing sales organizations in the software field. He enjoys skiing, hiking, playing pickleball and is also an inveterate biker (having pedaled in two dozen countries). But mostly, he prefers traveling—having visited 75 countries. He has volunteered to assist Narayan's Helping Hands group in both Nepal and Bhutan.

Preface

Looking back on my life, I've often wondered if I should highlight my work in a book. When people advised me to write an autobiography in the 1990s, I thought that I hadn't accomplished enough to warrant a book about my life's work.

After the 2015 earthquake in Nepal and the 2016 US presidential election, I began to rethink my decision, but I didn't start writing a book. Not yet. In 2015 and 2016, I witnessed how the earthquake devastated Nepal and her people. I felt the effect of the casualties and damage. It killed over 9,000 people, wiped out many villages, and leveled countless houses. Hundreds of my friends in Japan and the United States shared my feelings after the earthquake. They poured their love into Nepal through donations, supporting my wish to rebuild schools and build shelters for those who lost their homes.

The 2016 election left me feeling as though the people of the US were treated unjustly. Initially, some people believed that the election was going in the right direction, but it went in a different direction at the last minute. I stopped watching the news that night because the result was not the one I had hoped for. I couldn't sleep as I feared the election's impact on the United States and its democracy.

Sure enough, the ensuing four years negatively impacted the country, and we are now feeling the detrimental effects of that presidency. We are wounded, but I believe and trust that the American people have the willpower, commitment, understanding, and community to heal. We will soon be living together in peace and harmony. The United States is built for that. It is built to lead as it did for decades. The country is shaken but will come back again as a world leader, strong as before. Maybe even stronger.

I aim to inspire future generations, showing them the power individuals have to make a difference in the lives of others. For many years, I focused on helping people in Nepal, Nicaragua, and Bhutan via health and education infrastructure. In 2017, I organized many trips, including one with Montessori teachers and students to Surya Boarding School in Khandbari, Nepal.

That group of 23, led by me and two Montessori teachers—Metta King and Devon Warn—was comprised of exceptional individuals. Notably, a family of five participated in the trip—Carl and Caroly Nadelhoffer and their three daughters Rose, Lila, and Teka. The Nadelhoffers and the other members made valuable contributions to the group and the schoolchildren. The Alexanders, Dr. Scott, Ph.D. , and Laura also played a significant role.

Caroly approached me during the trip and said, "Wouldn't it be nice to write an autobiography about yourself, Narayan? I had no idea that you had done so much until I traveled with you to your birthplace. Now I see that your life is remarkable and worthy of a book. My daughter, Rose, can help by typing up your memories as you dictate, and we can find someone to edit it."

Once Caroly urged me to write my autobiography, I was convinced that I should. After our work in Nepal, the group returned to Colorado. In the summer of 2018, I felt compelled to start the book, so I called Rose, and we began writing. As a high school junior, Rose was applying to colleges and eventually left in 2019 for college, leaving the project unfinished.

Jeff Pinkerton, a humanitarian, donor, builder, and dear friend, approached me and urged me as Caroly had to write a book.

I responded by saying, "I don't know how!"

Jeff said he'd find a ghostwriter for me, and with his lead, I found Ann Tinkham to ghostwrite my autobiography for me. We signed a contract and started working on my book.

Helping Hands Health Education, Old Tibet, and the Semester in Nepal program are the pillars of my success. My other accomplishments include the many restaurants I opened and my other business ventures.

During my life, I always wondered in which direction my work would go. I often sought a philosophical path, mainly through religion, but I was not satisfied, perhaps because of my focus on helping others. Or perhaps because I believed helping others was my religion. Regardless, I still felt an emptiness no matter how much I did to help others. That emptiness was only filled when I discovered the Shumei philosophy. I realized that it was the guiding philosophy I had been looking for in my life. The Shumei philosophy made sense in my life for what I had done, what I am doing, and what I will do tomorrow. Shumei fulfills my desire for spirituality, Natural Agriculture, respecting others, and appreciating the glory and beauty of art. It teaches us to align our lives, to balance dignity and integrity, and to walk into the future. I thank the teachers of Shumei philosophy from the bottom of my heart, who traveled with me throughout Nepal, Japan, and the US. I deeply bow toward the members and staff of the Shumei institution and greatly respect their honest, kind, and helpful ways of doing things. They have taught me so much. Most of all, they taught me that to receive respect, you must respect others first. If you are interested in learning more about Shumei, I urge you to explore this philosophy for yourself. Visit the Shumei website (shumei.org) to learn more.

When I think about my life, I always think of my parents, born and raised in a town with hardly any modern technology. I was born and raised in the same village, and although I experienced a better life than theirs, I still grew up in a rough, poorly developed town. There were only ten of us in my school, and we had to read and write without books, paper, or pencils. I learned to read and write with a wooden board as paper, a stick as a pen, and dirt as ink.

Coming from that experience to the United States in the '70s and living in a discriminatory environment in Dallas encouraged rather than discouraged me because I like to think positively. That attitude brought me to Colorado, which I claimed as my home. To be honest, Coloradans and Americans are the most extraordinary people, and I can never thank them enough for what they have done for my success. America and her people are the best in the world. The American people and government care deeply about developing nations.

Without their support, the people in developing countries would struggle even more than they do.

By writing this book, I wish to convey my appreciation for the United States. I want people to know how much this country has to offer. The US makes the impossible possible. Here, there are many ways to live happily, but you must take the initiative and do it yourself, imbued with hope and courage. People call America the land of opportunity and the promised land. I say, indeed, it is a promised land. It made possible my life of giving. Without the love, support, and trust of the people in my life, I could not have succeeded.

I don't know what I would have done if I had stayed in Nepal, nor do I know what my family would have done. Ninety-one of my family members are here, and thousands of villagers live in the United States because of my efforts. This is what I call success. This is what I call opportunity. There is room for everyone who comes to the United States seeking a better life. America is not only the promised land; many people coming here from other countries call it heaven.

But we have lots of work to do in the United States. For the people that come here to live, please appreciate what you have. And, similarly, for those born here, please appreciate what you have. You cannot imagine how many millions of people live in situations far worse than here in America, yet those people are happier than many of us. We, the citizens of the United States, must accept what we have and be grateful for the opportunities available to us in this country.

Many times, Americans have endured sadness, frustration, disappointment, and suffocation. But through all that, we continue to believe in law and order, the justice system, and truth. This helps us tolerate, understand, and wait with patience for the moment to confront injustice and restore democracy, valuing truth over a cascade of lies. This is how America started its democracy 225 years ago. It has long been the world's leader of democracy and remains a beacon of hope. America seeks truth, and the truth will always win. In the long run, evil never prevails.

In closing, the greatest thing in my life—that I cherish every moment—is the blessing I received from my parents. No matter what I did, whether with them in Nepal or away from them in the US, they blessed, praised, admired, and trusted in my work. They said I was their hope for raising the family they gave birth to. Their blessings turned into a reality.

Similarly, I want to share my pride for my children. My son, Anu, and daughter, Regina, are adorable, kind, compassionate, and motivated. They wish the best for everyone and want to live in peace and harmony. And finally, I cannot close this preface without sharing my honest and deepest love and gratitude to Sreejana Shrestha.

CHAPTER 1

Diamond Horse

I dreamt of a place far, far away, where fathers could provide for their families, where mothers weren't ashamed, where their children didn't have hungry bellies, and where sisters-in-law weren't treated like lowly beasts.

A T 24, I WAS A LUCKY YOUNG MAN, having landed an enviable job of my dreams—the Station Manager of the Royal Nepal Airlines at the airport in Tumlingtar, Nepal. I handled the arriving flights, took care of passengers, sold tickets, and collected and deposited the money. I had a very handsome salary of 1,300 rupees per month, equivalent to $130 in 1972. In my district of almost 200,000 people, I earned the second-highest salary with just a 10th-grade education. It afforded me a lavish lifestyle by Nepali standards—a horse, five assistants, and flights to anywhere in the region. My friends and family envied my life.

A Circle of Darkness

By day, despite my good fortune, I was filled with unhappiness and dread. To the world, I looked like the happiest man alive, but inside, I was overwhelmed with sorrow. By night, my sleep was fitful and tortured, my dreams tinged with disaster for my family. While I wanted to ride the wings of my good fortune, my parents, Surya Bahadur and Chhanda Kumari Shrestha, and eight siblings in my village of Khandbari in Northeastern Nepal were drowning in debt and despair. And there was nothing I could do to save them. As my family grew from 19 to 26, all living in one house, feuds frequently erupted as the resources became scarcer. My father's inheritance and earnings were slipping through his fingers like sand pouring through an hourglass. My great-great-grandfather had been a tax collector, and, over time, he became the richest man in Eastern Nepal. He distributed the land to his children, and they to theirs until the fourth generation, my dad's.

My father sold much of the land he had inherited to feed the growing number of hungry mouths. My brothers and father borrowed money from whomever they could—the bank, friends, and neighbors. Our family's once noble standing was slipping into disgrace.

As I lay awake in bed at the airport, I thought, *What am I going to do? I am the only one with a job. I don't like this town. I don't like this place. I don't like this society. I don't like my family. I don't like anyone, not even myself. I need to escape.*

A circle of darkness was closing in on me, the remaining light a mere flicker, a candle about to go out. I stared into the darkness, but my eyes were unable to show me the way. I imagined only one path forward. I ventured outside towards the grassy runway of the airport and crossed the barbed-wire fence. My diamond horse, Hire, a white stallion, grazed on the grass as I headed for the suspension bridge. I planned to fling myself off the bridge into the rushing river below, where my limp body would be pulled by the currents, away from this godforsaken land. And all my troubles would be over. I wouldn't have to watch my family slip into poverty. I wouldn't have to see worry lines appear on my mother's long-suffering face. I wouldn't have to witness my father's pride vanishing, and I wouldn't have to see my siblings disappoint my parents. In an instant, I would be swept away from our family's humiliation. Forever.

As I sauntered, the moonlight sparkled on the landscape, but I didn't notice because darkness had overtaken me. When I tried to cross the runway, Hire charged as if he were going to attack. It startled me. Standing in front of me, he stomped his forelegs and reared up on his hind legs. "Eeuuu, euuu!" he cried out. I tried to get around him, but he blocked my passage. I commanded him to move, yelling, "Get out of my way, Hire. Let me get by!" We struggled, locked in an impasse for ten minutes. But he was much bigger than me, and he simply would not allow me near the river. I skulked away, thinking, *Today is not my day.*

The next morning, I awoke to Hire's cries. "Euuuu! Euuuu!" *I hadn't asked my assistant to bring him to me this early.* I opened the back door to feed him. *Maybe he was hungry.* I recoiled when I saw him. *Oh, my goodness!* His chest was torn open and bloody flesh hung down in a grotesque flap. I thought he had been attacked by a tiger and perhaps had run into the barbed-wire fence trying to escape. I cried out in a panic, "My horse is going to die!"

I was so depressed, thinking Hire was doomed. There was no known cure for my beloved horse. We didn't have veterinarians in our region back then. My assistants took turns shooing the flies away. But the flies were relentless and laid eggs.

After a week, despite our efforts, Hire's wound was crawling with maggots, and I didn't know how to save him. My helper said, "Let's try giving him tree bark."

"What's that going to do?" I asked, thinking it was too little, too late.

"It's worth a try—no?" My helper stripped bark from a nearby tree and chopped it up into my horse's food. I was skeptical of the folksy remedy; it seemed like a feeble attempt in the face of a mortal wound. But with each passing day, more maggots dropped off, the pus and ooze lessened, and his skin turned a healthy pink. After a month, his gory wound healed—a miracle for my grand white stallion.

We saved Hire, my diamond horse, who had saved my life.

I had no way of knowing the life of my dreams awaited me. I had no way of knowing my universe would soon open worlds away from here. I only knew the world I had come from was crumbling. Nepali society was getting worse. I had seen it with my own eyes—humans treated in ways no human should be treated.

My sisters-in-law did most of the housework, helping my mother cook, clean, and take care of everyone. Awakened at 3:00 am when the roosters crowed, their chores started with sweeping the floor with cow dung—to rid the floor of bacteria. They slaved away for hours, and according to Nepali custom, were always the last ones to eat—with no exceptions. They were sometimes beaten with a stick because they didn't work quickly enough or because they snuck a little food to ease their hunger pangs while working. *How could they be productive with empty tummies?*

I witnessed this injustice and felt such deep sympathy for their wretched lives. I wondered, *Why are some people given a lower status than others? Aren't we all equal as human beings? Why are my brothers' wives treated as servants? Shouldn't marriage be joyful and an equal partnership?*

I promised my sisters-in-law I would one day make money to hire someone to lighten their burden so they could live less back-breaking lives with their heads held high. They shook their heads in disbelief, not seeing a way out of their grim existence. I didn't know how I would keep my promise, but I was determined.

When I went to the fountain in the morning to wash my face and brush my teeth, I overheard the village women as they gathered to collect water for their families. They set their containers down next to the fountain and took a little time away for themselves while they gossiped, criticized, and cursed. They swapped stories of worry and hardship. The fountain was their place to expel their anger and frustration, whatever it may have been. One woman didn't have enough rice to feed the entire family, another had lost her baby in childbirth, a third had a useless child with a deformity, and a fourth had a deadbeat, alcoholic husband. Once cleansed of their burdens, they filled their water jars and lugged the heavy loads on their backs with a strap pressing against their foreheads, navigating the sometimes-treacherous trails back to their homes.

Next, I went to the tea shop where the men gathered to talk politics and nonsense. They gossiped, cursed, and criticized other people. The women and men shared one thing in common—they had no dreams. How could they?

Opportunities were scarce. Most were struggling just to fill their children's tummies.

But I had dreams. I dreamt of a place far, far away, where fathers could provide for their families, where mothers weren't ashamed, where their children didn't have hungry bellies, and where sisters-in-law weren't treated like lowly beasts. I dreamt of a place with streets of gold and gigantic, sparkling buildings filled with people and their dreams coming true.

We were lucky enough to have a radio in our home, and I clung to the airwaves. I traveled to distant places in my imagination. Radio announcers spoke of President John F. Kennedy of the United States of America, Prime Minister Jawaharlal Nehru of India, and King Mahendra of Nepal. Of the three, Kennedy impressed me most. I paged through magazines, stopping to admire photos of President Kennedy. I could tell what a likable, successful fellow he was. I thought, *One day, if I become a really smart man and I get lucky, I'll go to America to meet him.*

As early as age seven, my siblings and I became animal herders. While our parents plowed the fields and took care of the land, they tasked us with taking care of the buffaloes, cows, and goats. We cleaned the animals' barns, milked them, and tended to them before taking them to graze.

When my buffalo, Chapala, died, my oldest uncle, Chandra Bahadur Shrestha, said, "Don't cry. I'll replace your buffalo." He was well-respected, and people in my town often asked him to mediate a fight or quarrel. He took care of me when I was in trouble, such as when I had fights with friends.

While the animals grazed, we would play games in the field such as marbles with Rudrakhya, round fruit that looks like blueberries. My friends and I played another game with grapefruit. We took it out of the skin, and when we pinched it, the juice sprayed. Whatever direction the juice sprayed was the direction you were destined to go. Even though sometimes my grapefruit pieces sprayed east, I always picked Ammrika, our pronunciation for America.

On November 22, 1963, we were in school when the headmaster interrupted our class. We were completing an assignment by writing on Nepali rice paper with our bamboo pens with ink made from soot that had collected on the ceilings inside our homes.

He said with a booming voice, "President Kennedy of the United States of America has been assassinated in Dallas by an unknown shooter. School is officially closed for the day. You can all go home."

The news grabbed me and shook me to the core. My first thought was, *My idol is dead!* And for a moment, I feared that my dream of going to Ammrika had died with him. I watched as the other kids ran out to the playground and to swim in the river, elated that school had let out. But not me. I went straight home, up to the room I shared with my siblings. I was inconsolable and cried myself to sleep. My siblings didn't understand. They thought, *Who cares about a man who's worlds away in Ammrika?* But it wasn't far away to me; it was in my heart from the very beginning. I promised myself, *If or when I go to America, I will vote for Kennedy's family.* I was only 11 years old.

A Prophesy of Promise

At that age, my parents saw something in me that I didn't—something they didn't see in my siblings.

At night when my father was in a good mood after a long day in the fields, we gathered around and listened to his stories, his pearls of wisdom. He said, "Among the nine of you, I have hopes that one will become rich and famous, and the rest will be fine. All I need is one." He looked at everyone's eager face, not singling me out. I knew everyone had high hopes for me because I led the pack, showing the earliest promise.

Despite showing early promise, my college years were a bust academically. I was more interested in my social life, getting to know as many people as possible. In that area, I excelled. After I flunked out of college twice, I came home feeling like an aimless drifter.

One morning, my brothers Bashu Dev, Ram Bahadur, and Dharma Raj, and I were sitting in our front yard talking to my father. None of us had jobs or even any prospects. There was finger-pointing and arguing, each of us thinking the other should step up and help my father.

My younger brother said to my dad, "Why does all our family's money go to Narayan's education? He flunked out twice. It is such a waste! Why should we put up with this?"

Before I lost my temper, I took off in frustration. I needed to cool down, or I might say or do something I regretted. Plus, I wanted some distance from my family to think more clearly about my next steps. I was so caught up in my thoughts that I didn't notice my father following me.

He called out, "Narayan, stop. Come sit down next to me and let's talk."

We sat down in a terraced rice paddy. I feared he might chastise me, might shame me for having let him down, for having let the family down. I braced for my much-deserved rebuke.

With his eyes squinting against the blinding sun, he said, "Narayan, I still have hope in you. You are my son with guts. You can achieve things. I don't see nearly as much promise in my other children. I have heard from so many people that you are amazing. The young women tell me at the fountain, the men in the tea shop, and the old women in the village. I don't care that you flunked out of college. You have lived up to our family's name by being someone, by being known across the land. I have faith in you. If you feel you can't do it alone, remember I believe in you. But don't think about us, think about you. Be somebody." And with his words, I knew he would let me follow my destiny.

I'll never forget a conversation with my mom at the fountain. I was sitting cross-legged, and she looked at the birthmark on the sole of my foot and said, "You are so lucky!"

"Why, Mom?" I never thought the mark on my foot was anything special. I saw it as a blemish.

"You will not have to walk as far as most people, plodding the treacherous rocky trails between the downtrodden villages. You will walk carried by your dreams only. You will always want to give and make others happy before you."

I had no way of knowing that her blessing was like a prophecy.

CHAPTER 2

The Man on the Moon

America is a vast, dark ocean, but I will find the light, dive in, and discover a big, shiny pearl.

ONE DAY IN THE SPRING OF 1977, travelers were milling around, buying tickets, and waiting to catch a flight to Kathmandu from the Tumlingtar Airport. The airport had just one runway, perched on the largest mesa in Nepal, on which a few flights departed to and arrived from Kathmandu and Biratnagar. We had just received a batch of mail that I was sorting through, and I noticed a thick letter addressed to me. I guessed it was a stack of administrative documents from my boss on a new process or procedure.

The Invitation

I tore open the letter, and to my delight, it was an invitation from my Peace Corps friend Douglas Brown to visit the United States. For a couple of years, I had delivered mail to him and three other Peace Corps volunteers in my region of Nepal. I jumped on top of my desk and started dancing. I didn't care if the travelers thought I was crazy. *I'm going to the United States!* Of course, I hadn't yet secured my visa or plane ticket. But I truly believed I was going to America!

I immediately arranged for someone to fill in for me and headed to Kathmandu to secure my visa and airline ticket to the United States. I requested a ticket to New York but was denied. I decided to go to the US Embassy and apply for a visa anyway. In those days, nobody visited the US

Embassy because it intimidated most Nepalis. Plus, the journey to the US was too far and much too expensive for people accustomed to subsistence living.

When I strolled into the embassy, my steps echoed down the tiled hallway. There was just one customer service window, and I was the sole customer. If you were denied in those days of strict bureaucracy, you would never have the opportunity again. I might have been intimidated by the process had I not believed the embassy would approve my request. With an invitation from a Peace Corps friend, I thought it was a sure deal.

With an air of confidence, I pushed Douglas Brown's invitation letter toward the balding man behind the window and explained that I was requesting a visa to the United States. I waited at the window for the stamp of approval.

A few minutes later, he pushed the document back toward me and said, "Denied."

What?! Why?! What did I need—a letter from the President of the United States?

I shuffled around Kathmandu with a heavy heart. I told myself, *Think, Narayan. Think of another way. What about going to the Peace Corps office?* For years, I had helped the Peace Corps volunteers in Nepal with all kinds of requests.

I walked an hour to the Peace Corps office to speak with the director. *What do I have to lose?* I told the director, whose name was Virgil Mideema, that my visa had been denied. He picked up his phone, dialed, and spoke so quickly, I didn't catch what he said.

"Hop in the car," he said.

I didn't understand the meaning of "hop in the car." But I followed him.

"Where are we going?" I asked when we got to his car.

"To the embassy."

"But they just denied my request an hour ago." I didn't have high hopes.

When we arrived, I felt the shame of denial and truly believed it was a fruitless exercise. But a little part of me held onto hope that my time helping the Peace Corps volunteers counted for something.

Virgil escorted me behind the window into the consul's office. He was the very same guy who had coldly rebuked my request and killed my dream of going to America.

The consul said, "Please have a seat. Would you like coffee or Coke?"

Coke?! Coke was a very fancy American drink that I had never had the chance to try. "Coke, of course!" I said.

Virgil opted for coffee.

The consul served us our drinks, and as I sipped the sweet, carbonated beverage, he said, "Give me your passport." He stamped my passport, granting a visa. "Welcome to the United States!"

I grasped the passport and held it up to the light in disbelief. I held the key to the magical kingdom!

I realized then that luck couldn't help you if you don't know how to use it. Everybody has luck, but you need to be able to see and pursue it. If I had not used my brain and worked around the obstacles, how would I have been lucky?

Once I secured my plane ticket, visa, and $200, the time had come to break the news to my father. One evening after dinner, I took him aside. "Daddy, I have bad news for you. I mean, it's good news to me, but I don't know how you'll take it."

Confusion fell over his face like a cloud obscuring the sun. "What are you talking about?"

"I'm going to America!" I said, having to restrain myself from jumping up and down.

He peered at me like I was delusional. "What? Don't tease me."

"I'm serious." I couldn't contain my smile.

"How? With what? How could you go? What is your proof?" He fired questions at me, not waiting for answers, as if his incredulity would make it untrue.

I showed him my ticket and visa. Even though his face registered sadness, he quickly put on a brave face as if he had always known this moment would come.

This was my only opportunity to be somebody. The United States was a vast, deep, mysterious ocean that I would dive into and find a pearl. *I know it is dark, but I will find the light, dive in, and discover a big, shiny pearl.*

The Send-off

My village hosted a send-off ceremony with banners, flowers, a feast, offerings, and blessings for good luck. Over 200 people accompanied me to the airport, chanting as we went. Close friends and family members cried. I think the only person in my immediate circle not crying was me. My dad gave me $300 worth of Nepali rupees, and I had $200, so a total of $500 to my name.

When the incoming plane landed and the passengers stepped off, the time came for me to go—to leave my homeland. My sadness was wrapped in a cloak of excitement for all that awaited me.

As I strolled away from my community and toward the aircraft, an old lady called out from the middle of the crowd. "Hey, Narayan, sonny, come here. Come here!" She was my father's former neighbor, an 82-year-old woman.

"Why? I have to catch a plane," I shouted back. I wondered what could be so important that I might miss my plane.

"Come! Come!" The old lady motioned to me. "I'll bless you."

I ran over to her. *I don't have time for this.*

I knew that Neil Armstrong was the first person to step foot on the moon in 1969. Everybody in the world knew that an American had walked on the moon. People in my village listened to the radio in wonder as Armstrong set foot on the barren landscape. He famously said, "That's one small step for a man, one giant leap for mankind."

But not everyone saw it that way, particularly Hindus, who worship the moon and believe she is the Goddess of Peace. Stomping on the face of a sacred goddess was blasphemous and simply out of the question.

The old woman with her crooked back, weathered face, and wrinkled eyes said with conviction, "We are here to bless you. Sonny, Ammrika is not a good place."

"Why is it not a good place?" I wondered.

"The people from there walk on the Moon Goddess. Don't go to the moon!" she warned, her brow furrowed in concern for my well-being.

I laughed to myself. "Okay, Grandma, please relax. I will make sure that I don't go to the moon. Let me go now."

As I scurried back through the crowd to the plane, my father was waiting at the foot of the steps to say goodbye. As I climbed onto the steps, he turned his face away from me.

"Dad, what's going on? You're not supposed to cry," I said.

"Don't worry. It's not tears. It's sweat from my heart that will help you come home. Go! Go!" He bravely gestured for me to leave.

En Route to America

Because I had dear friends in Newcastle, England, I decided to stop there en route to the US. My friend was a doctor in the small town of Rothbury. At one time, he was the only doctor. I had met Dr. Hugh Pelly and his wife, Jane, in Nepal in 1974 when they visited my village, Khandbari, and Chainpur. The British Nepal Medical Trust appointed him. This organization went to Nepal to provide medical services.

I caught a train from London to Newcastle, where Jane was to meet me at the station. As I waited outside the station, people scurrying in and out, I kept an eye out for her. A brunette woman with her hair pulled into a bun, pushing two children in a baby stroller, approached me. *This isn't Jane. Is it?*

"Narayan?"

"Oh, my goodness. Are they your children?"

"Yes," she said, proudly gazing down at her squirmy kids, who clearly didn't want to be strapped to a stroller.

"I guess you've been busy—huh?"

She chuckled. "Oh, yes, never a dull moment with these two! I figured you might be ready for a little babysitting."

My eyes widened, and I reluctantly nodded.

"Just teasing you, Narayan. We're so happy you came to visit us before heading Stateside!"

She took me to their home nestled in the quaint English countryside. She showed me to my room, a bright, cozy bedroom, and offered me a spot of tea with biscuits. As I enjoyed the tea, she whipped up a delicious meal of shepherd's pie, which we enjoyed when her husband, my good friend, came home. It was such a lovely reunion.

They were the quintessential tour guides, chauffeuring me to cities and towns, lovely beaches along the rocky coastline, majestic castles perched on cliffs, and north to Scotland on windy roads through sheep-dotted pastures. Several times, meandering sheep herds stopped us in our tracks, bleating as they went.

I'll never forget my friends' hospitality and warmth. I had never felt like such a special guest.

Riding Alligators

I landed in New York with just $500 to my name. I collected my luggage and waited for my friend Douglas, who never showed up. *Where is he? What's going on?* I didn't know how to call him. After an hour, I approached the baggage counter. "I'm supposed to meet my friend here. Should I wait here?"

"Yes, you can wait here in baggage claim or go outside. Where is your friend coming from?"

"Chicago."

He laughed. I didn't understand why Chicago was funny. *Did I mispronounce the city's name? Is it my accent?*

"Okay, young man, do you have a $100 bill with you?"

What is a bill? I understood $100, but not bill. "No, I don't think so."

"Do you have $100?"

"Yes. Yes, I do!"

"If you give me $100, I'll send you to Chicago."

"Chicago is another place?" I thought New York City *was* the United States. I had no idea America was so vast.

"Yes, in fact, it takes about an hour to fly there."

"Okay!"

When I landed in Chicago and retrieved my luggage, I asked a stranger to help me call Douglas. I had never seen a payphone before. Then I needed help to get my luggage upstairs to meet Douglas at a restaurant. I approached a skycap, who was a tall black man. "Excuse me, sir."

"What can I do for you?"

"Can you help me take my luggage upstairs?"

"That's why we're here. Follow me. I'll take you to the elevator."

I didn't understand the word "elevator." Instead, I heard "alligator." I knew this word because we had alligators in the flatlands of Nepal. "I don't want to ride alligator!" I exclaimed, hoping that I said it before he summoned the scaly beast with sharp teeth.

He laughed. "No, no. I said elevator."

Once again, I thought he was saying, "alligator." *What kind of country is this? You go upstairs on an alligator's back? It must be a very large alligator!* I said, "But I don't want to ride an alligator!"

"It's an elevator! Let me show you."

I expected an alligator with its sharp teeth and pointed tail to appear, wondering how, in heaven's name, we would ride one without getting chomped in the process. But when I followed the man, we stopped in front of a shiny glass door with buttons. He pushed a button, and the door opened.

Oh, a lift! I was only familiar with the British word "lift." I had ridden in one in Kathmandu.

Then two young girls—one blonde, the other brunette—approached me with big smiles. "We found him! We found him!"

I thought they might have been my friend's sister and her friend because he couldn't come to get me. They were pushing a cart.

"I already have my own cart. Why did you bring it?" I asked. Then I noticed their cart was filled with books.

"Oh, you're from India?" one of the girls asked.

"No, I'm from Nepal. Didn't my friend tell you?"

"Oh, good. Hindu?"

"Yes."

"Oh, look at this book. It's about Krishna." The blonde girl handed me a book.

I looked at it. My gosh, Krishna's book is in English. "Wow! Yes. It's my God!"

"It's yours to keep. It's a book for you."

I put the book in my luggage, thinking, America is such a great place. People just hand you books at the airport!

"See this? Do you have some of these?" She pulled $50 and $20 bills from her pocket.

"Yes."

"Come to eat Sunday in our temple. The more money you give, the more money you make in America."

Great, I thought, and I handed her $10, reluctantly, because it was a lot of money for me. For some people in Nepal, that's more than a month's salary.

I went to the restaurant and waited for Douglas Brown. When he showed up, I was so happy to see him! We warmly greeted each other, and he asked how my trip was. I told him it was long but uneventful.

Then I said in Nepali, "I just got shafted by two Hari Krishna girls. They made me give them $10."

"What? How did that happen?" He was furious. "Oh, don't worry. We'll get that back."

"How?" I asked. "They're gone."

"We'll go every Sunday evening and eat their food. And it will be paid off."

Great idea, I thought.

We walked to his car, stowed my luggage in the trunk, and we were off. It was so good to be with Douglas Brown in America. There were moments on my long journey when I doubted that I would ever see him. When we arrived at his apartment, he pushed a button, a door opened, and he drove his car inside the apartment.

Cars go inside apartments in America? It was the craziest thing I had ever seen.

Before we went to dinner the next night, Douglas said he had to get some money, so he walked up to a wall, inserted a piece of plastic, pressed some buttons, and cash magically appeared.

"Holy smokes!" I said. *Money just comes out of walls in America! The old lady at the airport was right when she said I was going to the moon.* "Is there a person behind the wall giving you the money?"

He chuckled. "No. It's a mechanized process. Banks have ATM machines that dispense cash when you input your code."

I stayed with Douglas for three weeks. It was a crash course in American life and culture. One time while we were driving, I was munching a shiny red apple. When I was down to the core, I rolled down the window and chucked it out on the highway. Another time after a coughing fit, I spit out the window.

Douglas explained in no uncertain terms that both behaviors were very rude and would offend fellow Americans.

The other thing I did wrong was to stay with Douglas for too long. But I had no idea this was considered impolite in American culture. In Nepal, whether a host likes it or not, guests stay as long as they want, eating as much food as they wish. They never ask, "Am I giving you any trouble?" In the case of Douglas Brown, I definitely overstayed my welcome.

My acquaintance in Nepal, Peter Skafte, a professor from Dallas, Texas, suggested that I go to Boulder, Colorado. He thought I would like it because it was so much like Nepal. He said if I didn't like it, I could visit him in Dallas. When working at Tumlingtar Airport, I had done Peter a favor that he never forgot. In return, Peter had arranged for me to stay with his friend Joe O'Laughlin.

So, I took a bus from Chicago to Denver for $35. I was down to $350. As I climbed the steps off the bus, I did a doubletake. The person sitting in the driver's seat was a woman! *Is this our driver?!* I noticed so many different people, black, Hispanic, white, and Asian. One guy had a machine that played music (a boombox), and whenever he got out of the bus, he'd crank the tunes. There were machines that people fed coins into at each bus stop, and food and drinks would appear. I searched for the person behind the machines, but there was no one—more evidence of magic afoot in America.

As we traveled the ribbon of highways, I admired the networks of roads and freeways with their expansive bridges. I thought, *This is truly heaven.* I knew I wanted to make America my home, but I didn't know how to make my dream come true.

During that bus trip, I would doze off, and whenever I awoke, my mind would return to Nepal. America was such a heavenly paradise in contrast to my country. I thought about everything my family had been through. I prayed constantly. *God, help me. If there's any way I can stay in this beautiful country, I don't want to go back. I'd rather have a glass of water and a slice of bread and merely survive in*

America than return. I vowed to save money and send it to my family. *Do I want to go back and get stuck in the mud again, or do I want to swim in the clean water and find all kinds of fish? I could finally see sunlight.* But my love for my family and the memories of our beautiful celebrations and the good times made me cry.

Visiting Boulder

At the Boulder bus station, Joe's mother, Nina O'Laughlin, greeted me. I stayed with Nina one night, and the next day Joe picked me up to head to his place. After having seen Douglas Brown's parents' lovely home with a kitchen, dining room, living room with a fireplace, and a basement bar, I anticipated lovely accommodations, especially since Joe worked with the athletic department at the University of Colorado (CU-Boulder).

We whizzed down the highway and turned onto a bumpy dirt road with no buildings, no houses, nothing, just a prairie with blowing grass. Joe pointed to a three-story house in the middle of a field. "That's my house! You'll be staying on the third floor."

As we drove up to the house, I didn't see any glass. I didn't see any walls. I didn't see anything but a naked structure with pillars and a roof. Parachute ropes were tied from the roof to the ground to hold the house together. I was shocked. *This is America?*

Striding up the steps to his place, he said, "All the plugs work. We've got pots and pans, so you can cook whatever you want. See those tents? Pick one for your room." Around 20–25 tents were folded and stowed on the first floor. "If you get cold, take as many sleeping bags as you want."

I asked, "Where's your toilet?"

"You came from Nepal, Narayan. The toilet is the ground. You should feel right at home. It's a beautiful resort for you. Don't you think it's better than Nepal?"

I wasn't so sure.

There was no running water to drink or take a shower at the house. After about ten days, Bob McNelly, a guy who was staying on the first floor at Joe's house and a student at CU-Boulder, asked me if I wanted to use the facilities of the University of Colorado recreation center. In Nepal, I was accustomed to taking a shower every Saturday, and when staying with Douglas Brown, I could take a steaming hot shower whenever I wanted. I didn't know that people lived like this in America.

I said, "Of course!" I felt filthy and couldn't wait to be sparkling clean.

We walked inside an impressive building with floor-to-ceiling picture windows and a pool. At the entrance, Bob pointed and said, "Narayan, the men's locker room is this way and the women's that way. I have to warn you: you cannot go to the women's area, and women cannot come to the men's area."

"Why not?" In Nepal, men and women, dressed in proper clothing, took showers together at the fountain.

"Well, here, everybody takes showers in the nude," he said matter-of-factly.

"What? No clothes? Not me!" I exclaimed.

"Trust me, just do what everyone else is doing. If not, they'll think you're weird."

I thought, *No way am I going to do that.* Wearing underwear, I turned on the shower, scrubbed my body with soap and water, and heard people snickering. I stared at the tile floor and didn't make eye contact with anyone. I quickly rinsed off, dried myself, and ran outside. That experience was horrible for me—one of the hardest of my life.

For three weeks, Joe was a gracious host and shared everything he had with me. For that, I was truly grateful. On the evening before I was to leave for Dallas and meet up with Peter Skafte, Joe asked me to join him for dinner and a movie. He explained that he didn't make much money, so that he couldn't complete his house. Before dinner, he said we'd each pay for ourselves, proclaiming, "Every dollar counts!"

We went to the University of Colorado cafeteria. Immediately, I noticed a blind man taking money behind a counter. I was shocked. *Not only is a blind man out in society, but he has a job! Even blind people have a way to make money in the United States. What a fabulous country!*

In our village, there was a blind person who would walk up and down the streets with his stick. He had an extraordinary voice, but nobody gave him the opportunity to sing for a living. He was a singing beggar. After you introduced yourself once, he would remember you. That day if he met 100 people, and three months later, I asked, "Do you remember me?" He would say my name. His family couldn't care less. "He's useless," they said. In Nepal, families relegated blind people to the corner of the house with the goats and cows. Blind people were seen as a burden.

The blind guy at the cafeteria instructed me to take a tray and order from the menu. I looked at the prices and ordered what I could afford—a bowl of soup for 75 cents. Joe told me that crackers were free with the soup, so I grabbed a handful of crackers. The blind guy took my dollar and gave me 25 cents change. *What a wonderful country! I'm in the right place.*

Immediately we sat down to eat dinner. My change remained on my tray. As I wolfed down my soup, I noticed Joe's hearty dinner—a sizzling steak, potatoes, mixed veggies, and a buttered roll.

"Narayan, it was very nice having you here. If you ever come back from Dallas or need anything else, maybe my house will be finished. You're always welcome!"

"Oh, thank you. Thank you so much for your hospitality," I said, polishing off my last cracker. I knew I'd be hungry because my meal was so small.

Joe said, "Is that enough food for you?"

I said, "Of course, it's enough," eyeing his half-eaten mashed potatoes and juicy steak.

"If you're still hungry, you can have some of mine. I'll have leftovers for sure." He looked at my tray and laughed. "Narayan, you know in America, you are eating dinner with pocket change. Your meal was under a dollar, and still, you got money back." He picked up the shiny quarter, held it aloft, and proclaimed jokingly. "This money in America; it's nothing for us."

His comments pierced my heart like a dagger and made me feel deeply inferior. I felt his words revealed his true opinion of me and my worth. One should never underestimate the power of another human being, especially a young person, who has their entire life ahead of them to succeed.

His words bothered me all night. I thought, *Every human who comes to the United States of America to make a living will do better. This is the land of opportunity.*

God help me. One day this man will work for me.

CHAPTER 3

Bless Your Heart

Sometimes, you have to go in the wrong direction to discover the right one.

I HOPPED ON A GREYHOUND BUS from the Boulder bus station for Dallas with $90 in my pocket. Of my original $500, that was all I had left. I watched as the snow-covered mountains shrank and disappeared out of sight. I had no idea what to expect from life in Dallas. The only thing I knew about the city was that my favorite American hero was slain there. Little did I know that I would face foreboding situations in my own life in the city renowned for John F. Kennedy's assassination.

Pulling Strings and Pushing Buttons

Peter Skafte met me at the bus station in Dallas. "So damned good to see you, Narayan! You must be tired from your long journey. I'll take you straight home so you can get some sleep. And we'll regroup in the morning."

As we strolled through the parking lot, I said, "Actually, I have a favor to ask. Are there any memorials to John F. Kennedy here?"

"As a matter of fact, lights burn in his memory at the Kennedy Memorial Plaza. It's an open tomb that symbolizes the freedom of JFK's spirit. But it's nighttime, Narayan. You won't be able to see much."

We arrived at his silver Audi sedan, and he loaded my suitcase into the trunk.

"That's okay. I would at least like to see the burning light," I said as we climbed into his car.

"I'm curious as to why this means so much to you," said Peter.

"I'd like to pay my respects to a great man." I shared my admiration for President Kennedy and my shock and grief when I learned about his assassination.

Being a kind and generous friend, he took me there. The walls were comprised of concrete columns, which seemed to float above the ground with no visible support. The lights created the illusion that the light itself supported the structure. The elements of the structure seemed held together by an unseen, invisible force.

"The architect's intention for this monument was to memorialize JFK's charisma and larger-than-life persona. What do you think of it?" Peter asked.

I imagined a great leader's life cut short and a vision for America buried with him. I tried to hold back my tears, but they came, nonetheless.

Peter rested his hand on my shoulder. "You're a good man, Narayan, just like JFK."

If I could live even half the life of this great man gone too soon, I will feel that I have truly lived.

Peter and his wife hosted me for a month, and I overstayed my welcome in true Nepali style. He made possible my admission to the University of Texas (UT-Dallas) by translating my transcript for the registrar. He also found me a room with his friends Peter and Nur Harlow.

With $90 left, I didn't know how I'd pay my tuition. Peter explained that if I landed an on-campus job, my tuition would be less. So, we went to the employment office on campus. Peter did all the talking.

Dorothy, the woman at the employment office with big bleach-blonde hair, bright red lipstick, and long pink fingernails, flipped through a binder, shaking her head like she couldn't help us. But she stopped on a page, glanced up, and said, with a thick Texas drawl, "You're in luck. I've got one opening."

"Doing what?" Peter asked.

"Dishwasher."

"For how many people?" I asked.

Without missing a beat, Dorothy said, "Oh, I don't know, sweetie. Sometimes 300. Sometimes 500. It depends on how many students and faculty eat in the cafeteria on any given day."

"Oh, my God. I can't wash dishes for that many people!" I thought about my sisters-in-law washing our family's dishes by hand. But we only have 26 people in our family. Five hundred people would take me all day. *How will I have time to study?*

"Not a big deal. You just have to collect and wash."

"There's no way one person can wash for hundreds." I was adamant.

Dorothy chuckled. "Bless your heart." And she lingered over the word "heart" for several seconds in true Texan style.

I had never heard that expression. *She must like me if she's blessing my heart.* I smiled.

"Come with me, young man. I'll show you how it works." She took us behind the cafeteria where there were two huge machines and an automatic conveyor belt going around and around, carrying trays of dishes that fed into a window.

"You separate the cups, glasses, and plates. If you can't get to them in time, you just let them go around again. Your job is to fill up the tray. When it's full, you push this button, and it washes and moves to the other side for drying. Not so bad—right?"

I relaxed, thinking, *Americans have buttons for everything.* "No problem," I said, having learned that Americans loved this expression.

"So, are we all set?" she asked.

I didn't understand "all set," but Peter said, "Yes, thank you!"

"Bless your heart," I said to her as we walked off, wanting her to know I appreciated her.

When we were out of earshot, Peter said, "That's not the right way to use that expression. Even though it sounds kind, it's an insult. It means you're too dumb to know better."

I felt at that moment that I would never understand Americans.

Thirty Days and Counting

Peter helped me enroll in courses he knew I could handle, given my limited English—anthropology, pottery, English, and theater. He said, to enroll in the theater class, I would have to audition. I had never heard this word before. He explained that you had to read lines from a play and act them out in front of people evaluating your performance. Since I wasn't shy, the only part of the audition that intimidated me was reading English aloud.

I practiced my part at home and mastered the English. I auditioned in front of a panel of people with clipboards, looking over their glasses, and was accepted into the class—a minor miracle! Our class did a production of Neil Simon's *The Good Doctor*, and I was given the part of a Russian park manager, which required an accent. Of course, a Nepalese accent is worlds away from a Russian accent, but what Texan knew the difference? They could, however, hear that I didn't speak with a Texas twang. I goofed up a couple of times in the performance, and the audience got a kick out of it. I thought, *Who cares as long as they are enjoying it? Wasn't that the point?* When I spoke the line, "I should have done it," I couldn't pronounce the "sh" sound, so it came out as "sould." More snickering from the audience ensued. I was a bit of a ham, so I didn't mind one bit, even if the joke was on me.

Adjusting to life in America wasn't easy. I was juggling my dishwashing job, my college courses, and trying to master English. To make matters worse, things in the house with Peter and Nur were rocky. They constantly fought, sometimes breaking whiskey bottles, drank, and smoked. I would eat as much as possible during the day because Nur didn't like the smell of Nepalese cooking at night. One time in a fit of fury, she dumped my dinner into the trash. Sometimes, my dinner was just soup and an apple. Often, I went to bed without dinner.

I also had to deal with my visa renewal—the change of my visa status from a visitor to a student. Five minutes before my visa was set to expire, Peter and his wife, Diane, rushed inside the immigration office; the officer completed all the documents and applied for renewal. A month later, I was denied. I appealed the decision to the upper court, but a couple of months later, the lower court's decision was affirmed, and I was denied once again. A darkness fell over me when I received an official letter from the US Citizenship and Immigration Services ordering me to leave the country in 30 days. I felt the heavy hand of government bureaucracy. My new world was closing in on me, and the prospect of returning to Nepal haunted me. I made desperate appeals to my circle of friends, hoping they could pull strings for me.

Peter Skafte accompanied me to the registrar's office and made a compelling case. The registrar, a skinny, freckled young man with red hair and protruding ears, said I couldn't continue to study in the US without a visa. "Terribly sorry, I can't help you. I'd like to, but the law is the law." He threw up his hands and shook his head.

I imagined with dread being forced out of my adopted country, having never launched the life of my dreams, returning to work in the rice paddies, and surviving in cramped quarters with my family, living on rice and lentils.

As we turned to go, the registrar said to Peter, "Hey, maybe your friend should just cross the border and come right back with a new visa."

Peter twisted around, and his face lit up. "Really? He can do that?"

"Yes. I'll call the US Consul's Office in Matamoros, Mexico, and make an appointment for him. He's an acquaintance of mine. Your friend should go to Brownsville, Texas, cross the border and head to the consul's office."

"How much time do you have left?" he asked me.

"Eight days."

"Oh, so this is a rush job. You should fly down there. I'll schedule your appointment in six days—enough time for you to arrange your flight and get your ticket."

I received the ticket on the morning of my appointment. If all went well, I'd fly to Brownsville in the morning, drive to Mexico and return to Dallas in the evening.

I was uneasy about the plan. *I'm a lucky guy, but what if my luck runs out? What if there's some kind of snafu? What if they deny my return once I'm in Mexico? I'll have to fly back to Nepal.* My head was spinning with worst-case scenarios, and my stomach was in knots as I flew to Brownsville.

Once there, I hailed a taxi for my border crossing. A friendly American fellow picked me up and drove straight across the border. There was no checkpoint to confirm my Mexican visa, which was required for Nepali passport holders. The taxi driver dropped me off at the consul's office. I pulled open the heavy door to discover a line that snaked through the lobby. I joined the line and played with the camera around my neck that I wore to look like a tourist.

A skinny guy at the counter called out, "You, hey you!"

I looked up. I didn't know which "you" he was referring to.

"Yeah, you with the camera." He motioned for me to come to the front of the line.

I thought I was perhaps in trouble for something—maybe for not having a Mexican visa. I coached myself to remain calm, even though I could feel my racing heart against my camera.

He introduced himself as Jacob, invited me into his office and closed the door. "Would you like any coffee or tea?"

My heart slowed because I figured if he offered me a drink, I probably wasn't in too much trouble.

"Coffee, please."

Jacob grilled me about how I planned to earn money to pay for my tuition. I said I had an on-campus job that covered my expenses, and if I came up short, my professor friend, Peter Skafte, would pay. He furiously took notes as I spoke.

I nervously sipped my coffee, hoping nothing I said could be used against me. I prayed I was saying all the right things, but not knowing much about American immigration law, I wasn't sure if I had stepped on a landmine.

Biting his lip, Jacob wrote for a long time after I stopped talking. *Is he evaluating the information I gave him? Should I retract or revise anything?* My eyes darted around his office, trying to figure out what I said that might've incriminated me, and how I might fix it.

He glanced up. "You know you can't work more than 20 hours a week? And if it looks like you intend to stay in this country after you complete your degree, your visa will be denied?"

"Yes, sir," I said, even though I had every intention of staying.

He put his pen down and folded his hands on his desk. "I don't know the registrar personally, but I trust him. He said he really likes you. He also said he has been to Nepal. Your country is beautiful, and I, too, would like to go there one day."

"Please come." I smiled.

"But you're here. How could I go without you?" He teased. "May I see your passport?"

"Sure." I slid it across the desk.

He opened my passport and granted me a student visa, a change of status. "Welcome to our country!"

I thanked him profusely and quickly caught a cab to the border. The Mexican border officer grabbed my passport and leafed through it with a furrowed brow. "You only have a Mexico to US visa here. Where's your Mexican visa?"

"I just came this morning from the US," I said.

He took my visa and airline tickets and disappeared.

Just when I thought I was in the clear, I may have hit another insurmountable hurdle.

The border officer reappeared, handed me my documents, and said, "Okay, go, go!"

Phew! Such a close call! I could have gone to jail if the border officer had arrested me for coming to Mexico without a visa. My luck was holding out.

Then I went through the American Border Patrol Office Immigration office at Brownsville. As my heart raced, I waited for his questions, but they never came.

The officer said, "I've been to your country. It's wonderful! Welcome back to our country!"

Don't Mess with Texas!

After I secured my visa, I settled into my life. I traded in Hinduism for Christianity, attending church every Sunday and Bible study on Wednesday. Learning about the gospel of Jesus made me hopeful that I would be accepted as a Christian and an American. But I noticed a troubling tendency. Baptists said good things in the name of Jesus at church, but it didn't stop them from sometimes doing bad things, like not welcoming dark-skinned people into their homes. Even though I was baptized as a Baptist, they never accepted me as one of them.

Christian circles weren't the only places I experienced the sting of discrimination. One night, a friend Maggie and I decided to have an after-dinner drink. Maggie said she knew a great neighborhood place that was cool and cozy. I was becoming a hipster American with longish hair and a goatee.

A bouncer blocked the entranceway. He was tattooed, with big muscular arms and a cowboy hat that he wore so low you could barely see his eyes. But I could see enough to know he eyed us suspiciously. He was missing a couple of teeth, which made him look gnarly; if he needed to knock someone out at the door, he wouldn't hesitate, even if it meant losing more teeth.

"What's the cover charge?" I asked, pulling out my wallet.

"No cover charge, but you ain't allowed in." He crossed his arms, so his tattooed biceps popped, and the right arm read—*Don't mess with Texas!* with the graphic of a pistol underneath. To my friend, he jerked his head toward the door and said, "Go ahead on in."

Maggie said, "What do you mean? I'm not going in without him. Why can't he go in?"

"Just can't. That's all."

"Hold on a second," she said. "This is a public bar. You can't discriminate."

"Excuse me, ma'am, if you don't want to go in, no one's telling you that you have to."

"But what's your reason for not letting him in?" asked Maggie.

"Reason is he has a goatee and long hair. Okay, lady?"

I glared at him and said to Maggie, "Never mind. Let's go." As we hightailed it back to the car, I said, "It's not the first time, and it won't be the last. They just see my brown skin and think I'm from south of the border. Honestly, they don't care where people with brown skin are from. We're just not welcome. Even if they let me in, they're not happy about it. They want me to go back to where I came from."

At another time, I wanted to buy a goat to prepare a delicious Nepalese dish for my American friends visiting from Colorado. I found a goat farm near my home, and I drove my pickup there with my friend in tow. When we pulled in, we noticed the grazing area with brown, white, and black goats chomping on greens. Compared to goats in Nepal, they were robust and healthy—no protruding ribs. We hopped out of the truck.

The goat farmer squinted against the sun and said, "How much goat you looking for?"

"I'd like a whole goat, please," I said confidently.

"Head, too?" His face was blank, but the lines and creases formed a map of worry.

"Yes. What's that going to cost me?"

"Twenty-five bucks," said the farmer, removing his soiled baseball cap and scratching his bald head.

Wow! That's a deal.

"Interested?" he asked, speaking to me but looking at my friend. For some reason, he wouldn't make eye contact with me. I felt like an invisible man.

"Yes, please."

"Let me go fetch the goat for you. Wait right here."

My friend and I watched the goats chomp on greens. Most were oblivious to us, but one young, frisky, curious, brown-and-white goat jumped up, shrieked, and stuck his tongue out. We loved the kid show, and the more we laughed, the more animated he became.

The farmer came back, hauling a shrink-wrapped goat. "Back there?" He motioned to my truck bed.

"Yes, thank you." When I opened the truck bed, he threw the goat in with a reverberating clang.

I handed him $25. "Oh, may I please use your restroom before we head out?" I asked, looking toward the farmhouse.

"Be my guest. There's plenty of space over yonder." He pointed to an open field.

I looked around to see what he meant by over yonder. "I don't see a restroom."

"There's plenty of open space for you to do your business," the farmer said, losing patience.

"What? He has to go outside?!" exclaimed my friend.

"Yes, ma'am. What do you expect? I'm not going to let *him* inside my home."

I jumped onto the bed of my pickup and hurled the goat to the ground. I asked for my money back. As we drove off, it hit me. *I'll never fit in here.*

My Schoolmate Sue

A few semesters into my bachelor's degree, I fell for a charming American woman named Sue. She was attentive, bright, worldly, and gave me a crash course in English and American culture. We married a year and a half later. Her parents, prejudiced Texans, opposed the marriage because I was an Asian. In the early days, Sue fought valiantly for me against the bigotry of her parents. Hearing her describe the battles she waged, I assumed her love for me was undying. I felt protected and cherished.

But on our wedding night, I was inconsolable, longing for my family back in Nepal. I wished I had married in the traditional way with my family gathered around and celebrating. I was a hero to my people, but I married like I was a nobody. As I cried on the couch, Sue offered no sympathy and no words of comfort, which hurt me more than anything. She just walked past me and went off to read a book in bed. I wondered how someone could be so heartless, especially on a day so sacred. I wondered if Sue wasn't who I thought she was.

As I worked hard, earning my bachelor's degree, Sue's behavior became increasingly troubling. This was particularly problematic because she was pregnant. She read and slept all day with intermittent periods of drinking and smoking pot. When I suggested she consider our child's health and adopt a healthier lifestyle, she rolled her eyes and escaped into her romance novel.

Our son was born on January 27, 1981, in the middle of the night. We named him Nathan Albert Shrestha and brought him home in a little blue bundle. When I gazed at him in his bassinet, at his shiny brown eyes, his upturned nose, and his curious mouth—an angel sent from heaven—I felt the weight of the world on my shoulders. *Will I be a good daddy to you, Nathan? Will I help you find your way in the world?* I promised him I would.

CHAPTER 4

Whistling Up the Wind

My baby bird with broken wings, we're in this together, son. You have your daddy's fighting spirit and determination. I will wait until your wings heal and you're strong enough. I'm not going home without you.

THREE WEEKS AFTER NATHAN'S BIRTH, I was engrossed in accounting class, studying income statements and balance sheets, when someone rushed in and handed the professor a note. I had discovered a knack for numbers and changed my major from anthropology to business finance. The professor glanced up at me with concern. "Narayan, you need to go home right away."

Tiny Fractured Heart

Holy smokes! What happened? I raced home to find my in-laws slumped on the couch in our living room with long faces. My mother-in-law was wringing her hands.

"What's going on?" Neither Sue nor Nathan was home, so I presumed one or the other was in trouble.

"Nathan is in the hospital. You need to go immediately," said my mother-in-law.

"Is everything okay?"

"No. That's why you must go," she said.

I sped to the hospital to find Sue falling to pieces in the waiting room. When she saw me, she peeled herself off the chair and collapsed on me.

"What's going on?"

At first, she was so hysterical; she couldn't start or finish a sentence. She just cried and cried.

"Okay. Breathe, and slow down."

She whisper-cried, "His pulmonary valve is so narrow that the blood can't flow. That's why his lips turned blue."

Panic seized me, but I held myself together for Sue and my sweet boy. *What good will it do for both of us to fall apart?*

A grey-haired man with round glasses and kind, blue eyes appeared in the waiting room and introduced himself with quick handshakes as Dr. Edgar Newfield, cardiologist. In a calm, measured way, he explained that he needed to open Nathan's tiny heart valve. "Of course, there are risks, but we will work to minimize the risks. In order to proceed, you must sign away liability."

"And if we choose not to have the surgery?" I asked, thinking it sounded too risky.

Dr. Newfield's face fell. "In truth, he might be okay for a short time, but in the long run, his prospects aren't good."

We agreed to sign, and Dr. Newfield strode off as an administrator appeared with documents on a clipboard. We signed the necessary paperwork. Then we white-knuckled it in the waiting room for what seemed like an eternity. I held my breath the entire time.

Five hours later, Dr. Newfield appeared, relaxed in scrubs, with his surgery mask pulled down beneath his chin. When I saw his smile, I started breathing again.

"Your boy's a little champ. We fixed his heart valve, and the blood is pumping through his heart at full capacity."

"Oh, thank God," said Sue, looking up toward the heavens, her hands together in prayer.

"Do you want to come see him?" asked Dr. Newfield.

We nodded and held each other as we tried to keep up with Dr. Newfield's brisk pace. I don't know who was holding up whom. But it didn't matter as long as we stayed upright.

Nathan's face was flushed, his wispy dark hair matted to his head. He was hooked up to breathing tubes, a heart monitor, and an intravenous (IV) tube, everything tiny, as though it was a miniature-world toy hospital. A bandage and tape covered his rib cage. I imagined the scar beneath, a forever mark over his heart. His little hands were wrapped in gauze and motionless next to his head. Just looking at him as a tiny science project made my heart sting. But I had to be Nathan's strong daddy, like I promised, and not fall apart at the first heartache.

"When can we bring him home?" I asked, bracing for the answer.

"It depends on the speed of his recovery," said the doctor. "Let's see how he does."

Two days later, Dr. Newfield explained, haltingly over the phone, that half of Nathan's body was paralyzed, requiring a longer hospital stay.

When I visited him in the neonatal intensive care unit (NICU), I whispered, "My baby bird with broken wings, we're in this together, son. You have your daddy's fighting spirit and determination. I will wait until your wings heal and you're strong enough. I'm not going home without you."

Nathan spent the next month in the NICU. He needed a second surgery during which he lost a lung. I was heartbroken, but I had to be strong for my baby boy. I tried to visit every day, but sometimes my work precluded it. Sue's visits were sporadic. We fought about it, but she said it was too traumatic for her.

When we received word that we could finally take our son home, I was relieved but worried. He was still recovering from his surgery, so he needed even more attention than a normal infant. His first night home, Sue poured herself a glass of wine and said, curling up on the couch, that she wanted to go back to work as a teacher.

Now? When our son needs so much care? This woman is out of her mind. My hope for our little family was vanishing with each passing day.

Nathan could barely function. He was unable to move his hands and legs. He also couldn't move his eyes. We hired an in-home occupational therapist to work with him. Whenever she had time, Sue would practice the exercises that rewarded him with toys and treats. His sessions often ended with him bawling and needing comfort. To say I was discouraged would be an understatement. I imagined a lifetime of disability and dependence for my sweet boy.

One evening after a long day at work, Sue and I were bickering about the teaching offer she had received. Nathan was on the floor nearby. My peripheral vision registered movement. I spun around and witnessed Nathan picking up a little toy gun, a gift from his grandfather.

I dashed over and hugged him. "That's my boy!"

A few months later, I noticed his eyes following the spotted cows orbiting around a moon in the mobile above his crib. I grabbed my baby bundle and held him aloft, then brought him in for a kiss. The medication and therapies for his eyes had finally worked! It had been an arduous road, but I now had hope that my son could live a normal, healthy life.

Protecting Our Family Name

In late 1981, when Nathan was a little less than a year old, I received a letter from my father with the happy news that my sister, Shanti, was to marry. I rejoiced that she had found a suitable husband until I read further:

> *We have no money. When you come, if there's any way you can bring money, you'll save my name and our family's prestige. We're in worse financial shape than before you left. Please know that you are our only hope.*

I took the news hard, knowing that Nepali weddings were elaborate celebrations fully funded by the father of the bride. If I couldn't help, my father would have to swallow his pride and beg someone else for the money, tarnishing his reputation in our community.

I tapped the bulk of my savings, and when I arrived in Nepal for the wedding, I took the money to Bangkok, Thailand, and purchased everything for the wedding—clothing, jewelry, and gifts. I financed the feast and festivities.

My mother said, "Bless you, son. Bless you. If you hadn't come to attend your sister's wedding, we would be in desperate circumstances. Because of you, we can hold our heads high."

The wedding was a traditional Hindu ceremony, a festive occasion with an elaborate feast, live music, and dancing. My sister, radiant in a shimmering red-and-gold dress and veil, was adorned in jewels and bangles. Henna art decorated her hands and arms. My seven brothers and I carried Shanti across town like a goddess in a golden carriage. As we bade farewell to her and her husband, Shyam, the villagers' weeping echoed in the hills. Many attendees said the scene was one they would never forget. Everyone in the town knew that I made the wedding possible. They patted my back in gratitude. And our family's standing in our community remained intact.

My brother Surendra, the second from the bottom, was 16 years old when I returned for my sister's wedding. He was a thoughtful brother. Because I showered every day in the US, he made sure I received a shower, even if it was Nepali-style. He would boil water over the hearth every day, bring the bucket, and blend it with cold water until it was the perfect temperature. Then he'd pour it over my head as I sat in a chair and bathed.

As the cleansing water flowed over me, he said, "Brother, is there any way you can bring me to the United States so I can complete my education, like you?"

"No. You're too young. Besides, I have so many problems right now. I need to be in a stronger position. Only then can I help you, brother."

He tipped a second bucket and let it wash over me. "I promise I will not give you trouble. I'll be a good boy, a very good boy. I'd really like to come."

Every day he would pour and plead. "Brother, are you going to bring me?"

I finally said, "I'll see what I can do." While I had my hands full, I liked the idea of having a family member with me in Texas. More importantly, I wanted to help my brother escape the fate of a Nepali man—struggling to make a meager living, living off the land with no dreams of his own.

After returning home and getting Sue's nod, I brought Surendra to live with us.

Trouble Brewing in Texas

In 1983, Sue and I purchased a lovely, three-bedroom house near her school. Our new home was modern, spacious, and had an expansive yard. I was pleased we were moving up in the world. My brother, still living with us, switched schools, and enrolled in my wife's school. He and I hand-built a handsome fence around our yard for protection and privacy. I was proud of our handiwork.

I landed a good job at a company called Irrigation Technology, an hour away. Typically, I wasn't home until 6:00 pm. One night when I arrived, neither Sue nor Nathan was there. I sped off to the childcare center to discover Nathan sitting alone in the middle of the floor, sucking his thumb. The director was fuming and confronted me in a harsh, accusatory tone. "You're supposed to pick Nathan up at 4:00! You're two hours late! What kind of parents are you?"

I apologized and made an excuse for my wife, who always left work at 3:30 in the afternoon. I picked up Nathan, who glanced around, saying, "Mama, mama, mama." Even he knew she was supposed to be there.

My doubts about Sue as a wife and mother mounted. She abruptly demanded that my brother move out of the house. She said, "It's either him or me. Honestly, I don't care who goes."

I was forced to choose between my brother and Sue. And while my loyalties were shifting toward my brother, I felt bound to Sue, but I resented her for making me choose. My brother moved in with friends six doors down.

One Fourth of July, Sue's father and mother, Al and Dorothy, invited us for the weekend. We accepted even though holidays with her family could be tense. Her father, a Navy vet, had never pretended to be fond of me. One time during a Thanksgiving dinner, as he passed the turkey to Sue, he said, "Give Narayan dark meat only."

Their family got a good laugh at my expense. I wanted to say, "I don't want your darned turkey, you old coot," but instead, I served myself a hearty portion of white meat.

On the second night of the holiday weekend, the four of us sat at the dining-room table, and Nathan, who was three, played on the floor with dinosaurs and trucks. The dinosaurs were being transported by pickup trucks, apparently incapable of walking anywhere themselves. His dinosaur noises were hard to distinguish from the truck noises.

Dorothy and Sue were setting the dishes of barbequed pork chops, coleslaw, and potato salad on the table, on top of a patriotic tablecloth. Dorothy said she had a dessert surprise. Sue guessed it was a red, white, and blue cake. And her mother, with a self-satisfied grin, said, "Nope. You can guess all you want, but you'll never guess it."

Nathan's highchair was set up for him next to the table, but he had no interest in being strapped in, especially when there were dinosaurs to transport.

I tried several times, "Nathan, c'mon, let's eat."

"No, I want to play," he said, zooming and varooming his trucks.

Just as I squatted to scoop him into my arms, my father-in-law said in a commanding voice, "Leave him alone."

I twisted around to glare at Al. "We want to teach him manners from an early age. He needs to know that we eat meals together. So, don't tell me what to do. He's my child."

"And this is my house," he barked with a flushed face and rigid posture.

"So, you want us to leave him on the floor while we eat?"

"Yes. He's my grandson, so he belongs to me, too. Now, shut your trap. You'll do what I say when you're in my home."

Sue and Dorothy said nothing, trying not to exacerbate my father-in-law's rage which could be triggered by just about anything.

He pointed his index finger at me and pulled the trigger of an imaginary gun with his thumb. "Bang! I can do this to you."

I thought he was kidding. "Shoot me? You have the guts to do that?" I laughed.

"Want me to prove it? Okay, you got it." He scooted his chair back, got up with a groan, and escaped to his bedroom. He returned carrying a shotgun like he was a hunter moving in on his prey. He opened it, rolled in two shells, flipped it up, and said, in a John Wayne cowboy drawl, "Narayan, I'll take you out in the garage."

"Are you crazy? I'm not going out there."

"It's my house. I'm ordering you," he shouted.

"You cannot order me to die!" I shouted back.

"Oh, hell, yes, I can!"

Dorothy intervened when she saw her husband's idiocy escalating to the point of ridiculousness. "Aaah! Are you out of your mind? Drop the damned rifle. Whether you like it or not, he's our son-in-law. And your grandchild is watching you, you old fool."

Al said, "He doesn't have to see any of this," and he headed toward the garage. Dorothy jumped up and ran after him, with Sue following.

I stood up and went after them. "Leave him alone. Let's see him try to shoot me."

The foolish bravado was contagious and could've led to a July Fourth garage execution. Thankfully, the ladies had enough sense and strength to wrestle the gun from him. Dorothy emptied it, shoved the shells in her pocket, and hurried to empty the rest of the guns in the house. It was Texas, after all. It wasn't uncommon to have a gun in every room. Before this incident, I had seen guns as Texas décor. Now I realized Texans meant business with their guns. Dorothy held onto the ammo for fear of her husband losing his mind again.

I grabbed Nathan, who had started whimpering, and comforted him. Without his guns and ammo, Al had lost his bluster. He went to bed.

We had lost our appetites, so Dorothy shoveled our special Fourth of July meal into Tupperware and stuck it in the fridge with other leftovers. No special dessert, either.

Although we went to bed early, I couldn't fall asleep with my thoughts spiraling to a dark, dark place. Perhaps Sue had shared her unhappiness with her parents, and they were thrilled that she saw the light. Maybe the truth was she was just unhappy with me. *Had my wife's family conspired to bring me here and kill me? Shots fired on the Fourth of July would be mistaken for fireworks, and no one would be the wiser. Don't think such crazy things. Sue's dad is just a crazy, right-wing cowboy.*

After trying everything to fall asleep, I realized it wasn't happening. At 2:00 am, I said, "Sue, are you still awake?"

She said, "Yes."

"I've got to get out of here. I don't want to sleep here tonight."

We gathered our things, grabbed Nathan, and hurried out of there. That was the last time I visited their home. That incident was the last straw and destroyed the relationship with my in-laws. I said to Sue, "Do you want them or me? You choose."

One day, I came home early from work, and Sue wasn't home. When she finally appeared later that evening, she was tipsy and disheveled. I asked her where the heck she had been, and she said nonchalantly, "Having margaritas with my friends." She ran and locked herself in the bedroom. When I knocked, she said, "Go away!"

That night something shifted in me. Looking back, it may have been that I could no longer tolerate the way her family treated me or Sue's seeming indifference toward our son. Or perhaps, I had just fallen out of love with her.

The next day after I tucked Nathan into bed, I told Sue I had had enough and was considering divorce. She once again locked me out of our bedroom.

I slept with Nathan that night. For hours, I listened to him breathe and stared at the glow-in-the-dark stars Sue and I had stuck on his ceiling when anxiously awaiting his birth.

The next day, Nathan poked me at 6:00 am, saying, "I'm hungry, Daddy."

Groggy-headed, I said, "Go wake your mommy. Maybe we can have breakfast together."

He skipped out of the room in his footed PJs covered with superheroes. When he returned, he said, "Mama won't move."

"What do you mean she won't move? Did you shake her?"

"Yeah, I said, 'Wake up, Mama. Wake up.'"

"Try again. Maybe shake her harder this time."

He scurried out and returned seconds later, looking confused and scared. "She has something gross in her mouth."

What does that mean? I picked up Nathan and hurried into the bedroom. *Oh, my God!* She was face-down on the floor with foam coming out of her mouth. *What the hell happened?*

I grabbed the phone and dialed 911. I detected a putrid odor emanating from the bathroom. I set Nathan down in the living room by his toy chest. "Stay right here—okay?"

I ran toward the bathroom to investigate. The foul smell was so overpowering; it made me lightheaded. The toilet and floor were splattered with vomit. An empty 100-pill Tylenol bottle sat on the sink.

The EMT team arrived in a flash, took Sue's vitals, strapped her to a stretcher, and whisked her off to the hospital.

After my initial panic subsided, I was seething. Angry that she would do this to us, especially Nathan. *What was her plan? To leave him a motherless child?* Or maybe she had no plan. She just wanted out. She just wanted the whole thing to be over. This was her easy way out. I knew there was no going back for me. But what about Nathan? She was clearly unfit to mother him, now, and maybe forever.

Following her overdose, Sue was admitted to a psychiatric hospital. My in-laws moved in with me, and Al was civil, but I knew it was an act. He suggested I file for divorce.

I said, "Beat you to it. Sue can have whatever she wants in terms of assets." But I couldn't, in good conscience, give her Nathan. "She can't have custody of Nathan, not in her condition."

"It's her son, Narayan."

"He's just as much mine. Can you say with confidence that she'll take good care of him?"

"She shouldn't get him, and neither should you. We, his grandparents, should."

The love between Nathan and me was the greatest love. Fueled by affection for my son, I spent a year and a small fortune locked in a custody battle. In the end, three-way custody was granted, and I was permitted to see my son every other weekend.

When I thought about the career path ahead of me, I reflected on what I loved so much about being the station manager at the Tumlingtar Airport. I realized it was the freedom to be my own boss. It made me think I'd like to pursue entrepreneurial ventures where I could call the shots. I also wanted to make a difference in the world, but I didn't know what that looked like yet. At various points in my marriage, I shared this with Sue. I said I hoped God was speaking through me. When I revealed my dreams, she just ridiculed me.

I thought, *I must escape this darkness. I don't know how, but I will find a way.* I needed to start over, but where did I belong? One thing was certain: I had to leave Texas. And, sadly, my son.

My tough times in Texas helped me to find my way. Even though I was in turmoil, Texas and Sue taught me how to see the positive things in life. I was thrown out of the darkness into the light.

I believe God is with me whether I'm having a good or a bad time. Humans struggle and must learn and grow from their problems. God created pathways, and it's up to us to choose which one is good, which one is bad. I'm in the best place on Earth, the United States of America. A person can be successful by thinking, when a door is closed, other doors open.

With just $5,000, I set off for Boulder, Colorado, a town that felt more like home, a place where people welcomed you into their houses, no matter your race or nationality, a place where you could climb mountain peaks and reach Heaven on Earth.

CHAPTER 5

Flying Dollar Bills

Hurdles are just stepping-stones in a river you must cross to get to the other side.

I F I HAD EXPECTED SOMEONE to hand-deliver my livelihood, I could have been waiting for my entire life. I knew I must create my luck and good fortune. Fueled by my dark days in Texas, I was determined not to squander my fresh start; instead, I planned to chart my future. I wasn't entirely sure what it would look like, and yet I trusted it would come to me.

But would it, really?

Starting Over in Boulder

In November 1985, I rented a trailer home for $250 a month in Eldorado Springs, a lovely canyon town outside of Boulder, Colorado, and a world-class climbing area. The friendly community, nestled next to a meandering creek, was affordable for newcomers like me. Surendra had come with me to Boulder but was restless and talked about returning to Texas.

Even though I was starting over, I wasn't discouraged. I was finally free from the forces that had held me down. I had learned so much from my trials in Texas. They had not beaten me down but rather had lifted me so I could discover my path. Although there were plenty of hurdles, I had begun to see them as stepping-stones in a river I must cross to get to the other side.

I didn't get disheartened because when I reflected on my family and community in Nepal and the difficulties they faced, my problems were nothing. I thought of my father and mother with so many children and grandchildren—barely surviving and trying to make the best of what little they had. They didn't realize that life could be so different—that they could experience the abundance and prosperity of their wildest dreams. They hadn't seen what I had—ribbons of highways, towering buildings, gas stations a-plenty, grocery stores chock-full of fresh produce and meat, and shopping malls filled with treasures. They hadn't seen Americans thriving with good jobs that afforded them homes, cars, and leisure time. They hadn't seen that, in America, when one door closes, ten more doors open. They hadn't seen because their vision was blocked by endless toil and worry while struggling to survive.

Even in my old beat-up trailer home in the dark of the night, I used to think, *In the morning, I'll wake up and see the sun!* I felt newfound hope and believed I'd discover an opportunity in my new community. I saw dollar bills flying everywhere—like leaves on a blustery autumn day, they were there for the taking. All I had to do was reach out and grab them! But I needed a ladder, a strong ladder, so that I could catch the flying dollar bills. Who would build the ladder? I knew the answer was: only me.

Besides a handful of American friends that I met through Joe and Peter, I became friends with Damber and Kalpana Nepali, an engineering graduate student and his wife, hailing from my village. One December day, when the snow was pummeling my trailer, and I was entertaining the Nepalis with lunch and tea, I served up an idea.

To Kalpana, I said, "You are like a sister from my village. Can you help me out? I can't predict what's going to happen tomorrow, but you need to believe in me."

"Tell us what you want. We'll see if we can do it," said Kalpana.

"This is a huge request, but I'm going to run it by you anyway."

"Go ahead, brother," said Damber.

"I'm alone. My younger brother Surendra lives with me now, but he wants to go back to Texas to complete his education. I would like your family to move in with me. Damber, you will commute to Fort Collins, and Kalpana will help me settle in Boulder. You guys can take the bedroom, and I'll sleep on the living room sofa."

"And then what?" asked Damber.

"I am looking to launch some kind of business. If you can help me, I can freely pursue opportunities. I'll pay Kalpana a monthly salary and food." I had $5,000 in cash and a little credit remaining on my credit card.

They generously agreed that Kalpana and their toddler son would live with me during the week, and Damber would join us on the weekends.

Even though I was a newcomer to Boulder, I decided to reach out to the community with some offerings to test the waters. My ideas included Nepali language and culture classes. I asked Kalpana if she would be interested in teaching Nepalese to Americans interested in traveling to Nepal. She agreed.

Being a determined guy, I placed an ad in *The Denver Post*, a daily newspaper in Denver. Language and culture classes for people wanting to travel to Nepal. For just $25, come learn to speak a little Nepalese over a delicious meal! The ad generated some buzz, and six people registered for our ongoing Nepali dinner and language lessons. I considered this only a moderate success, but a success, nonetheless.

Riding a wave of audaciousness, I decided to throw a Nepali-themed party on January 2, 1986, for my American and Nepali friends and acquaintances. I wondered how many people will gather for a Nepali-themed party? My guestimate was just a few dozen.

I rented a church at Pennsylvania and Baseline and had use of the kitchen, the great hall, and the stage. My Nepali friends helped me prepare a delicious feast. Drinks were on the house (aka me). Damber and Kalpana volunteered to perform a traditional Nepali-style dance for the event.

A Sherpa from Texas, four Nepali families living in Denver, and three Nepalis from Fort Collins attended. Peter, Joe, Diane, and other Boulderites came, many of whom had been to Nepal. I made so many friends that night.

All told, around 200 American and Nepali friends gathered for the festivities. My party was a smashing success! I spent $600 on the event, but it was well worth the expense. Not only was I thrilled that my event had exceeded my expectations, but I was also gaining insight into my new community at the foot of the Rocky Mountains.

On the heels of my party, my second oldest brother, Ram Dai, wanted to visit. He planned to stay for a month, expecting me to play host and show him a good time. Preoccupied with kicking off my life in Boulder, I sometimes left my brother in the trailer home, recommending that he explore the breathtaking Eldorado Canyon. He told me he didn't want to see boring, old mountains and instead hoped to see exciting things like high-rise buildings, superhighways, and glitzy shopping malls—things we didn't have in Nepal. I took him to Texas. My house was on the market but hadn't yet sold, so we stayed there. I introduced him to my son, Nathan. I also took him to NASA in Houston and Galveston, where we dipped into the waters of the Gulf of Mexico.

One day, we had tea in our hotel room, and the mood grew somber when the conversation turned to our family. My brother reported that our family wasn't doing well, that our father continued to sell off land to survive. I thought, *What happens when there's no more land to sell?* It made me determined to help. *But how?* I didn't have anything to share with them. I was starting from scratch.

The next evening, we were driving back from dinner at a Thai place, and Ram Dai said, "Hey, brother, we've driven so many roads and highways, but I've never seen cops zooming around. I've heard if you do something wrong, they will come and grab you. I'd like to see that!" His eyes sparkled.

"You don't want to see that happen to me. Do you?"

"No, but I'd like to see it happen to somebody else."

"Well, let's just say if it happens, it happens," I said mischievously. I pressed the gas pedal and throttled the car to 75 mph in a 60-mph zone.

And in a flash, I heard the approaching screech of a siren. Glancing in my rear-view mirror were red and blue revolving flashes. "Oh, great. Now I'll get a ticket."

"What is a ticket?"

"Hold on. We have to pull over now." I pulled to the side of the road, wondering how much damage I had incurred.

"Driver, step out of your car!" blared the cop's speaker.

I got out and looked toward the cop car. His spotlight was blinding.

"Passenger, step out, too!"

I leaned into my car. "You have to get out, brother." Ram Dai was grinning. Clearly, this was the cop show he had hoped for.

"Give me your license," said the cop, who then drew a line on the pavement. A second cop posed in a bicep-flexing position but said nothing. "Now, walk this line, please."

I walked the line. No problem. Thank God we hadn't been drinking.

The cop finished his paperwork, returned my license, and handed me a ticket for $65. "Might want to watch your speed, there, buddy," the cop said, stating the obvious. I figured his sidekick had no role other than to double the intimidation of the stop.

"Yes, sir," I said, sufficiently respectful.

Ram Dai and I returned to my car. I shoved the ticket into the glovebox.

"What is that paper?" Ram Dai asked.

"It's a ticket, which is, basically, a fine," I said glumly.

"How much is it?"

"$65." I tried not to think that I was losing money with each passing day with no income and now was paying a superfluous fee.

"What? Oh, dang it! If I knew it was going to cost money, I would not have asked. You should have just given me that money. I could've bought a Citizen Watch!"

"Yeah, no kidding. Well, you'll get your watch anyway."

He seemed delighted by the cop action-Citizen Watch pairing. Seeing him happy was perhaps worth the price of admission.

The time came for Ram Dai to return to Nepal, and a heaviness fell over me. Among my seven brothers, we were the closest. He never treated me like I was inferior just because I was younger. He never minded eating together from the same plate, unheard of for an older sibling. He was such a lovely guy.

I went to the American Express office and bought my brother a one-way ticket back home. I also picked up little gifts to send home with him, but no cash. He would show up empty-handed. Anticipating my family's disappointment made me despondent. But what could I do? I had to save myself first.

The Birthplace of Old Tibet

Following Ram Dai's departure, I fell into a pattern of staying awake until the middle of the night, drinking coffee, wondering, *What am I doing here? What is my direction? What is my purpose?* On most days, I languished in my trailer. My money was about to run out. I had a little credit left on my credit card, but that was someone else's money anyway. I had food and rent expenses, child support, the mortgage on my Dallas home, and I had blown so much money entertaining my brother. Although I probably could have found one, I didn't want a job. I wanted a business, a way of life, a calling.

This went on for weeks until, one day, I grew sick of it and told myself, *Enough! It's time to get out of my trailer and make a life!*

I decided to go in search of *For Sale* signs. I strolled down Pearl Street, a popular pedestrian-only shopping area. There were no *For Sale* signs anywhere. I walked one block south to Walnut, which didn't have as much foot traffic as Pearl. I was about to give up my search when I came across a store called Vision of Tibet. *Sounds interesting!* When I entered, I was delighted to discover it was owned by two brothers who were Tibetan refugees. I stayed for a while to chat with them, drink tea, and observe their customer volume and flow. When a few customers trickled in, the owners didn't interact with them at all. Instead, they stayed behind the counter and spoke to each other and me in Nepalese. I could see they weren't natural salespeople, and I suspected their store wasn't making it.

A middle-aged woman was browsing and came up to the counter to check out the sunglasses in the case. She pointed to a pair she was interested in. As the owner removed them from the case and handed them to her, I saw they were selling for $50. She slipped them on and checked herself out in the mirror from various angles, like modeling for a photoshoot. She looked a bit like Jackie-O, glamorous, sophisticated.

"How much?" she asked.

Pretending to be a salesman with the figures at my fingertips, I said, "$150." I glanced over at the owners, whose eyes widened.

When the customer hesitated, I wondered if I had aimed too high. I thought we might lose the sale as a result.

She set the sunglasses on the counter. "Okay. I'd like these."

On a hot streak, I sold jewelry to another customer for $50. That night, the owners treated me to Chinese food to celebrate. They were giddy with excitement having never made $200 in one day.

The next day, I returned to Vision of Tibet. One of the owners asked if I might be interested in buying the store. They were tired of the United States and wanted to return home. They told me the store averaged $1,800 per month and rent was $200. They offered me a discount on the inventory.

"If you give me 50 percent, I will negotiate with you," said the owner.

I was interested. I invited them to dinner to discuss the deal.

We painstakingly counted the inventory for two days—the statues, sculptures, tapestries, clothes, jewelry, trinkets, and keepsakes. The owners offered me the store for $25,000 with $12,000 up front. I asked Ellen O'Laughlin, Peter Skafte's attorney friend, to prepare the documents. I promised to bring cash the next day. The only problem was I didn't have the money. Not even close.

That night, I couldn't fall asleep until very late. Kalpana with her son, Darshan, came to the kitchen and fixed me a cup of coffee to calm me down. I kept thinking, *What are you doing? Are you out of your mind, Narayan?* I finally fell asleep at 3:00 am. When I woke up in the wee hours of the morning, a phone number flashed in my mind. I recognized the area code—Austin, Texas. I thought, *Maybe I should dial it and see what happens.* When I called, a familiar male voice answered.

"Who is this?" I asked.

The guy said, "You called me. Who are you?"

"Narayan."

"Oh, Narayan! Hi. How are you?" It was my math professor, Dr. Don Fusell, from the University of Texas at Dallas, who had been a great help to me.

"I'm planning to buy a store in Boulder, and I was wondering if you could help me."

"Well, that's exciting news! I can certainly try. What do you need?"

"I need to borrow $15,000."

"By when?"

"Today."

He laughed. "You could've given me a little more lead time. I'm sorry. I can't help you."

"Well, just in case you somehow come up with it, here's my bank name and account number."

"The money won't magically appear, Narayan. You take care now, and next time you need a loan, please give me some warning. Maybe two days next time!" He chuckled and hung up.

I wondered who else I might tap for a loan, but I came up short.

That morning, I acted as if I had the money to buy the store. I asked Kalpana to go to the store, a five-minute walk from where we parked, while I went to the bank. I didn't cancel the attorney. Yes, I was slightly crazy in those days.

My heart raced as I entered the bank. It would take a miracle for the money to show up in my account. I marched up to the teller, an older lady with half-glasses and a crooked smile, and I gave her my account number.

"I'd like to know how much money I have in my account, but don't tell me. Instead, write it down, please."

I could only see the tip of her pen moving. If she writes three numbers, I'm dead. If she writes more, I'm golden! As the clock ticked, her pen kept moving. I concluded it was a five-numbered figure. *Yes! Thank you, God!*

She handed me the slip of paper with my balance. Sure enough, my friend had come through for me, and I had $15,100 in the bank!

I wanted to jump up and down right there in the bank lobby, but I refrained and instead said, "Thank you, thank you, thank you!"

The teller looked at me like I was slightly nuts, but I didn't care. I was soon to be the proud new owner of Vision of Tibet!

The owners signed the paperwork and agreed to a loan of $12,500. I would pay cash now and $1,000 each month for a year. The last month, I would pay $1,500. I wrote a check for $12,500 from the emergency loan I had received. Phew!

At long last, I had my own business! On the very first day in April of 1986, I only sold about $100. But I didn't despair. I hoped with time, I would become a first-rate salesman, and that Boulderites would fall in love with my store of treasures.

I wanted to change the name of the store—to make it uniquely mine. Diane Skafte suggested "Old Tibet" because we agreed that keeping "Tibet" in the name was a good idea. I secured a city and a state license.

I proceeded to sell $3,000 in two weeks—about $200 per day. Even though my sales were much better than the previous owners', the month was nearly up, and I had accumulated so much debt setting up my business and life in Boulder. I needed to replace the merchandise I sold and pay off the credit card debt. I fretted over my shortfall as the month's end approached, but I thought, *I am a dreamer and a doer, not a loser.* America is the land of opportunity—a place where the doors open when you knock on them, a place where whatever you touch turns to gold. I had to believe.

I raised the prices in my store, so they were on par with market value. Being the only Tibetan-Nepalese import store in the country, my products were unique. In the first month, I had my first $2,000 day when a woman bought a $500 jacket, and a man purchased a rug for $1,500. My store sales ebbed and flowed, but at least they allowed me to pay my expenses.

I had long been interested in leading trips to Nepal, and I was curious if such a venture would fly or if it were a pie-in-the-sky notion. If I were American, I would be interested in exploring Nepal's culture, mountains, delicious food, and getting to know the people. But what did I know? I was biased. I decided to survey climbers in Eldorado Canyon. I asked 100 people the following questions:

1. Have you heard of Nepal?

2. Have you been to Nepal?

3. Would you like to go to Nepal?

I honestly didn't know what to expect, but I thought Nepal could be an unknown country for many Americans. Of the 100 respondents, all knew of Nepal, and 85 wanted to visit! My survey made me realize that Nepal was renowned and admired in Boulder. This simple survey uncovered a rich business opportunity for me.

CHAPTER 6

Footprints Across Nepal

God, help me. If I can, I will help Nepal and her people in the areas of health and education. I'll dedicate myself to these areas.

O LD TIBET, WHICH OPENED IN APRIL, was struggling in the summertime in our Walnut Street location. It was just one block away from Pearl Street, the busy shopping street, but in contrast, there was very little foot traffic on Walnut. And, on scorching summer days, the store was so uncomfortably hot, customers would duck out quickly. Some days, I had zero sales, which made me very unhappy.

The Early Days of Old Tibet

I knew I needed to move the store to Pearl Street. As fate would have it, a woman named Madeleine Day came into my store that summer and said she had heard through the grapevine that I was looking for a new space. She had a place for rent. I locked my store, displayed the *Be Right Back* sign, and went to look at her space. It was 800 square feet for $600 per month, which was $400 more than I was paying on Walnut. I knew I could increase sales, but would I be able to meet all my expenses while tripling my rent?

In my business studies, I learned the first law of business success for a brick-and-mortar store is location. The second law is location. And the third law is location. Location, location, location. The rest depends on luck and talent. I decided to move to the Pearl location in November even though I planned to travel to Nepal that fall and not return until November. Back then, I was unbelievably aggressive, and I didn't worry much about what would happen next. I felt confident, never seeing the darkness ahead and seeing only brightness instead. But I knew I needed to make more happen with a new venture.

I was interested in starting a trekking company, so I made a little sign and posted it inside my store window on Walnut. But because it was illegal to display it outside the window, I put it inside. I knew nothing about trekking in Nepal. I had never trekked in all my life. But I had to infuse trekkers with confidence. I wanted to be the first connection to Nepal. I marketed Nepal by just walking down the street wearing a Nepali hat.

The sign said: *A Nepali native leads trekking trips to the Himalayas. For more information, please come in.* I included my phone number.

That afternoon a couple, Dr. Mark Frank and his wife Karen, a nurse, walked in and asked how much I was charging for my trip. I told them $2,800 per person, including airline tickets. They signed up and gave me a 50 percent deposit on the spot. Within a week, 14 people, eager to travel to Nepal, had signed up. I couldn't believe it! Our trip participants included Bud Holmes and his wife, and Peter Skafte, who would help me lead. Peter received a grant from *National Geographic* to do a story on shamans in Nepal.

I hadn't expected overnight success and hadn't planned for someone to watch the store. The truth was I couldn't go unless I found a stand-in. I asked Damber and Kalpana if they could manage the store during my one-month trip to Nepal knowing that I'd be in trouble if they couldn't help me. Thankfully, they agreed.

"Brother, you must go to Nepal," said Kalpana.

"Yes, brother, please go to Nepal. While you are in Nepal doing business, we will mind your business here while earning money for you," said Damber.

We were set to leave on September 24, 1986. I'd never been to the mountains of Nepal before, so I was excited but slightly nervous. I was eager to host my new friends from Colorado. I was hopeful that I would have enough money to help my family, yet I wondered if I could lead a trekking trip because I was an inexperienced trekker.

The departure date was fast approaching. I spent most of the money I collected from the trekkers to pay my debts. I paid for the airline tickets and hotels in Bangkok and Kathmandu in advance. I also purchased food for the trek. And I needed money to buy merchandise in Nepal for my store. To my new landlady, Madeleine Day, I paid a down payment—the deposit and one month's rent. I didn't have much money left. I wasn't doing well in business; sales were way down in summer. I couldn't make the rent or pay my other expenses in Boulder. I knew I needed to help my family in Nepal with so many mouths to feed. But the money simply wasn't there. I worried day and night.

One day in my apartment in Boulder, Damber and Kalpana approached me in tears. "Tell us what's wrong with you," said Damber.

"Nothing," I said, looking away, trying to be strong.

"No, there's something. We can tell. You're not fooling us," said Kalpana.

"I'm fine," I said, even though I wasn't. I didn't want to burden them with my troubles.

The next morning, they wrote me a long letter and left it on my bed:

Dear Brother,

We know there's something wrong with you. If you don't tell us what's going on, there's nothing we can help you with. You need to be upfront with us. Is it us? Is it you? Or is it something else? You must tell us, and then we can help you when you are gone.

Reluctantly, I told them I needed money. I explained how I spent the money from the trekkers, and how much I had left. I told them I had already paid off most of my debts with the money. I said that I didn't have enough money to cover all my expenses.

"I have some money," Damber said. "How much do you need?"

I told him how much I needed to buy merchandise and give my family a little as well.

"You know what? I'll loan you what you need," said Damber. Working as a research assistant under a professor at Colorado State University (CSU) in Fort Collins, Colorado, while earning a Ph.D. in hydroelectric engineering, he had stashed money away.

The next day, he lent me enough money to save me and my business. Damber and Kalpana were a pillar of support to me during that time. They were always there when I needed them, and I feel forever indebted.

Dr. Damber Nepali is now a Dean of Engineering at Kathmandu University in Nepal.

Days before I left for Nepal, Damber and Kalpana brought me a worshiping plate with rice and flowers to say goodbye and to wish me good luck on my first trekking trip. We were in the store standing around the display case with jewelry and trinkets.

Kalpana said, "Will you do one thing for me?"

"Sure, anything," I said.

"Will you find yourself a good lady friend?"

"I can't promise that. How can I know fate?"

"You can't, but if there's one thing I know. You need a good woman in your life." She blessed me.

I promised myself I would not marry another American woman or even a Nepali woman living in the United States. I was determined to marry someone from Nepal. I hoped to find a long-haired woman who was beautiful, skinny, and educated. And she had to be the only girl in the house. I couldn't afford to shower many sisters with gifts every time I visited, as was the Nepali custom. But how could I ever find her?

My First Trek

After staying in Kathmandu for four days, our Sherpas and trekkers headed to Khandbari. The head of the Sherpas, Pasang Sherpa, was our cook and organizer. He later became a member of the Nepali parliament and a philanthropist, having become wealthy through owning land and conducting business in Belgium.

Over a hundred people came to meet us at the airport after walking three hours uphill from my village. The few horses were used to transport the elderly folks.

We walked back to the village together. Everyone was so excited to see my trekking group and me. The villagers had never seen so many gringos. I put the trekkers up in my home and other village homes for two nights. It was festival time, and people celebrated by eating at each other's homes. Plates were in short supply, so hosts would serve food on makeshift plates of leaves, covered in dust and bugs. Naturally, the trekkers' digestive systems weren't accustomed to such things. After consuming bugs, dust, and Nepali food, they all came down with stomach problems and diarrhea. Even Peter, who was used to eating Nepalese food, got sick.

Oh no! This is a terrible way to start my first trek. I should have known better. Thankfully, Dr. Frank and Karen treated everyone with the medicine we brought.

While the trekkers were laying low nursing their Nepali belly problems, my older brother Bashu Dai took me aside and shared my family's continuing financial problems—my father's enormous debts, my older brother's and other siblings' debt. I gave them some money, but it wasn't enough to provide total relief.

Bashu Dai was separated from the family because his family was becoming a burden. His wife was responsible for feeding him, their six daughters, and herself. To that end, she sold handcrafted cigarettes supplemented with a paltry income from growing rice on land my parents gave them.

In addition to his financial woes, Bashu Dai's health was failing; his liver was in bad shape. Dr. Frank estimated he had just two years to live. The whole town assumed he was going to die. Thankfully, the community hadn't lost all respect for him because he was the first-born of my father, Surya Bahadur Shrestha, who was highly renowned in the district.

After a couple of days of sickness, the trekkers were ready to go. We set out for our first day of trekking, planning to have lunch in the next village of Chandanpur. It had rained all night, and the roads and trails were muddy and slippery. Dr. Frank and I needed to take a quick bathroom break, so we darted over to a grassy area with a little cliff. Dr. Frank jumped first and did his business. I followed him, trying to do the same. I jumped down the cliff with muddy shoes, slipped, and twisted my ankle. I cried out in pain. Dr. Frank came running over to see what had happened, then carried me back to the lunch spot. He gave me painkillers, which I readily swallowed with tea.

The Shaman with the Torch

When my father heard about my injury, he sent a Nepali shaman to heal my ankle. He knew our team included an American doctor, but he didn't believe in Western medicine.

The shaman, a wrinkled old man with missing teeth, wearing a long strand of mala beads, appeared at our camp. He was a *dhami-jhankri* shaman, carrying a drum (dhyangro), and wearing bells around the waist, long necklaces (mala) of rudracche and ritho seeds around his neck and shoulders, and a long white skirt-like garment (jama). Jhankris can counteract the power of the witches.

The spectacle caused quite a stir among our trekking crew, fascinated by the Nepali medicine man.

"What are you doing here?" I asked.

"I am here to heal you," he said, digging around in his pouch.

"It's a twisted ankle. How are you are going to heal that?" I asked, aware of the limitations of traditional Nepali medicine.

"You don't understand. I can heal you," he said, extracting a stick for fire from his pouch.

"How?"

"My assistant and I will hold your leg steady and burn your ankle with fire until it penetrates the injury. There will be a pop, which will release the pain, and you'll be healed. It will be a miracle healing session with chanting and prayer."

I didn't want him torching my ankle. "No, I don't want you to do that."

But everyone urged me to be brave and give the healer a chance. Despite my reservations, I agreed to go ahead with it. People gathered, and trekkers readied their cameras with flashbulbs poised against the darkness. The shaman approached me with his burning stick while his assistant chanted. Locals held me steady for the torching.

When I felt the flame close to my ankle, I cried, "Stop! I don't care if I lose my foot. I don't want you to burn my flesh. I won't be able to take the pain."

The shaman withdrew his small flame in a rage, ranting about my lack of faith in Nepal's ancient healing traditions. Even though I fed him and gave him plenty of Raksi, the local whiskey, he was still upset that I had rejected his approach. Instead, I continued taking the painkillers that Dr. Frank gave me, which took the edge off the pain.

A Small Miracle

During lunch on the same day as the shaman incident, a middle-aged woman wearing a purple scarf and a red dress approached us. She looked like she needed help.

"Didi, what can I do for you?" Didi is a term used by Nepali people, which means older sister.

"I have some terrible news. My 13-year-old son fell off a Ferris wheel and landed on a stick." She called her boy forward.

I winced when I saw the stick puncturing his chin and protruding from his mouth. His face was so swollen; his right eye was a slit in a sea of inflammation.

Dr. Frank rushed over.

"He can't swallow and hasn't eaten for a week. Can you help us?" The mother in distress joined her hands in prayer.

I strongly suspected if we didn't do anything right away, her son would die. The hospital in Khandbari was about a half-day away. But with no doctors or equipment, they wouldn't be able to help. We had Dr. Frank on our trip but very little medicine in our bags.

I asked, "Where's your husband?"

She called her husband over.

"Help us. You are our last hope," he said.

I asked Dr. Frank if he thought he could help this boy.

"I can certainly try, but without anesthesia and surgical tools, I'm not sure we will succeed."

I translated for Dr. Frank. "Your boy needs help right away. We're willing to work on extracting the stick, but there are no guarantees. If something goes wrong, you cannot hold us responsible. Do you still want to do this?" I asked the boy's parents.

They begged us to go ahead.

We took the boy to our tent. Dr. Frank said we would need five people to hold him down while he did the surgery—one to hold his head, two for his arms, and two for his legs. Dr. Frank pulled out his pocketknife, and one of our Sherpas sterilized it by burning and boiling it.

I was too squeamish to watch the extraction, so I ducked out of the tent. The boy's screaming and crying went on for four hours. As the cries of anguish continued, I nearly lost hope. My twisted ankle pain was nothing in comparison. Perhaps it was an impossible task with such rudimentary tools. At least we tried.

The silence of my despair was interrupted by someone exclaiming, "Yes! He took it out!" One of the impromptu surgical assistants burst out of the tent.

I hurried over to the makeshift surgery unit and watched as Dr. Frank carefully stitched the sutures. Although the boy's face was swollen, he was able to close his mouth.

We had saved the boy's life!

The boy's parents said their prayers had been answered—that we were brought here by God. His mother wept in gratitude and blessed us over and over again. We gave them bandages and two weeks' worth of antibiotics and sent them on their way. We would later discover, when our trekkers returned to Khandbari, the boy's wound was black and blue but healing well. He ran around, playing games—a completely different boy than I had first seen. I could tell he would have a scar, but he was alive to tell his dramatic story of being saved by a trekking crew from America.

That evening our team stayed in the same spot.

Forsaken Hills and Valleys

On the third day, I was still limping and walking with a stick. That morning, we crossed the bridge of the Arun River and walked uphill to Tamku, a village in northeastern Nepal with a population of around 3,000.

A petite woman approached our group, dressed in a flowing yellow-and-green *guniu*, carrying a large basket, and said, "Who is the person I can talk to?"

A Sherpa said, "So, this is our leader. You can talk to him."

"If there is any doctor in your group, I am carrying my daughter to the hospital, which is a day away."

I detected a foul odor. "What? You're carrying a child? How old is she?"

"Five years old," she said.

"What happened?"

"She fell from a tree and hit her head on a rock when she was cutting branches for our goat. It happened a month ago," the mother said.

"Why didn't you take her that day?" I asked.

"We didn't think it was necessary because the bump wasn't very big. But it's growing bigger and bigger, and now it's so smelly."

"Okay. Put her down, and I will ask our doctor to look at her." I called Dr. Frank over.

Dr. Frank peered into the basket, recoiled at the odor, and with sad eyes, said to me, "Her child is dead. She has been dead for a long time."

I inhaled for courage and translated his words in my head. *How am I going to tell her? How can I tell her that she is carrying a dead child to the hospital? I had to find the courage to tell her.* I said very politely with courage, "Didi. Your child is dead. You're carrying your dead girl to the hospital. There's nothing we can do. She's gone."

The mother's screams echoed over the hills and valleys. Her haunting bellows implanted themselves inside us. The echoing cries poured into the silence of the hills, mountains, and valley as if the mountains themselves were heaving in grief, as if the cries were a blanket of fog obscuring the peaceful setting.

Both experiences had a profound effect on me. In the first case, we were able to save the boy's life. In the second, because the mother had no access to healthcare, she lost her daughter. The contrast between the two inspired me to do something for my people that they couldn't do for themselves. It made me realize that timely access to quality healthcare made the difference between life and death. I was in pain for the entire trekking trip, limping up and down the hills, but seeing the health needs and interacting with village people took away my pain. The people gave me strength and inspired me to give back. I felt I had been sent to witness a deep need of the Nepali people.

The Shaman with the Feather

We arrived in a village with a cave, a lush mountainous village with less than 1,000 inhabitants. Five of us stayed while the rest of the group set out to climb the nearby Lamini Peak. Isabella Iverson was from Dallas, and Peter had a *National Geographic* project to write an article about shamans in Nepal. Even though I was skeptical, I hired another shaman to heal my ankle so I could help Peter with his project. I checked to make sure he would treat me with a soft touch, and I hired him.

With Peter shooting footage, the second shaman, with the same regalia as the torch-bearing healer, started the ritual with chanting, dancing, and drumming. His two assistants kept the drumbeat going as he touched my ankle with a feather. He invoked spirits and invited me to communicate with them. He applied medicine with the feather—using a light, soft, healing touch—on my swollen ankle. It was a magical experience for me.

The shaman asked me to get up from the chair. Clutching my walking stick, I tried to stand up. The shaman approached me, grabbed my stick, and flung it aside. "Stand up."

I stood up, expecting a shooting pain, but there was none.

"Walk."

I walked, thinking I would hobble, but I walked normally.

"How about now?" the shaman asked.

"No pain," I said.

"What?" Peter said. "Impossible."

"Seriously. No pain."

"Amazing!" Peter said. "I got it all on video!"

I gave the shaman money, whiskey, and food and thanked him for healing me. He and his assistants packed up their drums, feathers, and medicine and disappeared over the footpath.

Four days later, the group met up with us. After their incredible adventure in the mountains, they were exhausted but exhilarated.

Dr. Frank asked, "How's your ankle, Narayan?"

"No pain. The swelling is down."

"Oh, great, the medicine worked."

"I haven't taken your medicine for four days."

"What? That's kind of a miracle," said Dr. Frank, shaking his head.

I smiled, thinking maybe the rituals of the shamans in the Nepali hills worked after all. Before leaving Nepal for the United States in 1977, we depended entirely on shamans for healing. As a child, I believed in them. It made me happy to think that perhaps a little bit of trust remained.

After we set up camp on one of our last nights, a local teacher came and sat next to us in front of the campfire the Sherpas had built. Some trekkers were singing and playing music.

By the light of the fire, he explained that he was a teacher with three class levels in a one-room schoolhouse with no furniture. "I haven't been paid for five months."

"What are you talking about?! How do you eat?" I asked, appalled.

"I eat my parent's food. That's how I survive." He shrugged.

Holy smokes!

In the morning, the teacher joined us for tea and then gave me a tour of the one-room schoolhouse. There was a makeshift roof, but you could see the drifting clouds through the slats. The dirt floor was dust-covered. A locally made straw blanket was placed in the middle of the room for the students to sit on while the teacher presented the lessons.

I said to myself, *God help me. If I can, I will help Nepal and her people in the areas of health and education. People are needlessly dying from minor things. When I go back to the US, I must find people to bring over here and offer treatment. Children are being educated in rickety shacks with no furniture or school supplies. Maybe I can build a school.*

I was zeroing in on my mission, my reason for being. Thinking back on the boy with the stick, it felt so good to be able to provide life-saving treatment to my people. The needs in Nepal were so great, but if I could start by providing help in my corner of the world, I could expand from there. My life's work was beginning to take shape.

But still, something was missing.

Photo Gallery I

In this first of two photo galleries, I include photographs of my early years in Khandbari, Nepal, including the house in which I was born, my parents, and siblings.

My first professional job was to manage Tumlingtar Airport, where my horse, Hire, saved my life when I was ready to give up. When I left Nepal for America, I flew from this airport.

When I first settled in Colorado, it was in Eldorado Springs, a small town near Boulder in the foothills of the Rocky Mountains. From here, I launched my first business.

I returned to Nepal countless times, leading medical teams and building a school, Surya Boarding School. On one of these trips, I had a fateful encounter with two shamans.

Igor Gamow, a University of Colorado professor and the inventor of the Gamow Bag, helped me run my Semester in Nepal program, and joined me on many treks to Nepal.

During my life, I have met many influential people, including His Holiness the 14th Dalai Lama, kings of Nepal, US President Jimmy Carter, Sir Edmund Hillary, and other dignitaries.

My wife, Sreejana Shrestha, and I.

Our family photo taken in Khandbari in 1964. My brother Dharma Raj is on the left. I'm in the very back. Another brother, Dev Ananda (DN), is standing in front of me. My sister, Shanti, is to my right. My brother Bashu Dev is holding my brother Sunil.

My mother, Chhanda Kumari Shrestha, (seated) with her helper at her home in 1981.

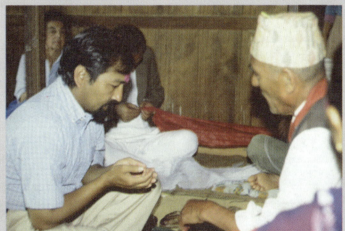

My father blessing me.

My father blessing family members during festivities in Khandbari in 1986.

Sreejana in 1993. Her beauty
still amazes me.

My sister, Shanti Shrestha,
in 1973.

(Photo credit: Peter Skafte)

My father in-law, Ayodhya Prasad Maskey, (standing to the right of car in
a white hat) saying farewell to his daughter, Sreejana, after our wedding.
Sreejana and I are inside the car. (April 20, 1987)

My elder uncle, Chandra Bahadur Shrestha, and his wife sitting in front of my birth house in 1973.

(Photo credit: Peter Skafte)

My uncle Chandra Bahadur Shrestha (in the center wearing a hat and facing away from the camera) mediating an argument about land between two groups. He was a respected leader in my village.

(Photo credit: Peter Skafte)

I purchased a horse and gave it to my uncle Chandra Bahadur Shrestha who lived to be 93. He was always good to me when I was a child. This picture was taken at the building in which I was born. Over 50 people were born here. (1991)

From left to right: My oldest brother, Bashu Dai, my father, my youngest brother, Jiban, my mother, and Peter Skafte. (1981)

(Photo credit: Peter Skafte)

I'm in front of my birthplace in Khandbari. Peeking through the window, you can see the dark room in which I was born.

The grade school I attended in 1958 built by my great-great grandfather over 100 years ago. My father brought a teacher from India to instruct a classroom of 20 students, including me.

My father blessing Håkan Wahlquist during the biggest Hindu festival, Durga Puja (Dasain) in 1973.

I'm with Hire, the horse that saved my life. (1976)

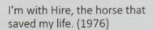

I'm posing while dancing at a picnic site. (1976)

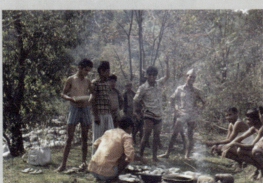

Khandbari is at the foot of Mount Makalu, the fifth highest in the world. Shaped like a chair, this is one of my favorite peaks.

Every Saturday, people come from the surrounding hills and villages to the Khandbari market to sell and barter vegetables, clothes, spices, oil, livestock, and meat. (1972)

The Saturday marketplace in Khandbari in 1973.

The Khandbari gateway in 1992.

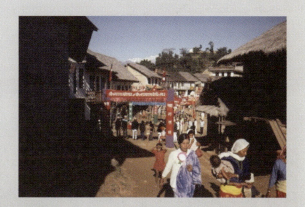

King Birendra was supposed to come to Khandbari but canceled his appearance. (1972)

When my Boulder friends and I visited Khandbari in 1986, a couple hundred people came to greet us. It was the first time that people in my village had ever seen foreigners.

When I visited in 1986 with friends from Boulder, the Sherpas living in Khandbari performed a dance to welcome us.

A team of trekker friends from Boulder posing with my parents in front of their home in Khandbari in 1986.

At 20, I held my first professional job at the
Tumlingtar Airport. I had the distinct honor
of being the first staff member.

The first charter plane
landed at Tumlingtar
Airport in 1972 while I was
the manager. Dr. Håkan
Wahlquist chartered a flight
to Num, where he was
assigned to earn a Ph.D.
while studying the Chhetri
tribe, a warrior/ruler caste.

Twin Otter aircraft preparing to take off from Tumlingtar Airport to Kathmandu in 1972.

The Tumlingtar Airport runway in 1972.   Waiting for a plane to arrive.

(Photo credit: Håkan Wahlquist)

For many years, the Tumlingtar Airport didn't have a communication system. The only way to
know when a plane arrived was to see it come in for a landing. We typically waited hours for
planes to arrive.

My good friend, Sukadav Shrestha, and I at the Tumlingtar Airport in 1975 when I worked there.

Greeting people from Khandbari at the Tumlingtar airport in 1999. The pilot on the left is from Chainpur of the Khandbari region.

(Photo credit: Peter Skafte)

This picture was taken from the plane at the Tumlingtar Airport in 1977 as I left for the US for the first time.

This is how we landed at the Tumlingtar Airport in 1992. We paid just $15 to get to Tumlingtar from Kathmandu. The airfield is now paved and modernized. The same flight costs $300.

The road that leads to the beautiful town of Eldorado Springs near Boulder, Colorado.

My remarkable first house in Colorado when I moved from Dallas to Boulder. This is the house from which I started my first business—Nepali classes paired with Nepali cuisine. I lived there from November 1985 to April 1986.

The Old Tibet store in Boulder. It has occupied the same location on Pearl Street since 1986.

The first customer purchasing merchandise at Old Tibet on our opening day, April 8, 1986.

In 2015, I spoke with the students of the Surya Boarding School, inspiring them with my story and talking about hardship and success. I guided them in the right direction by encouraging them to stay positive and to never give up.

The Surya Boarding School in Khandbari as it looks today. Currently, 900 students are served by 55 staff members.

An aerial photo of Khandbari in 1988. Every time I flew in and out of Tumlingtar to Kathmandu, I asked the pilots, who were my friends, to fly over my village.

The red boundary marks the 80 acres of land purchased from nine different families for the Surya Boarding School.

The first Surya Boarding School students in 1988 when we had only two teachers and 35 students in two rented rooms. A teacher from Cherry Creek Elementary School in Denver donated 4,000 ballpoint pens, 1,300 books, and a few thousand notebooks for its first library.

The opening day of the Surya Boarding School in 1988. It opened with three students and two teachers. Handwashing was the first lesson that the teacher gave the children.

A performance for Teachers' Day at the Surya Boarding School.

In 1986, during my first hike to Khembalung with 14 hiking friends from Boulder, I fell on a slippery path and twisted my ankle. My father sent a shaman to heal my swollen ankle, so I could walk without pain. The shaman, poised with a flame, planned to burn my ankle, egged on by my friends Dr. Frank and Dr. Skafte. But I refused to let him torch my flesh, which angered him. I gave the shaman local tequila, and he went to bed quietly.

The next day as we continued hiking toward Khembalung, Dr. Frank gave me pain medication. Unfortunately, it didn't completely alleviate the pain and I was waylaid by my swollen ankle. The local shaman performed a healing ritual, and three hours later, he applied a healing salve to my ankle. After that, I miraculously walked with no pain.

During our hike from Khembalung to Khandbari, we built our own bridge to cross the roaring river that blocked our passage. Mark, Bill, and Dok proudly and bravely crossed the bridge.

Igor Gamow's first mission to Nepal in 1987 experimenting with his invention later called the Gamow Bag. I arranged for him to be at the basecamp of Mount Everest in March.

In 1989, Igor Gamow and I led our first Semester in Nepal Program under the SANN Research Institute. We walked five days from the roadside to the hills, crossing swollen rivers with strong currents. We were afraid to cross barefoot with no luggage while the porters who carried our 80-pound loads had no problem crossing the rivers. We followed their lead.

The first group of seven students in the Semester in Nepal program are crossing the river to get to Khandbari. Jennifer Dingman is the girl in the red shirt.

A Semester in Nepal student during her ten-day village experience. Mount Manaslu is in the background.

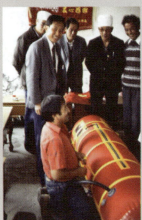

In 1990, I donated a Gamow Bag to the Boulder-Lhasa Sister City Organization. The organization gave it to the hospital in Lhasa, Tibet.

In 1992, a photographer friend from Boulder and I went to see Sir Edmund Hillary at his hotel in Kathmandu. I had previously met him in Boulder to help raise funds for his cause—the Sherpa people of Khumbu, a region in the Mount Everest area. After summiting Everest in 1953, he became devoted to helping the Sherpa community.

Sreejana and I with Sir Edmund Hillary and his wife, June, in 1993.

In 2001, my family traveled to India, Nepal, and China. We're pictured here at the Great Wall of China.

In 1992, I spoke in front of Prime Minister Girija Prasad Koirala and a few other Nepali ministers the day before our helicopter ride to inaugurate the Bandipur Helping Hands Clinic. This night, I presented medical equipment to the government of Nepal.

1992, The Minister of Local Development in Nepal, Mr. Ram Chandra Paudyal (standing center). Mr. Paudyal gave me a tour of the Bandipur hospital. That was the beginning of Helping Hand's involvement in Bandipur. Once the town was dead, but after working for 16 years on revitalizing Bandipur, the town was reborn.

Mr. Sher Bahadur Deuba, the four-term Prime Minister of Nepal, and I at his residence.

This scene is from the town of Hile, Dhankuta District in 2004. When I visit Nepali villages, they often give me a hero's welcome with a procession, including music and dance. Those gathered walk to the village medical camp or the host family's home.

After four camps in Bandipur, I got an invitation from the Royal Palace in October of 1994. The Palace sent a car and we drove all night to my hotel in Kathmandu. I met with King Birendra the following evening. He graciously thanked me for serving Nepal and her people. He said, "You are a son of Nepal who cares, even though you live far away. You've never forgotten your roots. I need ten Narayans, but I can settle for one." This was the first of many meetings.

On June 1, 2000, I met with the Crown Prince of Nepal, Dipendra Bir Bikram Shah Dev, for the first time to arrange for his education at the University of Colorado, Boulder. A year later, on the same day, the Crown Prince massacred the royal family.

King Gyanendra and I meeting for the first time on June 1, 2002. This was the same room in which I met the late King Birendra. I met the Crown Prince two years before to the date and the Crown Prince massacred the royal family a year before to the date.

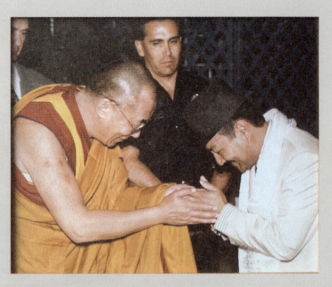

Meeting His Holiness the 14th Dalai Lama in 1997 at the Denver Pepsi Center. I was co-chair of the welcoming committee.

The 39th President of the United States Jimmy Carter, the president of Costa Rica and I at the University of California San Diego in 2003.

At a fundraising event in 2010 for Jared Polis (on the left) who was running for a second term as a congressman for Colorado District 2. He was elected governor in 2018. On the right is Congresswoman Nancy Pelosi, the first woman and a two-time Speaker of the US House of Representatives, the second time starting in 2019.

CHAPTER 7

My Good Luck Charm

Sometimes you don't know what you're missing until you find it.

AS I WRAPPED UP MY VERY FIRST trekking expedition, my sister, Shanti, was busy seeking good marriage candidates. In quick succession, I was introduced to six women and their families. My sister, friends, and I were invited to their homes for special tea ceremonies hosted by the parents. The homes sparkled from days of cleaning and preparation. The girls dressed for the occasion with jazzy clothes and eye-catching makeup.

The Inquisition

I knew the parents had already checked my background by talking to friends, neighbors, and acquaintances. Because I was independent, I researched the young women myself instead of relying on my parents to do it. And because I lived in the US, my sister, Shanti, was a big help.

In Nepal, arranged marriages are customary. The way it works is both sets of parents meet to determine whether their children are a good match based on each family's background and standing in their community. If the parents decide their son and daughter are a good match, the marriage proceeds. Families usually know each other and have their eyes on potential mates. Boys and girls typically have no choice in the matter; if they fall in love, they cannot marry until their parents approve. If the parents disapprove, it's not uncommon for the pair to run away.

Some of the women Shanti found weren't the right match for me. For others, I wasn't the right man for them. I eventually grew tired of the process and realized I would return to the US empty-handed. Oh, well, better luck next time, as my American friends liked to say.

Two days before I was scheduled to fly home to Boulder, I was having dinner at a friend's home. Mr. Deepak Bohara was the Minister of Transportation. My sister was also there helping the women prepare and serve the traditional Nepali gourmet meal.

She ran over to me. "I think we have a woman for you!" Clearly, my sister was working on more than just the meal preparation.

"No, thanks. I don't have time to meet anyone else. I'll come back next year." I waved her away and turned to resume my conversation with the dinner guests.

But my sister wasn't having it. "No, no, you don't believe me. She's exactly your type. You said long hair, slim, educated—right?"

I nodded.

"Only girl in the house?"

"Right."

"And do you mind if she has brothers?" Shanti asked.

"No, brothers are okay."

"Okay, I think we have a match!" Shanti said, more enthusiastic than I had seen her since she first met her husband.

"I'll meet her next year," I said, trying again.

"I'll arrange tea for tomorrow morning. Oh, and by the way, her name is Sreejana."

I laughed at my sister's persistence. Her optimism made up for mine, which was sorely lacking. "Well, okay, just tea."

The next morning, I hailed a taxi to Sreejana's home. I was still sporting my trekking look with long stringy hair, a goatee, and casual clothes. I took a jacket, but it was dirty.

Sreejana, who had apparently spotted me from the third-floor window, refused to come down to meet me. She told her family I was filthy, too short, and not her type. "Don't bother me," she said.

Dejected, I told my friend Pranti Sherchan she had refused to meet me.

"Of course, she did. She's no fool. Look at you!"

I hadn't looked at myself in a mirror since I had arrived in Nepal months ago. I looked wild after my trekking expedition. Wild and like a bum—like the hippies who had taken over Kathmandu.

Pranti said, "Get a haircut, friend. Shave off that silly goatee. Shave off everything, except for your mustache. You must wear a suit, tie, and nice shoes. And don't go by taxi. Take a private car."

I did as he advised and borrowed a car from a pilot friend, Captain B. M. Amatya.

Sreejana's parents had done their homework on me, reaching out to people familiar with my family and me. They discovered I hailed from a well-respected family. They knew she wouldn't have to suffer taking care of a large family because she would live alone with me. They saw that she would be the boss of the house. On the other hand, they knew that Sreejana would have to leave the country and would not be able to finish her master's degree in business law. Equally important was the 13-year age difference.

I arrived for my meeting a changed man, at least on the outside. On the inside, I was a bit nervous. I was ushered to the family room, where I waited to meet Sreejana.

Meanwhile, Shanti, Pranti's sister Darpan, and Pranti's older sister-in-law tried to convince her to meet me. I learned later that she was opposed to marrying an older man. But Pranti's older sister-in-law, married to a man 16 years older, urged her to give me a chance. They really worked on her, saying things like, "You don't have to marry him. You only have to talk to him."

After an hour and a half, growing more anxious by the minute, I asked Pranti for a shot of whiskey. He obliged, and I calmed down. Thirty minutes later, Darpan popped in and shared the good news that Sreejana had agreed to meet me. She and Shanti rushed upstairs to bring Sreejana down while Pranti and I waited behind closed doors.

The three ladies entered, then left Sreejana with me, Pranti closing the door from the outside. They tried to record our conversation but apparently forgot to press the Record button. Shanti and Darpan listened on the other side of the door.

When I first glimpsed Sreejana's elegance and poise, I was very pleased I hadn't waited another year. Another gentleman might have snatched her up.

Sreejana sat in a chair by the door, holding her face with a handkerchief. "Good evening," she said, pleasantly but formally, making quick eye contact and then casting her gaze downward. She sat with her legs and feet lined up perfectly.

"Good evening." I was seated on a couch, a good distance away from her. I was taken with her long shiny hair, slim figure, and stunning beauty.

She folded her hands in her lap and immediately got down to business. "I heard you were married once before."

Uh-oh. I shifted on the couch. "Yes, ma'am." Back then, many Nepali women would not consider marrying a divorcee. I tried to read her, but she had a darned-good poker face.

"How long were you married?" she asked.

"Four years. But I cried the night we were married. It was up and down the whole time, never a happy marriage."

"And you have a child?"

Wow. She's done her homework. Is this a deal-breaker? "Yes, ma'am."

"Son?"

"Yes."

"How old is he?"

"Nathan's five."

"Do you love your child?"

"Yes, ma'am. He's my son."

She shifted on the chair and looked at me more intently. "Child support is very strict in the US. Are you paying child support?"

How in the world does she know about child custody law in the US? "Yes, ma'am."

"On time?"

"Yes, ma'am."

"I heard you have a shop. Is it successful?"

"Yes, it is!" I was animated describing Old Tibet.

Her inquisition continued for about 20 minutes, as though she were deposing me in legal proceedings. Every question she asked impressed me. As she fired smart questions at me, I grew more attracted to her. Her intelligence was evident in her line of questioning. I knew that she was seriously vetting me because she would've excused herself if she weren't. This was a woman who knew what she wanted.

She paused.

I sighed, realizing I had been holding my breath because I really cared what she thought. She was nothing like the rest. She was in a league of her own. "Any more questions, ma'am?"

"No more." She glanced toward the door as though she were done with our session and ready to go.

"May I ask you a question?"

"Yes."

"Will you marry me?" As the words left my mouth, I thought, *Am I nuts? I just met this woman.*

Sreejana didn't answer, so I made my request more polite. "Will you *please* marry me?" I bowed.

She said nothing but nodded.

I wasn't satisfied with her silent consent, so I bent down on one knee. "Will you please marry me, ma'am?" I begged her. I knew there was something special about her. I knew in my heart she was the one.

She blinked several times. "Yes." She adjusted her dress and got up.

I wanted to throw my arms around her, but I knew it was not the time. Restraint was the order of the day. But restraint is, oh, so hard when your heart is singing.

I postponed my trip home to get married in court. Chief District Officer, Mr. Rameshwor Shrestha, a relative of both Sreejana and me, went to great lengths to expedite our marriage. Two days later, he officiated our official ceremony, where we signed the documents to get married. My parents and Sreejana's mother were among the witnesses who attended our ceremony. Her father, a stern government officer in land reform, was unable to attend because he was out of town. My parents were thrilled I had finally found a woman of substance and good character from a respectable family.

To my dismay, her parents would not allow me to take my bride on a date alone. We were legally husband and wife, but we couldn't see each other without a chaperone, and we were not allowed to kiss. After pleading with them, they permitted us to have dinner with some friends and my sister and her husband. We were given just two hours and a strict curfew.

While I was in Nepal, my trusted friends, Damber and Kalpana, moved Old Tibet to Pearl Street. I returned to a store that was set up and run beautifully. With the store in capable hands, I turned my focus to my new venture.

Given that I was the only Nepali in Colorado running a trekking business to Nepal, I decided my next move would be to generate media interest. To that end, I pitched my trekking business to *The Denver Post*. My story piqued a newspaper reporter's interest, and *The Denver Post* did a front-page article: "Nepali Native Leads Treks to the Himalayas." When it hit the newsstands, I grabbed several copies and read it with pride. But I wondered if there would be any interest in the piece.

The day the story ran, our phone rang at 10:01 am, the minute our store opened, and it rang off the hook for days! Trekking enthusiasts called from

Denver, Boulder, Colorado Springs, Aspen, and beyond. Kalpana and I could hardly manage all the calls and bookings.

On the heels of my success with *The Denver Post*, I reached out to Denver's Channel 12, who had an auction during their fundraising event. I donated a live auction item—two treks to the Himalayas in April.

I had picked April to coincide with our wedding set for April 20. I booked two groups: one was a wedding group of six people, the other a trekking group of five. The travelers and trekkers purchased full-price tickets through me, for which I earned a commission. I made money off the travel and trekking tickets.

My Wedding in Nepal

We had a lovely wedding in Kathmandu, followed by a huge party at a five-star hotel, where we spent our honeymoon. Our ceremony lasted all day and night. The next morning, as is customary, we went to Sreejana's home so she could say goodbye to her relatives. They were forlorn because she would be leaving their family for a new one.

In Nepali culture, when the groom prepares to take the bride away after the wedding, the bride's father must pay a dowry—money, property, or special gifts—to the groom or the groom's family. With this custom weighing heavily on him, Sreejana's dad pulled me into a corner of his home with tears in his eyes. "I can't give you anything. I have given you my daughter. I'm sorry I can't offer you more than Sreejana. Please take good care of her."

I said, "I don't need anything more. You have given me a jewel, a pearl, a diamond, a priceless human being. You have raised her perfectly, and I'm taking that perfect human being away from you. I treasure that."

I was supposed to bring Sreejana back with me after the second wedding. But, once again, I could not. I didn't obtain my citizenship on time. When I came back to the United States without Sreejana, it was so painful. We struggled mightily being apart but kept our love alive through letter writing.

With each letter, I fell more deeply in love with her. Her poetic words took my breath away; they were so lyrical and expressive. I read and reread her letters, crying on the second or third reads. I wondered when we would be together again.

Sreejana had the same feelings. Our love affair blossomed. Phone calls were difficult back then, so we spoke only once a week. When I received her letters, it was like winning a million dollars and carrying it in my pocket. I sometimes shared her letters with Damber and Kalpana, almost in tears. I thought, *This is what a man and woman's love is all about.*

Narayan's Gateway to Nepal

When I returned to Boulder in the spring of 1987, I opened Narayan's Gateway to Nepal travel agency for trips to Thailand and Nepal, and occasionally to India. I designated a room in Old Tibet as the office for my new company. My store was struggling, but it had given birth to my thriving travel agency. At the time, potential customers weren't interested enough in what I was selling in the store, including singing bowls, jewelry, and other Buddhist artifacts. One reason we survived was the influence of Trungpa Rinpoche and Naropa University. Rinpoche was a famous Buddhist teacher based in Boulder who converted almost 8,000 locals to Buddhism. In 1974, he founded Naropa, a private Buddhist-inspired university.

When I opened Old Tibet, Joe O'Laughlin was very generous with his time, helping me. He fixed shelves and drove me around. I offered him a job at my travel agency, and he accepted. Just as I had wished ten years earlier in the University of Colorado cafeteria, Joe came to work for me. That year, he joined my office staff, answering the phone, talking with clients, and delivering tickets.

Joe would come to my mobile home in Eldorado Springs and help in any way he could. For example, he would hand me water through my window whenever the pipes froze, and the mobile home door was frozen shut.

Joe worked for me for a year and a half, until he resigned. He was a big part of my life in Boulder when I was trying to establish my business. Over the years, Joe was always a good friend, helpful, and kind.

I continued advertising three-week trips to Nepal for two. I came up with an idea for Channel 12. I invited them to travel to Nepal with me to capture the vanishing culture of my village and make a documentary. They sent a crew with filmmaking equipment and titled the project: *All Roads Lead to Nepal.*

Another article about my travel agency appeared in the *Rocky Mountain News,* pulling in 18 people from Fort Collins, Denver, Boulder, Aspen, and Vail. I had cornered the market in Colorado for trekking in Nepal. To Coloradans, I was Nepal! As I strolled the streets of Boulder in my Nepali hat, many people recognized I was the local Nepali man.

Bringing Sreejana Home

In the summer of 1987, I went to the Immigration Office in Denver to interview for citizenship once again. I told myself as I drove to Denver, "Narayan, don't blow it this time!" I was jittery given how much was at stake. My wife was waiting for me at the other end of the world.

I arrived at the office with a shiny floor and high ceilings. The place was empty. I was the only one there, which is unheard of now. These days, hundreds line up for immigration services.

I tried to appear calm when I said, "I'm here for a citizenship interview," to the slender, black administrative assistant behind the window.

"Let me tell the officer." She buzzed his phone and announced my arrival.

The immigration officer, a silver-haired fellow with a thick mustache and smiling eyes, appeared at the door, offered his hand, identified himself as "Andrew Blythe," and escorted me toward his office. His strides were so long; it was hard to keep up with him.

We turned a corner into his office, and he said, "Okay, please have a seat." Andrew asked my full name and date of birth, which, of course, I aced. Then he asked, "What are the three branches of government?"

"Oh, that's simple. Educated, legislative, and judiciary."

He waited.

Oh, rats! I must've gotten it wrong. I racked my brain but couldn't figure out the correct answer for the life of me. I anticipated his cold rebuke. *Citizenship denied!*

But instead, Andrew said, "Do you know the name of the President of the United States?"

"Of course. It's Ronald Reagan." I smiled.

"Okay. Uh, and the name of his branch of government?"

"Oh, right! The executive branch!" *Phew!* I waited for more questions.

"Okay. You passed!"

"I did?"

Andrew handed me a certificate with a big smile. "Congratulations!"

"Thank you, sir!"

I was so excited I scurried out of his office and waved my certificate in front of the woman at the window.

She said, "Well, look at you! You did it! Congratulations!" And she smiled.

As I raced out of the office, something dawned on me, and I did an about-face. "Oh, but I have another problem." I explained that my wife was still in Nepal and that I needed to get a permit for her to enter the country.

"Oh, that's no problem. Please give me your certificate. I'll Telex a copy to the US Embassy in Kathmandu, and they will call your wife in two days."

"What? Really?"

"Yeah. She'll get her permit, and she can come in two weeks."

"Oh, thank you so much!" If there hadn't been a window between us, I would've reached out and hugged her.

At long last, my Sreejana came to America on September 1, 1987. I picked her up at Stapleton Airport in Denver and took her to my apartment in Boulder. As we drove westward toward the foothills, she told me about her final days in Nepal.

"Everyone cried except for me," she said.

"Why didn't you cry?" I asked.

"I don't cry during happy times. I was so happy. I was coming to see my love."

When we arrived at my—our place, she immediately exclaimed, "Oh, I love it!" and went straight to the kitchen to scrub the pots and pans.

I followed her. "Love, you've had such a long journey. You don't need to clean those. Now is your time to rest. We can take care of those tomorrow."

She twisted around to face me. "But I want to wash the dishes in my brand-new home!"

I laughed. "Okay, be my guest!"

The next day, we had some tea and fresh melon for breakfast before heading to Old Tibet. I couldn't believe Sreejana was finally with me. I couldn't believe this gorgeous, whip-smart, compassionate woman was my wife. I was one lucky guy!

I was anxious to show her Old Tibet and its treasures. When she walked in, she twirled around. "It's so lovely," she said, holding her heart. "I can't believe it's ours. It's like a dream!"

"Oh, good. I'm so happy you like it. By the way, I forgot to mention that I have an appointment this morning. If I show you the ropes, do you think you can take care of things while I'm gone?"

"Sure. How hard can it be?" she said, nonplussed but never having run a store.

I showed her how the sales process worked, including working the cash register. "Okay?"

"No problem," she said.

I probably should have been worried because Sreejana didn't know how things worked in America, but she approached everything with such understated confidence and competence, I knew the store was in good hands.

When I returned, she was handing a customer the purchase in an Old Tibet bag. The customer, a grey-haired hippy woman dressed in tie-dye with lots of beads and bangles, was pleased as punch; she practically skipped out of the store.

"How'd it go?" I asked.

She tossed her head back and laughed. "Well, one customer taught me about American currency. Another explained how checks work. And another gave me a little tutorial about credit cards, so I think I'm fully trained!"

"My clever bride," I said, beaming with pride. I slid behind the counter and, with a ding, opened the cash register. I couldn't believe my eyes! Sreejana had made a week's worth of sales in two and a half hours! It was then I realized she was my good luck charm with her poise, energy, and capacity for happiness.

"You know what? The customers were so honest. This is the kind of country I've always wanted to live in! Everyone is so trustworthy, cooperative, kind, and understanding. The very first day of my life in America made me so happy. Because of this, I believe my life here will go very well. People say, 'Morning sows the day,' and this morning was tremendous. This is my country!"

Overnight, she became utterly devoted to Old Tibet. It was almost like it was meant to be. She rearranged the shelves and store window and the case in the front to be more enticing to customers. She had ideas for new products that flew off the shelves. It was clear she had a magic touch.

I'll never forget calling her in the spring of 1988 from Nepal in the Public Communication Office, a telephone station.

"How's business?" I asked.

"Can you guess how much I sold today?"

"Oh, I don't know. $1,000?"

"Guess again."

"$3,000?" I said, thinking I was shooting too high.

"More," she laughed.

"Okay, $5,000."

"Not even close! I sold $12,000. Can you believe it?"

I froze with the phone in my hand, not seeing the goat herder chasing after a run-away goat in front of the telephone station. Sreejana had doubled the store's best-ever day. "Actually, I can't. Have I ever told you how amazing you are?"

"Oh, it's not me. The store you created is just so beautiful."

Of course, she would never admit it because she is such a humble person that even though I opened the store, she made it blossom like the rarest orchid that only blooms when conditions are perfect.

My Missing Link

Sometimes you don't know what you're missing until you find it. That was true with my love, Sreejana. She was everything from the very beginning. Unlike worrying about my many friends and relatives, I never worried about her. Sreejana is competent, wise, kind, and tolerant. She's also so beautiful, strong, and powerful. She never curses or gets angry. She never talks badly about other people or gossips. Instead, she praises others. She's humble and compassionate. She sees with positive eyes and heart. She views everyone as a friend, even people who speak badly about her. She doesn't believe she has any enemies.

Sreejana is the reason for my success. Once she came to the US, my ventures exploded with her support. She managed Old Tibet and my other businesses while also raising our children.

Sreejana is 13 years younger than me, but I have learned so much from her. She says, "If you want to do good for other people, you must first know who you are. If you want to do good for other people, you must first do good for yourself. If you want to do good for other people, you must learn to be tolerant and understanding."

We have many panhandlers and homeless people who come into our store. Instead of chasing them out, Sreejana is warm and welcoming. When they need cash for food, they ask her for a loan. She generously obliges. Amazingly, they return and pay her back when they can. That's the kind of trust and good faith they have in her.

One day, a grumbling, tattered panhandler shuffled into Old Tibet and swiped money from our change bowl. With handfuls of quarters, he walked toward the door.

"Sir, you're taking money from our store," Sreejana said.

"Yes, ma'am," he said, not making eye contact.

"Sir, you're not supposed to do that."

"I know. I need it, ma'am."

I was fuming and ready to stop him from taking our money. I had long helped people when they were in need, but I felt his coming into the store and grabbing money from under our noses was too much.

Sreejana said, "No, no. Let him go. He needs it more than we do." Her words touched and inspired me, a reminder that you must share what you can.

CHAPTER 8

Never Forget Your Roots as You Reach for the Stars

My heart has always told me that if I have enough, especially if I have more than enough, I want to share it with family and friends and those in need. We come to this Earth with nothing, and we take nothing with us when we die. So why hold onto everything?

EVERYTHING FELL APART FOR MY FAMILY in Nepal in 1987. That year, I learned that the lender had repossessed my father's house because he could not make the loan payments. The situation had become so dire for my family members that people refused to lend to them or help them anymore. I knew I was their only hope.

A Window into my Roots

That year, the Channel 12 crew accompanied my trekkers to capture Nepal's vanishing culture, which few were familiar with. I wanted them to film my childhood culture and introduce it to the West.

The trekkers and Sherpas headed for the snowy Himalayas while the Channel 12 crew stayed back in my village of Khandbari. I organized festivities every day for the filming—coordinating feasts and gathering people for traditional Nepali song and dance performances. Channel 12 captured everything on film, which later aired in a few states in the US.

One of my primary motivations for spearheading this project was to create a film to be shown in Colorado and elsewhere that highlighted Nepali villages, people, and culture, to drive business and facilitate Nepali-American connections. The more people knew about me, the more interest I would generate in my trekking trips to Nepal, and the more I'd be able to help my family and my village. Part of success is taking the long view. In other words, as you climb a mountain, you don't just think about the next few steps in front of you. You strategize to reach the summit and descend safely. You cannot be successful if you only look a few feet ahead.

Because the weather had turned dicey, I chartered a plane from Tumlingtar to Biratnagar instead of Kathmandu, our original destination. Whenever I brought trekkers to Nepal, I arranged for them to visit my village and family. I invited them to see my modest home. I wanted my village to be known to Westerners, especially Coloradans. They, in turn, brought those memories back to Colorado. Many said to me, "Look what you came from and look what you've become!"

I chartered a bus from Biratnagar to Dharan, which broke down twice on the way; it was rough going, and yet the group finally made it. The Channel 12 crew and the trekkers visited the home of my second oldest brother, Ram Dai, in Dharan and captured footage of his life. He lived in a wood house owned by my father, the one I stayed in when completing the 10th grade.

Ram Dai's family prepared a special dinner for the group—a local rooster cooked Nepali-style. With modest accommodations, it was a rough night for the members of the team. When the trekkers told me about their stay in Dharan, they were surprised by my brother's living conditions.

When the Channel 12 journalists returned to Colorado, they hand-delivered the video of my brother to me. Eight of them lived in a three-room house. There were slits for windows, a tiny kitchen in the back, and bed mats stacked in a corner of the home. As I peered into their world from my house in Lafayette, Colorado, pain gripped my heart, and tears welled up in my eyes. Seeing them living in such conditions crushed me. They had to endure such hardship. It only underscored how much Ram Dai needed my help.

Later, Ram Dai visited me while I was in Kathmandu buying merchandise for Old Tibet. When he talked about his life, it matched the stories from the Channel 12 reporters and my trekker friends. Ram Dai was a prestigious member of the municipality, but it didn't pay.

My brother's story touched my heart and made me realize I wanted to help him and my other siblings as best I could.

If Ram Dai had a good education, he could have been a minister or held any high-ranking position in Nepal. He was so charming, personable, and smart that he always won whenever he ran for office. I asked him to bring his family to Kathmandu and said I would rent a house for them. I promised him a job. He started crying, and we hugged. I rented a two-story house for him in Kathmandu. At the beginning of 1988, he moved there with his family to start a new life.

To help my brother even more, I set my sights on a position for him with the National Peasant's Organization, a political party representing agricultural workers. I thought he would make an excellent Assistant Treasurer. I spoke with my friends Mr. Poon and Mr. Giri, who were members of Parliament, and asked them to help my brother in his election bid. I financed Ram Dai's campaign. And, lo and behold, my brother won! He received a modest salary and money for travel.

My Philosophy of Giving

Some entrepreneurs stash money away to expand their ventures and elevate their lifestyle. As I became more successful, I never forgot my roots, my family whom I held dear, who continued to struggle mightily. With my businesses prospering and spawning new enterprises, I wanted to knit my family into my network and springboard their success. I could have invested and profited handsomely in real estate in downtown Boulder if I had not been thinking of Nepal and helping my siblings and the Nepali people. Was it my responsibility to take care of my family in Nepal? No. Did I have a duty? In a way, yes. But ultimately, it was my choice. I wanted to share my good fortune with my family in Nepal. I could have saved and invested all the money I earned. But we come to this Earth with nothing, and we take nothing with us when we die. So why hold onto everything? I vowed to make a difference, not only in the lives of my family members but also relatives, neighbors, and my village.

Some friends saw it as a weakness in me. They believed I should disengage myself from my family's unfortunate situation. But my heart always told me if I have enough, especially if I have more than enough, I want to share it with those who are less fortunate. Giving to others brings me more good fortune, but more than that, it brings me happiness. Giving to others makes me happier than any vast accumulation of wealth ever would.

When people are in trouble, you must see the world through their eyes, mind, and heart. Putting yourself in their shoes, you'll know how difficult it is for them. If everyone felt that kind of kindness for each other, the world could be a much better place.

Throughout our lives, Sreejana has always reminded me, "Any money we earn in America goes a long way in Nepal. If we can make a small difference in the lives of people in the villages, we should. As long as you help the children, women, and the poor, you are free to go to Nepal. I'll take care of our home life and run Old Tibet and the other businesses, so you are free to return to Nepal and do what you do best."

Without her, I might be a real estate tycoon in Colorado. Sreejana cared about my happiness and didn't push me to become a wealthy man. We supported each other, and she encouraged my ventures of giving. We had the same life mission.

I derived energy from my wife's encouragement and support and from helping the Nepali people. Seeing their need motivated me to generate creative ideas for lifting them up and out of hopelessness.

SANN Research Institute and High Altitude Enterprises

Sometimes opportunity just walks through the door. And sometimes opportunity looks like a cowboy. On a spring day in 1988, a young man wearing a cowboy hat and boots strolled into my store. My eyes were immediately drawn to his belt with a knife holster. He looked like he had just stepped out of a Western movie set.

He approached me with a cordial smile. "Are you Narayan?" He removed his hat out of respect.

"Yes, sir. Who are you?"

"I'm Dr. Igor Gamow. I teach chemical engineering in the departments of Aerospace Engineering and Chemical and Biological Engineering at CU-Boulder. Judge Holmes, a friend of mine, and his wife, June, went to Nepal with you in 1986. He says you're the go-to man for Nepal. He's very complimentary."

"Happy to hear that! What can I do for you, sir?"

"I have something that might interest you. I invented a portable hyperbaric bag, used as an emergency treatment for acute mountain sickness (AMS) from cerebral and pulmonary edema caused by a lack of oxygen in the blood. In later stages, it can be fatal. By increasing air pressure around the afflicted, the bag simulates descent down to 7,000 feet and relieves AMS symptoms. It's an inflatable pressure bag large enough to accommodate a person. The person is placed inside the bag, which is sealed and inflated with a foot pump. But I need to test it, and where better than Nepal? Would it be possible for you to plan a trip for me to Everest's base camp?"

As he spoke, something clicked. "I will help you if you will help me." I already had the idea for the Semester in Nepal. I had always wanted to introduce American students to Nepali culture. I suspected CU-Boulder students living at the base of the Rocky Mountains would be eager to go to Nepal.

"What do you have in mind?" Igor flashed a curious grin.

"Getting you to the base camp of Everest is a piece of cake for me. I want to start a venture and need your help. If you say, 'Yes,' we're in business."

"Go on." He cocked his head with interest.

"I'm looking to start a semester of study abroad in Nepal for American college students."

"How can I help you?" he asked.

"You said you're a CU professor—right?"

He nodded. "Have you heard of George Gamow?"

"No, I'm afraid not."

"My father is known for the Big Bang Theory of the origin of the universe. There's a tower at CU-Boulder dedicated to him—the Gamow Tower."

"What?! You're his son?"

"Yep. That's me!" He smiled.

"Then I definitely want to work with you. Together, you and I can launch a semester of study abroad in Nepal, perhaps starting in the fall of 1989. I can help you test and market your hyperbaric bag. What do you say?"

And the Semester in Nepal was born. I named it SANN Research Institute. "S" stands for Sreejana, "A" is for my son Anu, "N" is for my son Nathan, and the second "N" stands for me, Narayan. The program was housed in a single-family home in Kathmandu with Dr. Gamow as a chaperone, mentor, professor, and guide. The curriculum featured anthropology, religion and philosophy, the political science of Nepal, Nepali language, ecology, travel journalism, photography, and Igor's mandatory high-altitude physiology program. The program took off with the support and dedication of Igor after receiving accreditation from Tribhuvan University, a highly respected Nepali institution in Kathmandu, the only university in the entire country of Nepal at the time. Igor was instrumental in recruiting CU-Boulder students. The University of Colorado became my closest ally with the help of Dr. Gamow.

We ran three semesters a year and added short programs and faculty for a three-week to one-month program. After running several programs with

Igor, in 1994 and beyond, I reached out to other universities to partner with. Some years, the Semester in Nepal brought up to 200 students.

When Igor returned, after his hyperbaric bags performed beautifully in the Himalayas, he urged me to help him start a company to promote his bag. No one had bought his patent or produced his bags that could save the lives of skiers, high-altitude climbers, and trekkers.

We had lunch every week and had a deal that whoever showed up last had to foot the bill. One day, I sprinted toward the restaurant, thinking I would beat him, but Igor was already there and looking very amused. Once again, I was stuck with the bill.

Igor was so impressed with my connections and success, he gave me a lead and asked me to write and submit a business proposal to the DuPont Corporation. Soon after that, Jim Bower from DuPont contacted me to set up a dinner meeting.

During that dinner, attended by Igor, his wife, and me and Sreejana, Jim agreed to buy Igor's patent for a decent amount of money to Igor's great delight. We all toasted to Igor and DuPont's partnership.

I piped in. "Now that DuPont has agreed to buy and produce bags, I have a business proposal for you, Jim."

"What is it?" Jim asked, intrigued.

"Many climbers go to Nepal and, sadly, die. The hyperbaric bag could prevent needless deaths. Would DuPont pick up the tab for the three of us to go to Nepal to promote this amazing bag? We can invite 300 trekking and travel agencies to the demo."

Jim agreed, and the three of us went in the fall of 1989. DuPont gave Igor a first-class ticket to Kathmandu. I was already there with my family. In November, we presented the demo of the hyperbaric bag, now called the Gamow Bag, in a five-star hotel for 300 trekking and travel agencies and ambassadors from many different countries. I was the patient inside the bag for the demo. The attendees were so impressed that they broke out in applause and cheers after the presentation. The trip was a smashing success, and Igor signed on the dotted line to receive royalties.

After the demo, Igor asked me what part of the deal I wanted. I asked to become the sole agent for Nepal—the only one who sold to the Nepali market.

We returned to Boulder, created a company, and named it High Altitude Enterprises. Igor gave me seed money, and we worked with Doug Emerson and Julian Alexander to launch the company with a big promo splash. We started our venture with 35 bags. As a sole agent, I sold bags to trekking companies and rented bags to climbers and trekkers. In the end, we made more money renting than selling the bags. This was, in part, due to the emergence of a French company that started competing with the Gamow Bag and many agents selling competing products around the world. The market quickly became saturated, forcing us to close the company in 1995. We continued to send the Gamow Bag with mountain trekkers.

Empowering my Siblings

In 1989, the Nepali Congress Party (NCP), a pro-democracy group and the largest political party, and the United Left Front, an alliance of communist and leftist parties, launched a democracy campaign in Nepal. The NCP and leftist groups coordinated pro-democracy agitation. Street protests that were suppressed by security forces resulted in deaths and mass arrests. After the army killed protesters in Patan in early April, the movement gathered some 200,000 people who marched in protest of the monarchy in Kathmandu. King Birendra eventually bowed to the pressure and agreed to a new democratic constitution, and the multi-party People's Movement brought an end to absolute monarchy. In 1991, the NCP won the first democratic elections, and Girija Prasad Koirala became the Prime Minister of Nepal.

During this time, my brother Ram Dai, Assistant Treasurer of the National Peasant's Organization, lost his job. I wanted to make him the

Managing Director of the Semester in Nepal. During that time, SANN had seven students under the supervision of Igor Gamow. I believed in my brother—that he would excel in the role—and I was right. I also hired some of my other relatives to work in this organization.

Old Tibet gave birth to many companies. As Sreejana and I opened companies here in the US, we also launched ventures in Nepal, in large part, to help my siblings. We figured if we created and gave them companies, they would prosper. That was our hope, anyway.

We opened a mountain bike shop for my youngest brother, Jiban, in Kathmandu. It was called American-Nepal Mountain Bike Shop, the only one in the country at the time. To do so, I contacted Doug Emerson, owner of University Bicycles in Boulder, who agreed to a partnership and sent 35 bicycles to Nepal. He also sent an employee from Boulder to help run it. I spoiled Jiban by renting him a single-family home in the capital city and buying him a motorcycle. I couldn't help it. I had a tender spot in my heart for him, who was not married at the time. He was waiting for his green card to the US through my mother. Later, when he came to the US, the bike shop folded.

All my businesses were located on the thriving Thamel Street in Kathmandu.

To my sister, Shanti, we gave Tawache Trekking Company, and to her husband, Shyam, we gave High Altitude Enterprises.

During my first trip home in 1986, I witnessed how Shanti was living. She lived with her family in a tiny, one-bedroom apartment and ran a small shop that sold household items. She would sit in a chair and watch the door, waiting for customers to come in. Their store was struggling to survive. When I saw Shanti so gaunt and frowning, I wondered where my sister had gone. I moved her from that apartment to a much better home in Kathmandu with many rooms and a front and back yard.

I assumed my next youngest brother, Dharma, who worked as a government officer, was set, but when I visited his home in Kathmandu, his family of five was crammed into one room with a stove in the corner and a bed in the middle of the room. When I saw that Dharma, an honorable, hardworking man, was living in squalor, it crushed me. It prompted me to open a travel agency for him to run. Sreejana and I gave him Narayan's Travel Agency, the Nepali branch of our travel agency. Part of our thinking in setting up this branch was that we could legally bring my siblings to the US by applying for an intra-company transfer of employees.

We not only gave these companies to my siblings to create their jobs; we also saw that the only way they could come to the US was by transferring them via our companies.

To my brother Dev Ananda (DN), the sixth youngest, we gave a boarding school to manage. During my first trek to Nepal in 1986, I noticed the deteriorating condition of education in my village. I visited a local school, which inspired me in 1988 to establish the Surya Secondary Boarding School named after my father. Amy Newfield, the daughter of Nathan's surgeon in Dallas, became the first principal of the school. She stayed there about seven to eight months.

I thought DN would be a perfect manager for the boarding school. He was always a very devoted brother, working his hardest when I pushed him to achieve excellence. He hated to see me upset or to disappoint me. As I expected, he was fully committed to the school. Under my supervision, he has done fantastic work in Nepal and at the school. At one point, under his management, the school became one of the best in the region.

DN was always my greatest champion. In Hindu belief, just as Lord Ram had a devotee named Hanuman who never left Ram's side, always defended him, and obeyed his orders, my father once told me that DN is my Hanuman. DN wouldn't tolerate anyone saying bad things about me; he would give his life to protect me. I love him dearly and did everything in my power to bolster his success. Throughout, he was my right-hand man, but he didn't always realize the importance of his efforts.

To keep business humming for my siblings, my job was to recruit and send a steady stream of trekkers and tourists including climbers and hikers, as well as students, to Nepal. It worked like a charm; the travel agency flew the tourists to their destinations and offered tours of cities, towns, and villages. The trekking company took the trekkers to the mountains and provided Sherpas and provisions. The mountain bike company rented bikes to tourists so they could pedal around Kathmandu. High Altitude Enterprises coordinated with the trekking company to help trekkers treat any high-altitude sickness. All these enterprises earned enough income to more than cover my siblings' expenses.

When trekkers and tourists registered for the trips here in Boulder, instead of putting them in hotels, I thought, *Why not set up homestays in my siblings' and villagers' homes?*

As trekkers, climbers, hikers, and students participating in the Semester in Nepal settled into their homestays, they grew attached to the Nepali families that hosted them, nurturing connections between Nepalis and Americans. This opened up possibilities for Nepalis to come to America and start anew through sponsoring. The spirit of giving means coming up with creative ideas for helping others.

Although six of my siblings were set, I faced remaining challenges with two. My oldest brother, Bashu Dai, and the third from the bottom, Sunil, drank too much. Bashu Dai was such a severe alcoholic; I had him admitted to the hospital in Kathmandu for treatment. I also rented a house for him in the city. Despite my efforts, his drunken episodes continued, so I didn't feel comfortable giving him a business to run.

Later, Sreejana and I brought three of his daughters to the US and helped them as they got settled. When they began to earn incomes, they sent money to their parents in Nepal. Slowly, Bashu Dai started to improve.

This experience taught me not to underestimate humans and their ability to overcome bad habits. Most, if given an opportunity, will thrive. Bashu Dai became so happy, he no longer needed to abuse alcohol. Later, he became Chairman and CEO of our nonprofit healthcare organization in Nepal.

Sunil was helpful, kind, and handsome, but a troublemaker. He has never understood what life is about. No matter what opportunities were provided to Sunil, he never allowed himself to become a successful person. He's a fine human being when he doesn't drink, but no one could convince him to kick the habit.

After talking it over with Sreejana, I agreed that a good woman from our village could control Sunil's future and give him a better life. I trusted my wife completely. She had never given me bad advice. I also talked it over with my parents, and they agreed that Sunil should get married. They thought the same for Jiban.

I decided to focus on Jiban first because he was in the process of getting a green card, and he'd be leaving Nepal soon. At 19, he could get his green card through my mother. The window was closing. When he reached 21, he would no longer be able to get a green card through her.

One day, I approached him at my parents' house with what I thought was great news. "Jiban, I found a girl for you. She's educated, her family is well-off, and her father is my good friend. I can talk to his daughter. What do you say?"

He glared at me with a deep frown, slid against the wall, and collapsed onto the floor. He looked like he might cry. "No, I don't want to get married."

"If you get married, it will be easier for me to bring you two to the US."

"The only girl I'm interested in is Ganesh Dai's daughter."

"Who is she?" I asked.

"Her name is Renu."

"Oh, is she in Khandbari?"

He nodded.

"She loves you?" I asked.

He nodded again. A smile replaced his frown.

"Well, then you must get married now."

"Okay. I'm ready!" he said, perking up.

The next day, I went to Renu's grandmother's house in Khandbari, and she happily approved. A few days later, I bought jewelry and other wedding items, gave my mother money to cover the wedding costs, and Jiban was married to his sweetheart.

One down. One to go.

My mother told me that I must arrange a marriage for Sunil before heading back to the US. But I wondered who in God's name I could get, given Sunil's reputation as a troublemaker. There was a young woman named Meena, who we thought would be a good match. I was told if I went to the family's house, they would approve of the marriage because of my good standing in the community.

We didn't have to go far, as Narendra Bahadur Shrestha and his family lived right across from my parents. I took friends and relatives with me.

As expected, Meena's parents had serious reservations about Sunil.

To reassure them, I said, "Your daughter won't have any problems. If she does, I will take care of them. You have my word."

Narendra Bahadur Shrestha peered at me gravely. "We are saying 'yes' only because of you, Narayan."

The next day, they married and moved in with my parents.

In 1992, I moved Sunil and his family to Kathmandu and gave him a travel agency with airline ticket stock and Gamow Bags to rent. But, whenever people paid Sunil for tickets, he spent the money on booze. He didn't care about the company, only about financing his habit.

One time that same year, I sent 16 doctor friends from Colorado to volunteer in Nepal. After their medical service in a village, they planned to hike in Western Nepal. Sunil was supposed to have plane tickets for the whole group in Pokhara, but he was so drunk he had spent all their payments on booze. The group called me from Pokhara, stranded. Immediately, we arranged the travel back to their homes.

To keep the travel agency afloat, I took on debt. Sunil didn't give me a dime from the rented Gamow Bags. And to obtain loans, he would put up Gamow Bags and trekking equipment as collateral.

I moved Sunil and his family to another house without agreeing to help any further. I urged him to learn a better way to survive. But, knowing my brother's history, I didn't want to abandon him. I gave money to DN to give to Sunil when needed. I just didn't want Sunil to know it came from me.

Over my lifetime, Sreejana and I have spent so much money helping Sunil, bailing him out many times, all to no avail. As the old saying goes, you can't help someone who can't help himself.

All told, we opened six companies in Nepal for my brothers and sister: SANN Research Institute, American-Nepal Mountain Bike Shop, Tawache Trekking Company, Narayan's Travel Agency, and High Altitude Enterprises. We also opened Surya Boarding School. We covered all my siblings' expenses for years until we brought them to the US. After we taught them how to run businesses and manage their affairs, they launched successful lives. We lifted my family members from near poverty; we helped them to thrive. Regardless of who my siblings are and what they do, I love them all equally and wish them the best. As siblings we are knitted together closer than everyone else. When I see my siblings cry, I can't stop my tears.

Every time I traveled to my village, Khandbari, people greeted me at the airport with horses, lanterns, music bands, garlands, and gates. They displayed welcome banners all over town. Hundreds lined the streets, carrying worshiping plates of flowers and colorful rice and fruit. They wanted to make me feel like a special human being. I did not feel that I was such an important man.

CHAPTER 9

Health Trek and the Early Days of Helping Hands

Mahatma Gandhi's philosophy was about simple living and high thinking. His philosophy inspired me to live simply, talk less, do more, be with the locals, and help the poor and helpless.

I N NEPAL, HEALTH NEEDS ARE VAST. Maternal mortality remains one of the biggest public health problems. Lack of access to basic maternal healthcare, difficult geographical terrain, poorly developed transportation and communication systems, poverty, illiteracy, women's low status in society, political conflict, shortage of health care professionals, and under-utilization of currently available services are significant challenges.

Nepal's Valley of Need

The average life expectancy in Nepal is 65 years. The seven leading causes of morbidity are heart disease, chronic obstructive pulmonary disease (COPD), lower respiratory infection, diarrheal diseases, road injuries, strokes, and diabetes. Some disease stems from dirty drinking water.

Women carry heavy loads of logs, water, and rice, whether they are pregnant or not. This often results in prolapsed uteri.

The Birth of Health Trek

In 1987, I had opened a travel agency, sending trekkers, hikers, and bikers to Nepal. With the lessons I learned in 1986, after seeing the injured children and hearing the mother's echoing cries, I wanted to convert my travel company from a profit-making venture to a mission-driven organization. That way, our health treks would be funded by medical volunteers. The model I put in place back then—volunteers work for two weeks and trek in the mountains for two weeks—is still in operation today.

Considering my experiences while trekking and seeing these widespread health needs and the lack of access to modern healthcare services, I told my wife that I wanted to bring doctors, nurses, and other medical support to Nepal. She said, "By all means!" I told her if she met any doctors or nurses in the shop to send them to my office in the back of Old Tibet. Sure enough, in the spring of 1988, she introduced me to Dr. Ross Stacy, an anesthesiologist, and his wife, Jan, from Longmont, Colorado. Dr. Stacy said he wanted to go to Nepal someday. I suggested that he and I take a group of people to my village in Nepal.

First, we would need to recruit some medical folks. Dr. Stacy and I hosted a dinner at his home for 40 guests, during which I gave a slide presentation, and Sreejana cooked Nepalese food. I pitched an idea to Western doctors and dentists, who regularly paid good money for two-week beach vacations. I said, "Give me your Bahamas trip money, and I'll give you a month-long trip to Nepal where you can experience the culture, the beauty of the country, and also provide much-needed healthcare to the people of Nepal." With that approach, we generated lots of interest.

Of the 40 guests who came to hear my talk, ten medical professionals signed up right away.

A month after the dinner, in the spring of 1988, Dr. Stacy, Jan, and I went to Nepal on a scouting trip. I wanted to show them my village so they could recruit more people.

We decided to run our first health clinic program in Khandbari in the fall of 1988, with a departure date in September. For a time, we ran our mobile medical operation without an official name. We referred to it informally as "Health Trek."

Ever since I heard the cry of the mother with her dead daughter in the basket and saw the desperation of the boy with the stick impaled in his cheek, those memories had stayed with me and constantly tugged at my heart to do something. I felt I must go back and help Nepal and her people.

Health Trek in Khandbari

Throughout the summer, I advertised our upcoming health clinic in Khandbari. Not only did the nearly 20,000 people of my village know we were coming, but also the people who lived in the valleys across the rivers and mountains.

On September 24, 1988, we set out on our journey. It was the first trip I had ever made with an official medical team. I took a team that included ophthalmologists, opticians, anesthesiologists, dentists, a general practitioner, a physiologist, a pediatrician, and their spouses. We traveled under the umbrella of Narayan's Gateway to Nepal. We carried 8,000 pairs of prescription glasses and a brand-new autorefractor—a machine used during an eye exam to generate a prescription for glasses.

In Kathmandu, our team stayed at the Hotel Himalaya. We had so much luggage; it was piled up to the ceiling in the lobby. We couldn't lighten our load because we carried all our medical, dental, optical, and school supplies. All told, we had 19 team members, 100 porters' loads of medical and educational supplies, 70 pieces of luggage, plus food and provisions.

A month before our arrival, an earthquake had rumbled across Eastern Nepal, killing 1,200 people and leaving many thousands homeless. Despite an international relief effort, the Nepali army maintained an iron grip on the distribution of foreign emergency assistance. They blocked foreign humanitarian aid because Nepal's corrupt government wanted to hoard valuable supplies and selectively distribute them. Thus, the government would not allow us to take our team and equipment to my village. Instead, they wanted us to hand over all our supplies and equipment and go hiking in the Western mountains.

It's important to note that the government only limited humanitarian health interventions in times of emergency; after the earthquake was cleaned up, we continued our health treks without pushback from the government.

But, in the meantime, I had a big problem on my hands.

So, I plotted. *Who can I call to get us out of this bind?* I thought of my friend, the Minister of Transportation, Mr. Deepak Bohara.

When I called him, he said, "Narayan, quietly come to my quarters at 11:00 pm. We'll make a plan."

His place was very close to my hotel. He served me herbal tea, and we prepared to discuss our plan of action.

He took a sip of tea, deep in thought. For a minute, I thought he might not have a plan at all. But then he leaned forward and said, "Without telling a soul, send your people to the airport early in the morning. I'll have two airplanes waiting for them. I'll inform the staff that no one is permitted to reveal the destination of the flights. Have your team load all their luggage and equipment onto the airplanes. Then let everyone know you have a meeting at my office. While you're here, I'll put you in touch with the Health Minister. She may not cooperate, and she'll think your people are still here. But the planes with your team and equipment will be on their way. You'll go later, on a chartered plane."

That sounded like a great plan.

I went to his office the next morning while the planes with my team flew to Tumlingtar. As expected, the Health Minister, Ms. Sushila Thapa, refused to write me a letter. Thankfully, the Assistant Health Minister was a friend of my brother Ram Dai. He wrote Ram Dai the letter we needed, addressed to the Chief District Officer (CDO) of Khandbari.

It read:

Narayan Shrestha, citizen of Nepal and the United States of America, born in Khandbari, is responsible for this operation. Please allow his health clinic/mobile hospital to operate.

Our team waited for me at Tumlingtar Airport. When I arrived, we spent the night at the airport, sleeping in tents in the field. There was a downpour that soaked the earth and turned dirt into slippery mud. In the middle of the night, Dr. Steve Weddal, an anesthesiologist, got up when nature called, slipped, and injured his elbow. His injury required emergency stitches. Good thing we had so many capable surgeons on our team!

The next morning, we walked uphill for four hours to the ridge in the sunny, hot, and humid weather. We hired 100 porters who carried our luggage, supplies, and equipment on their backs.

We camped on my relatives' land. Then we set up our tent city right below the existing bare-bones hospital, including the kitchen, dining, sleeping, and toilet tents. We had 30 tents in all.

People from seven villages came to see our daily routine of brushing our teeth, Sherpas serving tea, and people playing music and dancing at night. It provided great entertainment for them. Each day, we had hundreds of spectators.

Typically, the Assistant Minister of Health's permission to the local government to bypass the federal government's ban would be honored. But the CDO and the local police officers had received an order from the Home Minister that no donations from other countries should be accepted without a government permit. All donations were to go to the central government, which was responsible for their distribution.

Without a permit, operating our mobile medical unit was in direct opposition to the order, and we were told that we could not carry on.

Holy cow! That's a huge problem. We've got a first-class medical team ready to go and thousands of patients who need help and had walked days one-way to see us, and they won't let us operate!

So, I thought I'd try a new approach. I asked my family to sacrifice a goat for a fancy feast. In Nepal, sacrificing a goat and offering a feast with liquor is paying the highest respect to someone.

I invited the CDO, a police officer, and other local officials for dinner at my house. We treated them to a meal of fresh goat and imported whiskey. When I saw that the CDO, who supervised the police officers, and the police officer were tipsy from the whiskey, I pulled a police officer aside. "I have a letter from the Assistant Health Minister approving my operation. Does this make it official for me to open tomorrow?" I thought of the thousands of patients waiting for us to open. "If you don't let me do it, I'm going to do it anyway. Are you going to arrest me or what?" I asked slyly.

"Do you have the letter?"

"Yes, indeed. Here it is." I handed him the document.

He grabbed it and slid it into his pocket without looking at it.

The CDO approached us and said to me, "Ah-ha! You just gave him a bribe. Why did you give him a bribe? Let me see what you gave him."

"No, you don't need to see this," said the police officer to his boss, emboldened by the liquor.

The CDO reached into the police officer's pocket and pulled out the piece of paper. He read it, looked up at me, and said surprisingly, "No problem. You can open tomorrow." The CDO was so drunk; he didn't even remember what he was talking about. He was out of control, yet I had him under my control.

Hooray! Success at last! I was anxious to get started.

Every day, we did a massive amount of work from daybreak to nightfall. We provided all the dental, optical, and medical services for free. We provided many other services. For example, we had one dentist, with no assistant, who was primarily pulling rotten and damaged teeth that caused pain. Patients in agony one day had no pain the next. Every two to three days, the buckets filled with teeth. At the end of the 10th day, the dentist grabbed the buckets full of teeth and was amazed to learn from a local volunteer that 1,700 teeth had been pulled!

We distributed thousands of prescription eyeglasses and gave patients medicine free of charge. In ten days, we saw a total of 3,000 people. The patients were so happy.

Well, the ones we could see.

Around 10,000 people showed up, but we only had the bandwidth to care for 3,000. That meant 7,000 people had to return home untreated. Some of them had walked for three days to get to our clinic. My heart felt heavy, and I thought, *This is not the way to help enough people. I'm just giving too many of them trouble.* My doctor friends reassured me that I was doing good things, but I felt terrible for the people we turned away.

When Health Trek started, Nepali doctors weren't going to remote villages to treat people. Our medical team discovered big problems as it went from village to village. Although the villages tried their best, their healthcare was sorely lacking. For example, in my village there was a so-called hospital for a population of 20,000. The beds were bare—no sheets or pillows—just hard, flat surfaces. And the staff was comprised of one nurse and two assistants—no doctors. What kind of hospital is that? In the villages, people had never even heard of dentists, so, naturally, their dental hygiene was nonexistent, resulting in many cases of gum disease, rotting teeth, and intense tooth pain.

The more I learned about the woefully inadequate healthcare in Nepal, the more it strengthened my conviction to expand Health Trek's reach.

Surya Secondary Boarding School

Given that my commitment to the Nepali people was to help them with health and education, the idea was also to open a school for children in my village on my first trip.

On the second day of our 1988 Health Trek operation, my younger brother DN approached me and said, "Brother, you wanted to open a school. On the hilltop, there's a school for sale with two teachers and 35 students. If we purchase it, your dream will come true. We can change the name."

Following his recommendation, I asked DN to purchase the school. I gave him 4,000 rupees, which was equivalent to $150 in 1988. A few months later, DN moved the school to my building in the middle of Khandbari with the two teachers and 35 students. It was the only private school that taught in English. I named it the Surya Secondary Boarding School after my father, Surya Bahadur Shrestha.

The school had a small library with books donated by Cherry Creek Elementary in Denver. A teacher from that school had read about my trekking operation in *The Denver Post*. She contacted me with the news that she had collected 1,300 books, 4,000 notebooks, and 8,000 ballpoint pens that she wanted to donate to Nepal. We carried those school supplies with us on that first trip. I also brought a carpenter to build a compost toilet on the school grounds to teach children sanitation and health.

The Surya Boarding School was the first investment in Nepal by Sreejana and me. It was launched before we had established High Altitude Enterprises, the American-Nepal Mountain Bike Shop, and the Tawache Trekking Company. Many more companies in the field of education were added later. Being an ambitious guy, I would've liked to open a better hospital as well, but I realized that my full dream was unattainable on my first trip. But a temporary medical clinic, once or twice a year, was certainly doable.

Blinded by Ideology

In 1989, Dr. Ross Stacy became the president of Health Trek. I was the international coordinator. Our board was comprised of doctors and other medical personnel. Dr. Stacy and I had a strained relationship, but I needed him to make the organization run. Or so I thought. The board members saw me as the one who was pivotal to the program. But Dr. Stacy believed he didn't need me, and our relationship became so difficult that I resigned in the fall of 1991. While he continued to run Health Trek in Khandbari, I was free to launch my own health program in 1992.

In the spring of 1991, Health Trek provided cataract operations for Khandbari. I hired Dr. Sanduk Ruit, a rising star ophthalmologist from Kathmandu. One of the ophthalmologists from Ohio, Dr. Chris King, noticed his brilliance. He said, "Dr. Ruit is such a talented and experienced surgeon. If I ever need eye surgery, I will fly to Nepal to have the procedure done by him."

Health Trek appeared on national Nepali television news; our work in Khandbari was featured. While our mission, plans, and intentions were well-thought-out, I had no way to anticipate the challenges that would arise.

Fortunately, Khandbari now had electricity, which our mobile clinic relied on for the cataract procedures. I was very pleased that the first two days of the cataract operations had gone smoothly. On the third day, the doctors were in the middle of surgery—ready to put a lens in—when the power went out.

What the heck is going on? Was Khandbari's power grid that fragile and unreliable?

Although we had a backup generator, we had no gasoline source in town. A communist family owned the only house with a supply of gasoline. Because we were an American-run organization and the US was vehemently anti-communist, they refused to give us fuel. This brought our cataract operation to a screeching halt. Panic among the medical team ensued. Everyone looked to me to fix the problem.

I had to think quickly. I knew of families with gasoline, but they were in a village an hour away on foot. Meanwhile, we were losing precious time.

My brother DN and his friend Shambhu Neupane, then mayor of the municipality, graciously volunteered to walk uphill for an hour to the village. They managed to secure almost 20 liters of petrol—about five gallons—and haul it back down. We restarted the operation with our generator. In all, our medical team performed 120 cataract operations on that trip.

Later, we learned what had caused the power outage. The communists had gone to the jungle, found the electrical wires, cut the trees, and knocked down the wires, damaging the whole system. Why did they do this? They were rejecting Western influence and American humanitarian assistance. They were so blinded by ideology; they didn't care that they were hurting their people. It made me dislike communism even more. They were expressing anger toward America and me. But their thinking was flawed. They were hurting the 120 Nepali patients, not the Americans.

The town went berserk when they found out what had caused the outage. The patients and their family members rose up against the communists, declaring, "We are very grateful to Narayan Shrestha. He's the one who gives us eyes. He's the one who cures our ailments. He's the one who lifts us up. This is the kind of person we need here, not people who don't care about us."

One Saturday after our cataract clinic, there was a bazaar where people gathered to barter as they did every Saturday. People from the surrounding valleys and hills poured into the marketplace to buy, exchange, and barter food and goods. I bought the entire market's supply of bananas, oranges, and other fruit to the sellers' delight. Over 300 people carried 700 bags of fruit to the patients, who were so happy to have fresh produce. Also, the local Nepali volunteers received fruit to take home to their families. It was good for the market, the patients, and volunteers—a thrilling moment for everyone.

Afterward, I went back to Kathmandu. We invited the Prime Minister of Nepal to speak in a conference room at our hotel. The Prime Minister stood up to give a speech and said in a commanding voice, "We need more people like Narayan Shrestha who lives in America, but who thinks of Nepal. He lives in America but helps Nepal. He lives in America, but his heart is still in Nepal. We need more people like him to make this country great."

I felt honored and, at the same time, humbled. There was so much work to be done; so far, I was only scratching the surface. I was not doing the work to be honored or humbled; I was doing it for the sake of the Nepali people because I had seen their suffering with my eyes. I had experienced their suffering. When I walked to the hills and valleys, I saw that people needed so much help. That is the reason I was committed to go back and help Nepal and her people.

Mahatma Gandhi's philosophy was about simple living and high thinking. His philosophy inspired me to live simply, talk less, do more, be with the locals, and help the poor and helpless. I would greatly help my village by being a simple coordinator, cultivating understanding, being kindhearted and tolerant, and respecting my American medical friends. Health Trek was the first program to bring medical teams to Nepal's villages, where they had never seen any doctors.

Helping Hands Health Education

After many successful trips, Health Trek folded in the fall of 1992, while I was working in Bandipur, and I gave our organization a new name, Helping Hands Health Education. I wanted to promote education in addition to healthcare. To create the logo, I traced the fingers of one hand on a piece of paper—the symbol of a helping hand.

Even though Helping Hands was a nonprofit organization, we did not have any formal fundraising activities for a long time. Each volunteer paid for their trip, and a portion of their trip costs went to buy medicine, cover transportation expenses for patients to Kathmandu, and often their hospital costs. For years, we chartered planes full of patients to be admitted to the Kathmandu hospital. We also sent busloads of patients and their families. If patients required extended stays in the hospital, we paid for their often months-long hospital stays, food, and medicine. The financing came from volunteers paying to go to Nepal and from my various companies.

Opening Narayan's Nepal Restaurant

Back at home in Boulder, I was cooking up more entrepreneurial ideas. The more successful businesses Sreejana and I had in the US, the more we could give to Nepal. To capitalize on Boulder's love of Nepal, we decided to open a restaurant. I already had enough on my plate, so I wondered why this idea interested me so much. I guessed it was because I wanted to corner the Nepalese market in Boulder. I did a little research and discovered there were lots of Indian restaurants, but the only Nepalese restaurant in the entire country was in Madison, Wisconsin, owned by a Nepalese language teacher. I asked if I could borrow his menu, and he happily mailed it to me.

I had three nieces in high school in Colorado who could work for me. I also had a partner in Denver named Bashu Shrestha. I was short on cash at the time because every dime I had funded my projects in Nepal. Bashu offered to put up some money, but it wasn't nearly enough to open a restaurant.

I started becoming friendly with Jay Elowsky, the owner of the very successful Pasta Jay's restaurant in Boulder. Jay had opened Pasta Jay's two years earlier, in 1988. One night, Jay offered me a beer at his place, and we sat down and talked. I shared my idea of opening a Nepalese restaurant. Jay was enthusiastic about the idea and encouraged me to pursue it.

It just so happened that just across the street from Old Tibet—at 921 Pearl—and right next to Pasta Jay's was a home that housed a Chinese restaurant. Occasionally, I would have lunch there and chat with the owner, an engineer and a cook. He gave up his engineering job to open a Chinese restaurant. The place was usually empty at lunch and dinner.

One day, I watched as the owner strolled outside, and he peered inside Pasta Jay's restaurant. He had no customers while Pasta Jay's was packed. He was probably wondering, *What is Pasta Jay's secret?*

I thought, *I'm gonna tease this guy. Maybe he will sell.* I walked into his place. "Um, hey, man, I want to eat lunch." I was the only customer. "Would you please come and sit down with me?"

"Sure. Why not?" he said.

"Would you like to sell your restaurant? I'm interested."

Without hesitation, he said, "Yes, I'd love to sell."

"Well, think about it and talk it over with your family. When you're ready, here's my card. Old Tibet is my store. Please come over and talk to me."

"You've got it," he smiled and got up to seat his second customer.

The very next day, he came into our store wearing a chef's apron. "Hey, man, I'm ready to sell the restaurant."

"Okay. What's your price?"

"Oh, I don't know. Give me whatever."

"No, not whatever. You tell me."

"Okay, how about $25,000?"

"No, that's too much. You have no customers, and your equipment is old. I will talk with the landlord to see whether he will transfer the lease to me. If he does, I'll let you know."

I went to talk to Robert Shonkwiler, the owner of the building. He had heard of me through my travel agency because he had bought tickets from my staff. I asked if he would rent to me. My credit checked out, and Robert approved a lease. It was only $600 a month, very inexpensive back then.

So, I offered the owner of the Chinese restaurant $10,000.

"No, you can do better," he said.

"No, I cannot. $10,000," I said. I still had a little wiggle room but not much.

"$15,000."

We decided to meet in the middle at $12,500, and we had a deal!

I got the money together and bought the restaurant. I told my partner, Bashu, I thought our place should have "Nepal" in the name. Then I further suggested that lots of people knew me because of my travel agency and Old Tibet. So, I said, "What about 'Narayan's Nepal Restaurant?'" My partner and friends agreed.

The minute we opened Narayan's Nepal Restaurant, a nice cozy place, customers poured in. Bashu wanted to leave the partnership in 1991, so I bought him out and became the sole owner. Little did I know that would be the first of many Narayan's Nepal Restaurants. In all, Sreejana and I founded 11 restaurants between 1991 and 1996.

In 1992, two years after opening my first restaurant, I hired an architect, obtained approval from the city, and completely renovated the basement. I called it Narayan's Club Makalu, The Climber's Bar.

In November of 1993, Sir Edmund Hillary inaugurated The Climber's Bar. He was the first climber to reach the summit of Mount Everest, with Tenzing Norge, his Nepali Sherpa guide, in 1953. Hillary's order of scotch and orange juice was our first at The Climber's Bar. I named it the Sir Edmund Hillary drink. I still have the framed dollar he used to buy the drink, which he signed.

I asked the owner of the Hotel Boulderado, Frank Day, to offer a suite to Sir Edmund Hillary and his wife, June. Frank graciously provided three suites for three nights, free of charge, to them, to Hillary's manager and his wife, and to me and Sreejana. With my request, whenever dignitaries or high-ranking people came to town, Frank would generously provide them rooms free of charge.

During Hillary's visit, we did a breakfast fundraising event as well as an evening fundraiser. At the time, I was the President of the Boulder Lions Club. We organized this event under the Lions Club. Around 900 people gathered in a ballroom at CU-Boulder to hear the story of his 1953 Everest climb, with a slideshow capturing the harrowing and triumphant moments on the mountain. All the proceeds went to his nonprofit organization, the Himalayan Trust, helping the Sherpas of Nepal's Khumbu Region. The organization is dedicated to improving the living conditions and economy of these people living in the Himalayas.

Hillary did a signing at Old Tibet, where he sold autographed posters, pins, and New Zealand five-dollar notes which featured him. Hundreds of people lined up for a chance to meet him and buy Sir Edmund Hillary merchandise. All the proceeds went to his cause.

Although Hillary will always be remembered for reaching the summit of Everest, his greatest satisfaction came from befriending and offering financial support to the Nepali people. In an interview later in his life, he explained, "My most worthwhile things have been the building of schools and clinics. That has given me more satisfaction than a footprint on a mountain." He was made an honorary Nepali citizen in 2003.

CHAPTER 10

Making Dollars Dance in Bandipur

Sometimes things happen in life that you believe are barriers to your success, but they're directing you to where you need to go.

I N 1991, HEALTH TREK WITH DR. ROSS STACY had the corner on healthcare in my village, Khandbari. Not wanting to compete with my friends and former associates, I decided to focus my attention elsewhere in Nepal. *But where would I go instead?*

Discovering Bandipur

I had a group of 16 Canadians, Americans, and people from the Dominican Republic, but I didn't know where I'd take them. Also, we had six Nepali medical doctors and dentists. I decided to go to Num, which is a 12-hour walk from Khandbari. We worked in Num for ten days, and the operation went very well. When we finished our work in Num, the group traveled from Khandbari through Tumlingtar to Kathmandu. Travel arrangements went very smoothly. Everyone got on the flight right away.

In contrast, Dr. Stacy's travel logistics weren't well-organized; in fact, he hadn't made flight reservations. His Health Trek volunteers were stranded and spent the night in Tumlingtar. They weren't guaranteed flights home the next day. The volunteers were distressed that the logistics weren't better organized. Although I was no longer with Health Trek, I made the travel arrangements to get them home. Sadly, because of that trip, Health Trek folded. And even though our friendship ended, I am forever grateful for Dr. Stacy's help launching Health Trek and Helping Hands.

The town of Bandipur first caught my eye one night in 1987 while watching TV in my hotel room in Kathmandu. Bandipur sits on a mountain saddle in the Mahabharat Range and is 89 miles west of Kathmandu. The news featured the once thriving and prosperous town that had fallen upon hard times and was on the edge of ruin. The government offices had moved from there to another town. The beautiful homes were neglected, dilapidated, and bug-infested. If nothing were done, it would become a forgotten ghost town.

One morning, in November of 1991, I received a call from the US State Department with news that Mr. Ram Chandra Paudyal, the Minister of Local Development, was visiting Breckenridge. He was in Colorado to study the mountain town, see how it was built and how it functioned. After Nepal became a democracy, government officials looked to fashion its towns after those in the United States. I was asked to host him after he visited Breckenridge.

That night, when I arrived at my restaurant, Mr. Paudyal was already eating. He was a skinny guy sporting a Nepali hat. We shook hands, and he asked about my ventures. I described everything I was doing. I was juggling Old Tibet, Narayan's Travel Agency, Narayan's Nepal Restaurant, SANN Research Institute, American-Nepal Mountain Bike Shop, Tawache Trekking Company, High Altitude Enterprises, the Surya Boarding School, and a health program focusing on the villages of Nepal. We recruited doctors and nurses and took care of trekkers, hikers, and bikers bound for Nepal.

Mr. Paudyal couldn't believe that a Nepali, especially one coming from a remote mountain village, had so many successes in America in such a short time. He was also impressed that I had a health program I took from village to village. Later that night, he asked me to help his village. I told him I preferred to go to Bandipur instead. He said the town was in his district, so he agreed.

On March 3, 1992, I traveled to Bandipur. To get there from Kathmandu, the minister, his guard, secretary, my secretary, and I endured five hours of treacherous driving with hundreds of potholes on a makeshift road. At times, it was touch and go, and we wondered whether we'd make it at all. Upon our arrival, a large crowd of people greeted us with colorful garlands and flowers. Mr. Paudyal was a member of the Congress Party and introduced me to the townspeople, explaining my importance to Nepal. Then he gave me a tour of the town. I said I especially wanted to see the school and hospital.

We visited the 15-bed hospital, which was far worse than Khandbari's— lacking so many of the basic necessities. If this were going to be a well-equipped hospital, it would need an infusion of investment money.

What struck me about Bandipur were the panoramic views of the lofty mountains and the sweeping horizon. The snowy peaks towered above me as if I could touch them with my outstretched hand. From my vantage point, I was perched so high, and yet the mountains towered over me. The deep valley stretched from Annapurna Valley to Pokhara. To the north were infinite mountains. The view in every direction was breathtaking.

I knew that Westerners and other tourists went straight to Pokhara and Chitwan National Park, never stopping along the way, never turning toward Bandipur. The town wasn't known to anyone. People didn't see the value and importance of this little, hidden town. But I could see its potential, importance, and value. I said to myself, *Someday I will make this place a better place to visit for Nepalis and tourists worldwide.*

Despite its magnificent setting, the town was very poorly maintained. The main street in front of the houses was muddy, filthy, and in shambles. Most of the houses were dilapidated and abandoned. After Mr. Paudyal and I toured the town for most of the day, we left to travel to the capital of the district, Damauli, where he had a meeting that evening. The government offices had moved from Bandipur to Damauli. He put me up in a rundown hotel there. I was nervous that I might get sick from the food they served. Instead, I opted for a dinner of crackers from my backpack.

As we left Bandipur for Damauli, I sat in the car's back seat with Mr. Paudyal when a crowd engulfed our vehicle. An old man approached my side of the car. It was clear he had something to say to me. I rolled down my window.

The old man whose name was Mr. Surya Piya, said, "The government neglected us, but today you appeared as an angel of hope. We don't know you very well, but you are our hope. We trust in you. You are our angel. You're going to give us something. We believe you'll be back to take care of us."

His words grabbed me and wrapped around my heart. I knew then that helping Bandipur was my fate. I knew that I had a lot more things to do in my life, in that country, every house I visited, every person I spoke with. The bottom line was that the country and her people needed help.

Once, people of Nepal said to me, "There are so many people in the world who are starving, but we are the hungriest." That was the only thing they knew. They didn't travel. They didn't read. They had no televisions. They had no window into the world outside theirs.

Wherever I go in Nepal, all I see is poverty. In every corner of the country, people need help with education, health, roads, and their drinking water supply. Whenever I travel back and forth, which is often, I compare the US and Nepal, and there is no comparison. My heart increasingly goes to Nepal and her people rather than the US. That's why I always say America is the greatest place to live. When you save a little here, it goes a long way in Nepal and elsewhere. A very long way.

One day, when I met the Prime Minister of Nepal, Mr. Girija Prasad Koirala, he said, "Yes, we have a problem in Nepal. The biggest problem we have is poverty. If we can eradicate poverty, we would be better off."

At the time, Nepal was shifting from a monarchy to a people-led system. The Nepali people were filled with hope that better days were ahead. With the advent of democracy, people became excited. But they didn't know how to translate that hope into action. They didn't know how the change would come. Under the monarchy, the rule of law was enforced through punishment. With democracy, the government couldn't control the people that way, therefore corruption and bribery became rampant. Law and order were maintained through either guns or money. Political party bias emerged. And thus, the Maoist Party was born in 1996, giving rise to communist insurgencies.

My Promise to the People of Bandipur

I returned to the US with dreams of transforming Bandipur into a gem of a town that the Nepali people could be proud of—a destination for Westerners traveling to Nepal. *What if it became a destination along the way to Pokhara?*

I drafted a handwritten letter to the people of Bandipur. Knowing that I wouldn't be back for a while, I sent it to my brother DN, asking him to get his ex-mayor friend, Shambhu Neupane from Khandbari, to travel with him to Bandipur. I said, "Please gather all the people of the town in a field and read this letter to them." I went to great lengths just to have my letter read and my words shared with the people.

My brother and Shambhu flew from Tumlingtar to Kathmandu and endured a six-hour bus ride to carry out my request. DN gathered between 500 and 600 people in July, the middle of the rainy season. He faithfully read my letter to the people of Bandipur. This letter is featured in the *Rebirth of Bandipur*, a book written about my work there.

In the letter I wrote:

I am coming to see you in the month of October 1992, between your festivals. I'll bring the Prime Minister of Nepal by helicopter, land in your town, and open his eyes to the beauty and incredible potential of your town. He will promise you, the people of Bandipur, to connect the highway to your town with a 13-kilometer road. I will also bring a group of medical people to take care of your people, your town, and the surrounding villages. We'll stay for ten days and provide top-notch healthcare services. And who knows what we can do together in the future? But at least I can do this. And please be hopeful. If everything goes well, I will arrive on October 10 or 11. The Prime Minister will be there to inaugurate our camp.

Everyone became so hopeful. Mr. Piya cried; he was so moved by my letter. He said, "Very much respect to you." But I had not yet talked to the Prime Minister of Nepal and didn't have his agreement or a legitimate plan for revitalizing Bandipur.

Making Bandipur's Dreams Come True

I arrived in Kathmandu with our Helping Hands team to fulfill my promise to the people of Bandipur. It was two weeks before the anticipated start of our operations; I had to secure an agreement with the Prime Minister. He agreed to go with us to Bandipur.

The afternoon before we were to go to Bandipur, the Prime Minister invited my team and me to his palace for tea, coffee, and treats. Our group from the US included a reporter/photographer named David Gulki from Boulder's *Daily Camera,* who captured all my work in Nepal. After David's trip to Nepal, I was featured on the front page of the *Daily Camera* with photos. The Prime Minister also invited the ministers of health, education, forestry, and homeland security. The ministers, staff, and our medical team gathered in the yard in front of his palace. Everyone was there, except for the Prime Minister and me. He gazed out the palace window anticipating my arrival. I was the guest of honor that afternoon, but I kept everyone waiting because my shoe broke at the last minute. Unfortunately, I was delayed by 30 minutes while buying new shoes for the event. When I arrived, the Prime Minister joined the gathering and spoke. Then it was my turn to speak. The event went very well.

It was such a lovely gathering and warm welcoming. I saw it as a harbinger of good things to come. But, perhaps, I drew my conclusions too quickly.

Later, I was informed that I had to pay to charter an army helicopter for our trip to Bandipur. My jaw dropped even though I knew the Prime Minister usually traveled in an army helicopter. *Why do I have to do that? Doesn't the Prime Minister's budget cover this state-sponsored business?*

Because this was such an important trip, I went ahead and paid. I figured I was chartering the helicopter so that I could fly my people in it. But I was told I could have only six seats out of 19. We had 18 members on our Helping Hands medical team—12 Americans and six Nepalis, so I had to arrange for most of the medical team to go by road for a six-hour drive from Kathmandu to Bandipur. Who knows if the money went to charter the army helicopter or into someone's pocket?

I took my brother Ram Dai and a few helpers to the airport. The six of us went early as we had been asked to do. Our helpers, my brother, and I stood in the road, waiting. A local official driving up to us, said, "Oh, by the way, Mr. Shrestha, the Prime Minister is going to be late. And we're going to be a little late taking off. Wait here while I go to my quarters to eat a meal."

The official, who was supposed to welcome us, demonstrated a lack of leadership, courtesy, and humanity. I was stunned. I expected him to say, "What can I do for you?" I did not like the official's attitude at all. If I were him, I would've hosted me in his home with respect and honor. I lost all respect for that man. *Is this the kind of leader who can make a country better? Absolutely not.* Countries will never change if people like this lead. Countries will never be in better hands if this sort of leadership is allowed to persist. Sadly, many have leaders like this and are heading in the wrong direction.

The Prime Minister was finally ready to go. People started climbing up the helicopter ladder. A skinny fellow with a snotty nose wearing flip-flops was one of the first to board.

As we waited our turn to climb the ladder, I said to the Prime Minister, "Who is this chap?"

The Prime Minister said matter-of-factly, "He's the official's son, sir," but with no explanation of why he was taking up a coveted seat.

I said, "Why is he going? He's not on my list of passengers."

The Prime Minister said, "I don't know. Ask the official."

"Why is he going?" I asked the official the obvious question.

"What can I say? He just wanted to go." The official shrugged like it was no big deal.

"Wait a minute, sir! Do we have enough seats? I have six people on my team," I said.

"Well, Mr. Shrestha, why don't you take one of your members off to make room for my son?" said the official, glaring at me.

"No, my people must go. Please send your son home."

"Sir," he insisted, "I cannot."

"His son will not obey his own father," said the Prime Minister.

I had to tell one of my helpers he couldn't go. I hid my mounting irritation.

En route, I noticed the helicopter was preparing to land before we had reached Bandipur. I learned the Prime Minister had ordered the helicopter to land near Manakamana Temple along the way. In preparation, the Nepali army was directed to cut down trees and clear cropland to create a helipad for a safe landing. Crops sprouting from the ground were destroyed.

When we got off the helicopter, the Prime Minister and his people raced ahead. I noticed a police officer trailing behind. I said, "Who's going to pay for this destroyed land?"

He said, "No worries! This is the way it is here."

"Actually, I *am* worried. What do you mean this is the way it is? We must take care of this. These destroyed crops are the farmer's food! What kind of leader does this?"

"We cannot pay for this," he said sternly.

The Prime Minister's people did not care about any damage they had done to the land.

I said to my friends, "We have to take care of this." I found the landowner, and with my helper, we determined adequate compensation for the damage. I paid the owner for his damaged land out of my pocket.

We went to the temple with an ornate stage. The flip-flop kid ran ahead of everyone, including his father. This entitled kid sat in the Prime Minister's chair and wore the slippers meant for the Prime Minister.

If a leader cannot discipline his children, how can he lead the country? How can he discipline the country? How can he help the country? This kind of leader can only help himself. I shared these thoughts with my helpers.

The helicopter finally arrived in Bandipur, where nearly 15,000 people had gathered. Initially, I was with the Prime Minister's group, who walked up onto the stage. Instead of inaugurating the camp, the Nepali officials spent hours giving speeches while sick and injured people, who had come from far away, were waiting for care. I could not bear to see that, especially since this kind of self-serving conduct among the leaders was the norm in Nepal.

I didn't stay with the herd. Instead, I went straight to the hospital and addressed the healthcare professionals on my team. "Don't wait for the inauguration. Please start working and seeing patients. We'll do the ceremony later."

Our doctors and dentists immediately started treating patients. Later, when I made the rounds, it pleased me that they were hard at work.

When the Prime Minister spoke, he praised my work. "If Narayan Shrestha were not here today, I would not be here. I am the first Prime Minister to be in this town. And because of him, I will pay to build a road from your town to the highway." The whole town started singing and dancing.

When the Prime Minister left, I saw that our contributions brought so much happiness to the townspeople. Their happiness, in turn, inspired me to do more. That happiness connected my spirit with God, with Divine Light. When I felt the Divine Light of God, it gave me energy, strength, and power to do even more for Bandipur.

I was particularly inspired by the old man, Mr. Piya, who gave a lecture to the people of Bandipur. He said, "Narayan Shrestha is a man who fulfills his promises. He gave his word, and he fulfilled that word. He gives hope. We can trust him. We don't need a leader who lies and doesn't keep his word. We need a leader who's not even from this town. Narayan wants nothing from us. He wants to give, give, give."

Mr. Piya walked with a cane. Whenever anyone said anything bad about me, he wanted to smack them with his cane.

We committed to going back to Bandipur because it desperately needed our help in the areas of the economy, education, and healthcare.

Our second trip included students from the Semester in Nepal as well as a medical team. Continuing to fulfill my promise to Bandipur's people, I gathered the townsfolk and spoke in a booming voice so everyone could hear me. "Once upon a time, rupees used to dance around this town. Now, it's so poor. Guess what? Your town is not poor. This place is still rich, but your mindset is poor because you cannot see what this town can offer you. You are blind to what this town can become. I'll tell you how to use your creativity and inventiveness to bring this town back to life. Look at those mountains." The crowd's gaze shifted toward the peaks. "Do you see the mountains?"

"We see them every day," declared a man in the crowd.

"That's why you ignore them. And you don't see the richness of the people and the culture of this town. I live in America, but I am Nepali, and I see the value of this town, and I captured it on film and made the images into slides. Back home, when I show the slides of these magnificent mountains, the stunning scenery, and the beautiful people and culture of your town, you know what happens? See these people?" I pointed to our medical team and our students. "That's how I recruited them. They fell in love with your town. This is your local treasure—soon to be our national treasure. Bandipur is a beautiful, heavenly place. All of you who've left town, please come back. Let's work together. Let's make this a great tourist destination."

We set up homestays for our students and medical teams. The medical professionals and students lived in villagers' homes, two people per home, and paid room and board. The homestays helped form connections between the locals and Americans.

We had students paint and restore the old houses, schools, and the hospital. If the houses didn't have a toilet, we had them install one. If there was open space, we asked them to plant trees.

Bandipur's high school of 500 students did not have a single toilet. The students and teachers had no choice but to do their business behind the school building out in the open. When I saw this with my naked eyes, I almost cried. It was an alarming sight to see. We paid workers to build six private compost toilets, three for the boys and three for the girls, and a water fountain.

My good friend, Bholaman Shrestha, often helped me. Once a member of the British Gurkhas, he was one of the nicest, kindest, and most trustworthy and distinguished men I have known.

From 1994 to 2004, he was with us at every village and camp. He would stay near my tent while I slept. The minute I woke up, he had hot water ready for my shower. He would take good care of me from morning to evening.

One day during one of our trips, I asked the locals to guide me to the hills. The local doctors, hospital employees, businessmen, and helpers were walking with me. When I was walking to one of the hills, I saw a plateau on the hill from which one could see panoramic views. I really liked that land.

"Who owns this land?" I asked.

A local doctor said, "I know the man who owns this. Do you want to buy this land?"

"Yes!" I knew if I bought the land and built a house, I would come back for sure.

"Okay, I will talk to the guy." That afternoon the local doctor talked to the landowner, and we came up with a deal. It was 17 acres of land at 4,000 rupees per acre.

"Can I put a deposit of 10,000 rupees on the land?" I asked.

He agreed.

Six months later, when we went back to Bandipur with another group, I learned that five local businessmen had bought the land away from me at 17,000 rupees per acre. They didn't want me to own the land.

Ram Kumar Shrestha, the ex-mayor of the town, was so upset, he came to me and addressed me as "Prabhu," which means God, even though he was older than me. "You were betrayed by idiots. They don't know who you are. I know exactly who you are. You are a giver, not a taker. You are something else. Don't worry. I want to offer you something. I have land right next to the land you like. I have five acres with 65 orange trees. I will give it to you as a gift."

"I cannot do this. I have to pay for this," I said.

"I call you God, Prabhu, because I want to give something to God. A God must not refuse."

"Please, let me get back to you," I said.

He would not let me go. "Tomorrow afternoon at 4:00, I'm gathering the townspeople. Please come, and let's have a talk then."

In the middle of the meeting with 150 people, Ram said, "Prabhu, I want to give you the land. Please say you accept. I will even pay for the title. And then I will throw a big party in your honor."

"I accept," I said.

He promptly went to the government office and transferred the land to my name. His gift was priceless.

I later added 11 acres, which I bought for 150,000 rupees.

When you do good things, people support you. Ram Kumar, Mr. Piya, and the whole town started supporting me. Because Ram Kumar, who was such a cherished friend, wanted a temple in his town, my siblings and I donated money for a temple in Bandipur. We established it in the name of my parents and siblings.

Meeting the King of Nepal

One day in 1994, I was in Bandipur, working with doctors and nurses at the hospital. A guy came running up to me. He was winded when he said, "The Royal Palace is looking for you. You need to come to the Public Communication Office (PCO) and talk to the Royal Palace."

"What do you mean, the Royal Palace?!" I asked, stunned.

"The King of Nepal asked me to reach out to you. He wants to see you."

The King of Nepal?! Birendra Bir Bikran Shal Dev? Oh, my goodness! I jumped a fence and ran up to the PCO, my heart pounding out of my chest. I spoke to the King's secretary, who said that the King wanted to see me at the Narayanhiti Royal Palace in Kathmandu at 10:00 am the next day. He said if I didn't have transportation, he'd send a car.

"Oh, and please dress well," the secretary requested.

"I'm terribly sorry, but I don't have any formal Nepalese clothes with me."

"Okay, since you are an American citizen, why don't you wear a suit and tie? But you should at least wear a hat (a topi)."

"Okay, that much I can do," I said.

The palace arranged for a driver to pick me up that evening at 8:00. We reached the Malla Hotel near the palace around midnight. When in Kathmandu, I regularly stayed at this hotel. They even had a suite—Room 307—ready and waiting for me. This high-end hotel suited me because of my allergies. I had to limit my exposure to pollution and dust and be careful about what I ate. I needed to stay healthy to do my work in Nepal.

The next morning, I took a shower, got a haircut, and put on my nicest suit.

A brigadier, a one-star general, came to pick me up and let me out at the west gate of the palace. It was the first time in my life I had entered that gate. I was thrilled to be a special guest of the King. An army personal guard led me inside, where another army general greeted me and then the King's secretary.

The secretary said, "This is your first time meeting the King, so you must greet him properly. Although you are a citizen of the United States, your origin is Nepali, so you are expected to know the traditions of our culture."

"Don't worry. I'll go the extra mile to greet the King."

He briefed me on the proper way to greet the King, and I thanked him.

His secretary announced me, and we both entered the ornate room in which the King waited for me. I greeted him and then tossed a one-ounce gold coin toward him, the traditional way to greet the King. After I threw it, he was supposed to pick it up and give it back to me. But the coin just sat there.

I thought, *I don't want to give him the coin. He doesn't need it.* Eventually, I retrieved the coin, and the King said, "Yes, keep it. It's yours."

I pocketed the gold coin and sidled up to the large coffee table between us. The setup was such that there were two coffee tables' distance between the King and his visitors. His secretary sat behind me, taking notes.

After we had talked extensively about our work in Nepal, the King said, "I've heard so much about you from the secretary, brigadier general of the army, and a few ministers. They all say good things about you. You know, Narayan, if you ever want to come back to Nepal and hold a ministry position, which ministry would you like? You let me know."

I said, "I would love to, but I have to check with my wife, Your Majesty. I don't know whether she would allow me."

"She allowed you to help the Nepali people. You've accomplished so much on your own that no one else has been able to do."

"Your Majesty, I will talk to her—okay? I will happily see you again. Just say the word."

"My secretary will be contacting you, or you can contact him, and if there's anything we can do, let me know, but one thing I will tell you..."

"Yes, Your Majesty?" I said.

"I need ten of you in this country. All I need are ten Narayans. You are a true son of Nepal."

I'll never forget that moment. His words touched me deeply. "But Your Majesty, if I were here, living in Nepal, I could not have done this much. I got the opportunity because I live in the United States, and I'm really happy living there. And I'm proud of what I have been able to do for Nepal and the Nepali people. If I were a minister here, I would be one of them. I cannot do that. But, still, if Your Majesty insists, I will check with my wife."

"Okay, let me know what she says. Thank you, Narayan."

When I returned to Boulder, Sreejana thought about it for a moment and then said, "I'd rather be the wife of the mayor of Boulder, Colorado, than the wife of the Prime Minister of Nepal. This place is heavenly."

A Promise Fulfilled

For 16 years, I worked to fulfill my promise to the people of Bandipur. Every time I visited Bandipur, I gathered the townspeople, including those who left the town for more prosperous cities. I asked them to return for my talks. They returned to listen to me because I was revitalizing their town. I shared my vision with the people gathered—to create a walking mall and turn their houses into hotels. I said that Westerners would come, and dollars would be dancing in their houses. Slowly but surely, everything I said happened. The town changed for the better, and every single day, so did each home in the town.

I kept an open dialogue with the extended community, asking them to come to Bandipur from Kathmandu, Chitwan, and Damauli, the headquarters of the district of Tanahau. I gave talks in which I offered recommendations about health and education. I stressed the importance of toilets for schools. I taught them about dental hygiene programs by bringing dental hygienists from the US to distribute products and to demonstrate their usage.

I visited the tourism department and asked them to come and see the transformation. I said, "Please advertise Bandipur in your government flyers. Promote the town to tourists." They listened to me because I knew the director of the tourism department. He had studied in the US and had always respected me. I believed and insisted that Bandipur could be a prized tourist destination, and I was right.

In 2006, I went back to Bandipur with a television crew. Ram Kumar and a reporter for a national newspaper were also there. The reporter authored *Rebirth of Bandipur,* a book about me written in Nepalese. The people of Bandipur made welcome gates and lined up on both sides of the street. I went through the gates, and they buried me with garlands and flowers. They had reserved a lovely hotel room for me, and they urged me to keep coming back.

Their words moved me. But I said, "My work is done here. All my goals and dreams have been accomplished for the Bandipur people who feel hometown pride and the tourists who clamor to visit Bandipur. Many of the locals who had abandoned the town have returned. Together we have westernized Bandipur but kept its treasured heritage. With a little touch here and a little touch there, we brought it back to life."

Bandipur began to appear on maps of Nepal. It became a tourist destination. The town has turned into one of the top tourist places from which to see the Himalayas' snow-covered peaks. Bandipur is a beautifully preserved village perched on a lofty ridge, its main street dotted with restored row houses. Ramshackle buildings found new life as restaurants and hotels. Temples and civic buildings have been pulled back from the edge of ruin. The trees planted by my students tower above the town. And the hospital is thriving. Most residents not only praise me as a good man, but they have a tremendous amount of respect for me.

I'll never forget, when I visited Bandipur in the 10th year, a woman approached me and said, "You are a god to me because you saved my life."

"I did?" I asked.

"I was sick, and no one could take me to your clinic. But you brought a doctor to my home. He took care of me, and you gave me medicine and supplies for one year. I got stronger and now I'm healthy. You came at just the right time and saved my life."

I'm proud of my legacy. Bandipur remains one of my most favorite places in the world. Helping Hands grew and prospered because of our work in Bandipur. If we had not started Helping Hands, Bandipur would not have turned around like that. Never. And the town would have been lost in the annals of history.

CHAPTER 11

Lessons from Ilam, Dharmasthali, and Chainpur

If you give, the recipient must be able to hold your gift firmly. Otherwise, when you release your hands to let go, the gift will pour straight into the ground like sand through a sieve and be lost forever.

N 1991, I HEARD THAT AN OLD COLLEGE FRIEND named Jhala Nath Khanal had become the Minister of Land Reform after the revolution, and democracy had come to Nepal. We had lost touch when he went underground because of his role as a Communist Party leader. I'd never been affiliated with any Nepali political party, including the Nepali Congress Party, the Communist Party, and the Royal Party. I'd never cared for the partisanship that plagued Nepal and so many other countries around the world. I went to see my friend. We hugged, shook hands, and talked about old times. It was such a beautiful reunion after 20 years.

Ilam

Later that year, he came to the US with six members of the Parliament, including two from the Royal Party, two from the Nepali Congress Party, and two from the Communist Party. They visited New York and Washington, and then they made a final stop in Colorado. For two nights, the US government put them up in a hotel in downtown Denver. I showed them the sights and fed them well in my Boulder and Fort Collins restaurants.

The night before they were scheduled to return home, I went to pick them up at the hotel to have dinner at my restaurant. I sat in the lobby, waiting for them. One by one, they joined me and slowly began to bicker. A Nepali Congress Party Parliament member, Mr. Bal Bahadur K.C., and Jhala Nath got into an argument. It became so heated they were nearly yelling. I was so embarrassed that I rushed them to my van, hoping they would calm down. I had to hit them to quiet them down, but they continued cursing at each other. I didn't know why they were fighting, but I didn't want to get involved.

After the meal, the State Department's escort took everyone but Jhala Nath and Bal Bahadur back to the hotel for a good night's rest before their long journey back to Nepal. My brother Dharma took Bal Bahadur to his house. Jhala Nath and I visited at my place, talking into the wee hours of the morning. At 5:00 am, I gave him a lift to the hotel. He had come to understand who I was and what I had done for Nepal. As we were saying goodbye, he asked, "Is there any way you can bring your medical team to my town, Ilam?"

I considered his request. I had refused many other ministers' requests, but I agreed to help the people of his town.

Ilam is a town in the Mahabharat Range on India's border. At that time, dollars were already dancing in Ilam. The fertile region produces some of the world's finest black and green tea and cardamom, a popular spice. Also, it grows potatoes and many other crops. Even back then, the people of Ilam didn't have to worry about the local economy's health. However, despite their relative wealth, they lacked healthcare services and quality schools.

In 1994, Jhala Nath Khanal lost in the midterm election, so he needed my help to boost his reputation. We took a 16-member medical team from the US and a 14-member team from Kathmandu to Ilam. Our volunteers included a man and a woman from the opposition party, the Nepali Congress Party. As far as I was concerned, no Nepali political party was superior to another. I didn't take sides.

Because Jhala Nath was a friend, I let him inaugurate the mobile clinic. But he did a sneaky thing, which I didn't learn about until later. He was supposed to leave after the inauguration, but instead he remained in Ilam. The volunteers from the Nepali Congress Party approached me in protest. They revealed that my friend made it widely known that he was the one who brought us. Although it was partially true, he had done it primarily to boost his chances in the election. The volunteers handed me a pamphlet claiming that only Jhala Nath had brought a medical team to Ilam for the sake of the people in the Ilam District.

It read:

Because I am your representative, I have brought Western medical help to our village. Please come and take advantage of this free service.

The pamphlet had been distributed all over the district with the wrong message. It was supposed to say that Helping Hands had brought the service.

I called Jhala Nath to my quarters and scolded him. I ordered him to leave immediately, but he refused. The next day, I called a meeting of both parties at the municipality building, and the opposition party gave him such a hard time, he finally left. I didn't have to say a word.

Ilam had a hospital with doctors and patients, but the facility was substandard and the medical equipment crude. I was shocked to discover that newborns who needed to be kept in the hospital were placed in a motor tire cut in half—the hospital's incubator! Like the hospital in Khandbari, the beds were makeshift, without sheets or pillowcases. The facility even lacked soap. I donated an incubator and other much-needed medical devices and supplies.

One of my most memorable moments was in 1995 when we ran our first medical camp in Ilam. I was speaking at a college and the students swarmed around me in the auditorium. For them I was a distinguished guest. It was the first time we brought American nurses, doctors, and surgeons.

In total, we ran six mobile clinics in Ilam. The first included medical professionals from Colorado and Alaska. Patricia Galaneck, a nurse-turned-photographer, photographed our medical team. We had eight doctors, six nurses, two physician's assistants (PAs), two dentists, two hygienists, and some dental assistants. Every day, each doctor saw 80 patients. Altogether, we saw

1,000 patients a day for ten days. We provided free services and medicine. However, we lacked an ultrasound machine. Without diagnostic equipment, the doctors could only guess at specific conditions and diagnoses.

Helping Hands did not have a hospital or clinic in Ilam, yet. We would collect 40-50 patients and ship them by bus to Kathmandu. We housed the patients and their families in a hotel and admitted them to a Kathmandu hospital. Once the patients were admitted, we fed them, bought their medicine, paid for the hotel, and covered the hospital costs for a month. Once people found out about this, I became so well known that they would watch me from windows and doors.

When I told this story to the college students, a young woman fainted and was rushed to the hospital. I went to the hospital to visit her. She said, "I don't care what I went through because it's unbelievable to see you here in person."

When I was in Ilam with our medical teams, Jhala Nath Khanal would visit me, and I'd advise him. "You should go from village to village with medical doctors and nurses, reaching the areas others cannot. With your party in power, why don't you take a helicopter full of doctors and surgeons and help the people? They will praise you, and you will lift them up and inspire them to do better, be better."

He took copious notes and implemented some of my ideas. After Helping Hands came to Ilam, my friend never lost an election again. And in 2011, he became the 35th Prime Minister of Nepal.

We did no fundraising whatsoever; we drew from my wife's and my income, plus volunteer contributions. We never raised funds until 2003. We didn't need to because, in the 1990s, our businesses were so prosperous. Not only did we support our extended family members and villagers, but we also funded the work of Helping Hands all over Nepal and in other countries. We shared our income with hundreds of thousands of people. We gave and became happier. My wife was always supportive, boosting my morale by saying, "Help the poor, women, and children. I will always work to fulfill your dream to help others."

Since we did no fundraising, for many years Helping Hands was primarily fueled by Sreejana's and my earnings, our ideas, and her encouragement. Support also came from the American volunteers who donated their money and expertise. The generosity of my American friends knows no bounds. So many of them donate money to NGOs, which goes to poor countries around the world. Americans are doing the right things by forming NGOs, collecting money among citizens, and giving to countries in need. I've always been blown away by the generous hearts of my American friends.

I'm particularly grateful to my very good friend John Power whom I met at Old Tibet in 2003. He runs several philanthropic organizations and understands the importance of Helping Hands. Not only is he a continuous donor, but he has taught me how to host fundraising events for Helping Hands.

It is beyond anyone's imagination how much Americans donate in the areas of health and education. Without these donations, the world would be significantly poorer. If Americans stopped thinking about other people in the world who need help, those people would suffer even more.

In later years after 2005, hundreds of my friends in Colorado and other parts of the country chipped in to support our causes. We could not have continuously supported our programs without the generous help of these donors. Those friends greatly inspired us to do more in other parts of the world.

I've discovered that you become richer when you give more to other people. You are the richest of all when you feel intrinsically satisfied. You harbor no internal pain. This is the richness of giving. When you keep giving without expectation, it's the purest kind of giving.

With great regret, we had to leave Ilam. The people there didn't hold onto our gift; they let it fall to the ground. I gave lectures to leaders, teachers, and students, which they intently listened to, but they dropped the ball the minute we left. Some people were individually successful, but they didn't care much about our services. I discovered that many people were just politically motivated, using our organization for political ends.

Ilam had fine educational institutions, but the hospital was run down. We went there for six years, but we realized we were wasting our time. My college friend became a renowned leader in the country and never asked us to go back again. If he had, we would not have gone back because he was too politically motivated. Helping Hands is a people's organization focused on people's development, not a tool for political gain.

Lessons learned: To expand Helping Hands' reach, we needed to fundraise. We had done so much with my wife's and my money, but it was time to move beyond self-funding. Our organization could grow and prosper even more with outside funds. Also, for doctors to effectively diagnose Nepali patients, we needed to invest in diagnostic equipment in our clinics. Back then, there was no diagnostic equipment in most hospitals and clinics in Nepal.

Dharmasthali

In 2003, I was invited to Dharmasthali by Buddhi Maya Ghimire, an older woman with a dream to open a women's clinic there.

Dharmasthali is a village, by a river, that is part of Tarakeshwar Municipality in the Kathmandu District of Province No. 3 in central Nepal. Mrs. Ghimire told me that many pregnant women going into labor in her village could not get to the hospital in nearby Kathmandu because there was no road. Women in labor would head for the city and not make it in time. They would squat down in the riverbed and give birth to their newborns. Sadly, some women died in childbirth when complications arose and there was no one around to help. Others survived but lost their babies. When I heard this story, it pulled on my heartstrings. I wanted to see the town and its people for myself—to hear firsthand accounts to understand their woes.

In 1998, my driver drove my Jeep to take me and a few others to Dharmasthali. The engineer who would do the drawings, and the young lady who introduced me to the village were with us. I knew we would be navigating rough terrain to reach the town.

No problem in a Jeep, I thought. I was seated in the passenger's seat on the left-hand side, and the driver was on the right—British driving protocols. As we approached the town, to our left was a cliff—a sheer drop-off—and on the right, a river. Because I felt nervous about driving so close to the cliff, the driver steered the Jeep toward the river, which streamed over the road. As he drove, the tires on the vehicle's right side began sinking into the mud. Then, he cut a little too sharply, and the Jeep veered into the river. If it had veered towards the cliff, we all would have died. Instead, we got soaked. With much difficulty, we escaped from the Jeep, but thankfully everyone was safe. The Jeep was partially submerged in the river and stuck in the mud. We waited by the river and watched as villagers tried unsuccessfully to push my car out of the water.

As we waited for help to arrive, many villagers—mostly women—approached me with a repeated refrain. "Please help us by opening a women's clinic here."

Later that evening, my staff from Kathmandu went to the river and retrieved the Jeep with a big, old crane.

After hearing so many women's pleas, I decided to open a small clinic in Dharmasthali and gave them my word that I would do it. The local people gave us land with the agreement that while Helping Hands ran a clinic, we could have that land. Instead of a small clinic, the people of Dharmasthali urged us to build a large healthcare facility. When an engineer gave us a design for a humongous building, I tried to reduce it. But in our absence, the locals dug a hole in the ground for the bigger building. I was living in the US and traveling to other countries and could not get there in time to stop them. By the time I visited, 23 towering pillars had been constructed, and there was no going back. The locals kept asking for money, which we sent, thinking that the project was viable and worthwhile.

We had no choice but to support the people. We were blinded and believed it would be a reasonably sized building with a bigger hospital. There was a building committee and two guys working to construct the building. They continued to have a money shortage. We struggled to keep up with the requests for money. We kept sending money. We discovered the full extent of the building only after one floor was completed. We had already invested a substantial amount of our money. And our enthusiasm drained. We couldn't send any more money.

The project stalled for three years. Eventually, we visited the uncompleted building and gathered the local people. They believed we were the only ones who could complete it. They wanted us to push one more time. The villagers encouraged us to add a second floor to accommodate more beds. We promised if they helped me, together, we could build a two-story building. They were very enthusiastic about the project, and I got caught up in the excitement.

To make it happen, we teamed up with a famous Nepali guru, Din Bandhu Pokharel, a preaching pundit who made appearances across the region to fundraise for the hospital. Before his speaking dates, we would announce Din's appearances, create advertisements, and go door to door, covering Kathmandu District's whole northern part. We went from village to village to promote the project, and we locally raised another $150,000.

For a week, Din preached six hours a day about Hinduism. This was called a saptaha, or seven days of preaching. Around 600 people gathered each day to listen to stories about Krishna. In 2013, we invited the first President of Nepal, Ram Baran Yadav, to a fundraising ceremony. He attended and spoke on behalf of me and Helping Hands.

Meanwhile, my wife took care of our children back home while I was thinking about the Nepali people. I called her every morning and evening.

Sreejana would say, "Keep doing what you are doing. I'm fine. The children are fine." Her words gave me the energy to keep going.

By the time the beautiful new facility was built and equipped, there was a decreasing need for our services, and it sat half-empty. During the four years our hospital operated, a road was constructed between Dharmasthali and Kathmandu. Now, villagers could go just six kilometers, a five-minute drive, to reach Kathmandu. Who would opt for a local hospital when a big city state-of-the-art hospital was so close?

Despite our best intentions, the project in Dharmasthali was the worst decision of my life. With the money spent to launch and run the big healthcare facility, we could have opened nine or ten clinics in other villages across Nepal, broadening the reach of Helping Hands. It was such a painful lesson, but one I heeded.

After 20 years, in 2018, there was a local election, and a new mayor was elected. We closed the hospital that year and gave the beautiful building to the town to use. The municipality now uses it for administrative purposes.

I am happy that Helping Hands' money went to help the Nepali people there. But we could have saved thousands more lives instead of ending up with a government administrative building.

Lessons learned: Don't make huge infrastructure investments unless the decision is carefully vetted with considerations such as community needs, access to other healthcare services, and competition for services. One should not be gullible when doing good things for others. One should listen, think, and make good decisions to impact as many people as possible. Helping Hands should invest in smaller healthcare projects to broaden its reach.

Chainpur

Once upon a time, Chainpur was the headquarters of the Eastern Region of Nepal. The town is a municipality in the Sankhuwasabha District in the Kosi Zone of northeastern Nepal. Sitting at an elevation of around 1,200 meters above sea level, Chainpur is at a vantage point where Mount Makalu, the world's fifth tallest peak, can be viewed to the north and the Arun Valley to the southwest. The world's deepest valley is home to 650 species of birds, 800 species of butterflies, 3,000 kinds of flowering plants, and 47 species of orchids.

In my youth, Chainpur was the only town in the region with a school. It was also one of the only towns with a thriving economy. But eventually, the economic boom shifted to Khandbari, and the businesses and government administrative services followed. The government announced that Khandbari would be the headquarters of that district. Its new offices were opened in Khandbari. Businessmen began losing faith in Chainpur. When the young people of Chainpur finished their education, they left in search of opportunities and never returned. Once they settled into their new lives, they sent for their parents, further emptying the town. The population was slowly dwindling, and animals began to emerge from the wilderness. In the middle of the day, jackals and other wild animals could be seen wandering the streets and into abandoned homes looking for food. The once-thriving town was dying.

I leveraged my knowledge and experience working in Bandipur in which I focused on one village until it experienced a rebirth. I decided to replicate my approach in Chainpur. I would start by introducing a healthcare program. Then, bit by bit, the locals would see the changes and be lured back.

Like so many places in Nepal, Chainpur didn't have a quality healthcare system. In June of 2018, Helping Hands introduced a healthcare program, opening a clinic in a rented house. Seven American healthcare professionals, mostly women, including Helping Hands board member Susan Mitchell, went to Chainpur. Also, long-time volunteer Peggy Milano from Fort Collins joined the team which included Dr. Jennifer Johnson, Mary Faltynski, and Sangya Dicky.

For five days, we offered free healthcare services, including X-rays and ultrasounds. A first-rate doctor from Biratnagar treated the patients, doing an excellent job of providing care. We also had a dentist who treated 1,600 patients, and we gave away toothbrushes and dental floss. A Helping Hands board member donated 20,000 pairs of eyeglasses. Initially, we distributed about 2,500 free. Each month, we had a camp called George's Village Medical Camp, and later we distributed more glasses. George Newell is another board member who donated money and eyeglasses and sponsored 18 camps per year throughout Eastern Nepal and Kathmandu Valley. Helping Hands donated to the clinic. Our final contribution was a digital X-ray that was part donation, part loan. After that, we didn't have to spend a dime. They kept it going on their own.

People poured into the clinic, and the patients and their families were thrilled with our services. Innovative Water Technologies, a company dedicated to researching and developing products for water treatment and purification, also donated a drinking water filtering system, and Helping Hands offered scholarship funds. Whenever I went to Chainpur, I held town meetings, gathering people, and spoke to them about education, healthcare, and tourism. I wanted to tempt the people who had abandoned Chainpur to return. I encouraged them to launch homestay programs for tourism as an alternative to the rundown, sometimes bug-infested hotels. Approximately 50 families signed up for the programs. I sent Japanese and American friends to stay in villagers' homes, generating income for the locals. This encouraged townspeople to fix up and decorate their homes. And everyone loved it.

Educating the townspeople to improve the quality of their lives didn't prove difficult. The challenge in Chainpur was that the villagers got jealous and tried to sabotage others' success. For example, when a Chainpur resident discovered that the child next door received a scholarship and their child didn't, animosity mounted, and strife fractured the neighborly relationship. The neighbor even tried to sabotage the other, figuring if their child didn't have access to a scholarship, no child should. The spiteful neighbor spread malicious gossip and made everyone miserable.

Instead of living in harmony, people sometimes lived in pain and strife. And it didn't just afflict Chainpur; it happened all over Nepal. Sabotage was a societal tendency—pulling each other down because of greed and envy. But it wasn't entirely the people's fault. Poverty breeds desperation and a survival mentality. If a person's stomach is empty, their brain is empty, and their heart is desperate. You must have enough food in your tummy for your brain to work. When your stomach is empty, your brain is focused on the negative aspects of life.

Seeing all the difficulties of Chainpur, I am focusing on building the town the way I helped rebuild Bandipur. But I see nobody who has left for Kathmandu, Dharan, or Biratnagar is returning to this town. They will not come back because they're already established in those big cities. Half of Chainpur is still empty. I am focusing on those empty houses and plan to reach out to people living lavishly elsewhere and bring them back to their hometown.

Helping to revitalize Chainpur is a worthwhile mission. My goal is to go to Kathmandu, Biratnagar, and Dharan, gather people who have left, and talk with them. I will convince them that just making money isn't the path to happiness. I know every property owner and family member of Chainpur who has left. I will request that they do something, like fixing up their abandoned properties to make their town a vibrant tourist town. From Chainpur, you can see the mountains of the east, the deep valley, and hills of the Eastern Region. It is glorious scenery.

When they played as children in their yards with the dirt, sticks, and pebbles, they saw the majestic mountains. If I can't do this in my lifetime, I want to send a message to the people of Chainpur:

Like your parents, never forget your roots. Our human duty is to make our backyards beautiful and lovingly grow our communities. Please don't forget to go back and make your abandoned home a place to live and prosper.

I will continue to encourage the people of Chainpur to be creative and carefully work and love each other and be prosperous.

Lessons learned: If you give, the recipient must be able to hold onto the gift firmly. Otherwise, when you release your hands to let go, the gift will pour straight into the ground like sand through a sieve and be lost forever. In addition to providing healthcare to communities, it's important to offer education so that the townspeople can make the necessary changes to enhance the quality of their lives.

CHAPTER 12

From Monarchy to Maoism

The work my medical team is offering in our clinic is for everyone. If anyone is wounded, we will be there to help, whether the patient is a Maoist or not. We won't discriminate.

I N THE LATE 1990S, KING BIRENDRA OF NEPAL invited me to his palace, the third of seven such meetings during his reign. He wanted me to help him with a problem close to his heart, his son, Crown Prince Dipendra. As always, it was an honor to be invited, and I hoped I wouldn't disappoint.

A Special Request from the King

After I properly greeted King Birendra, he asked me to please have a seat. He leaned forward in his chair and said with pleading eyes, "Is there any way you can help the Crown Prince?"

"In what sense, Your Majesty?" I asked. I had heard rumors that he was a wild prince, but that was really all I knew.

"I sent him to study in London, and his behavior problems worsened. When he came home, he was even more out of control. I wanted to see whether you could guide him in the right direction."

I couldn't imagine why he was asking me to help with the behavioral problems of his son. But I had become something of a solutions guy in Nepal. When people had a problem they couldn't solve, they would think, *Narayan Shrestha will solve it. He fixes everything!*

I earnestly gazed at him, wondering how one graciously turns down a king. "I would like to help, but I have so many other pressing priorities. If I don't continue my work, so many people in Nepal won't receive medical and educational help. Should I devote my focus to just one person when so many of our countrymen and women are in need? But, if this is an order from you, Your Majesty, I will certainly oblige."

He paused and wrung his hands. It was as if he had run out of options. "I really need your help," he said with a hint of desperation in his eyes.

I was no stranger to on-the-spot problem-solving; I always had to think on my feet. I proposed that the Crown Prince live in Boulder and study at the University of Colorado. The King agreed. But I would have to check with my friend, Dr. Judith Albino, President of the University of Colorado.

During this time, the Maoist insurgents, adherents to the political, economic, and social theories of Mao Zedong, had infiltrated many regions of the country in their ongoing attempt to seize power in Nepal. The rebels had been fighting since 1996 to overthrow the monarchy and install a communist government. By 2000, their influence had radically altered the landscape of Nepal. The Nepalese Civil War, known as the Maoist Revolution, was fought between the Communist Party of Nepal and the Nepali government. The Maoist insurgents were spread throughout the country, wreaking havoc and causing major disturbances. Travel warnings had been issued for Nepal, including from the US, who advised its citizens not to travel to Nepal.

Every time we sent a medical team or a group of students, we required them to register with the US Embassy. The people at the consulate were good to us because we sent so many people to Nepal at our risk. We weren't intimidated by the Maoists because we were doing good work for the people of Nepal. We were primarily concerned about the safety of American citizens, as the Maoists hated America. But we thought we could influence them so they wouldn't touch our people.

The Crown Prince

On June 1, 2000, I was invited to the King of Nepal's palace to meet with Crown Prince Dipendra. My first impression of him was that he was nothing like his father. He seemed surly and had no light in his eyes. But I thought nothing of it—just that he was a rebellious fellow. The minute we sat down to talk, he lit a cigarette. I asked him if he could refrain because I was allergic to smoke. He shot me an irritated glance while extinguishing his cigarette. We talked about the plan for him to study political science at the University of Colorado in the fall of 2001. Mostly he wanted to know how much freedom he would have. I told him that he would be under my watch and would have to stay focused on his studies. He seemed amenable to the plan. We had our picture taken together, and the deal was sealed. Everyone was pleased, especially the King.

I had many meetings with Dr. Albino and Dr. Richard L. Byyny, University of Colorado Chancellor. We struck an agreement that the Crown Prince would study there and reside in an on-campus apartment. We discussed the possible need for the Secret Service and decided we would arrange for a security detail if needed. Dr. Albino gave me an official invitation and books to deliver to the palace. The Crown Prince was to be admitted to the University of Colorado in August 2001.

On June 1, 2001, I was in Philadelphia speaking at the University of Pennsylvania, having been invited by a doctor who had worked with Helping Hands in Nepal. He arranged for me to speak to medical students and residents about my work.

After my talk, which was very well-received, my wife called me at the Holiday Inn where I was tucked in for the night, sounding panicked. "Did you turn on CNN?"

"No, what? What's going on?"

"There's a disaster in Nepal." My wife always kept her cool, so I knew something was terribly wrong.

"What do you mean?" *Is it a natural disaster, a crisis with the Maoists, or something personal?*

"Turn it on, turn it on!" she cried.

I switched on CNN and saw the headline: *Nepalese Royal Massacre*. I stopped breathing for a minute, felt dizzy, as if someone had punched me in the gut. I watched as the news anchors reported the story and showed footage of the unthinkable tragedy. I witnessed the scene 7,526 miles from my country of origin—the royal families' dead bodies, flies swarming, and absolute chaos descending upon the country. Nepali citizens were weeping and shaving their heads in mourning, schools were closed, and curfews were set.

Crown Prince Dipendra had opened fire at a house on the grounds of the Narayanhiti Royal Palace, the residence of the Nepali monarchs, where a party was being held. He shot and killed his father, King Birendra, his mother, Queen Aishwarya, and seven other royal family members—including his younger brother and sister—before shooting himself in the head. In the massacre, he had wiped out most of the line of succession, so he became King while in a comatose state from his head wound. He died three days later.

This was the same Crown Prince I was supposed to help. The Crown Prince who was going to be my charge. The Crown Prince whose life I had hoped to turn around.

The terrible scene devastated me. I knew I had to get home as quickly as possible. My flight was scheduled for June 3, but I returned on June 2. I mourned for seven days, crying my heart out. Hundreds of people gathered in front of Old Tibet to mourn with me. Everyone burned a candle, and I gave a small talk.

I had become a close friend of the King who entrusted me with the care of his son, the Crown Prince. And in one horrific, bloody moment, so many people and their dreams were dead. Was it a sinister foreshadowing for the future of the Nepali monarchy?

The New King of Nepal

The King's brother, the new King Gyanendra, assumed the throne of Nepal. There were rumors that he was involved in a conspiracy to take over the throne. I don't believe those theories. I believe the Crown Prince was crazy. Even the cigarette I had asked him to put out had looked funny, like he had rolled it himself, and smelled funny, like it wasn't tobacco.

About a year later, when I was in Kathmandu, I got a call from a two-star general, Mr. Tika Dhamala, King Gyanendra's bodyguard at the palace. "Mr. Shrestha, King Gyanendra wants to see you."

"Whoa, that's wonderful!"

I met the new King in the same room as his brother. He sat in the same chair as King Birendra.

He said, "My brother, King Birendra, and you had such a good relationship. I understand you were very close to the Palace, so I'd like to continue that tradition. Can we become friends? And perhaps you can help me, also."

"Your Majesty asked me to come, and I came. Whenever you need me, I'm here for you."

King Gyanendra and I became very good friends. Whenever I wanted to see him, I wrote him a letter, and he said, "Come on in." It was that easy.

During one of my visits, King Gyanendra asked me to listen to a speech he was planning to make and give him some feedback.

"Your Majesty, you are now the King of Nepal; however, you have no power. But I want the legacy of the King of Nepal to remain forever, like the King and Queen of England. They have no power, but they are highly respected among their people and the world, as is Hirohito, the Emperor of Japan. The prime ministers do all the work, and the king sits in the palace and enjoys the title. You should do that. I want to advise you, Your Majesty, to believe in me, as King Birendra trusted in me. Go village to village, especially the western side of Nepal, and reach out to the people of Nepal. When you touch someone's life, and they express their troubles, call on your assistant to help address that person's problems. Then, you will be an effective king."

Three months later, he did as I advised and started reaching out to the people in the villages in his attempt to become a compassionate king. But he didn't continue to follow my recommendations. As a leader, you don't ask villagers about their problems and needs unless you intend to follow through, which he never did. The people of Nepal began to mock the new king.

His cabinet ministers were all corrupt; each person he picked was dishonest or went to prison for bribery or attempted murder. He selected them because when he was the Prince of Nepal, they were his supporters. In the end, the Nepali people did not like the rule of King Gyanendra.

Helping Hands Clinic in Phalebas

A man named Mr. Bhola Sharma from Phalebas, a retired high-ranking government officer, had heard about my work. Back then, I was well known for my work in Nepal. He wrote me a letter in the early 2000s asking me to meet him in Bandipur. I could see he was a very sincere, loyal, honest man who wasn't angling for a political position. He had devoted his life to his people. He impressed me so much I invited him to become a Helping Hands board member. I appointed him the Board Secretary of the Nepal chapter. During that meeting, he invited me to visit Phalebas.

Not only did I visit, but I also brought a Helping Hands mobile clinic with me.

The village is located approximately 92 miles west of Kathmandu, in the Midwestern Region of Nepal. But there was a sticking point, one that would've stopped most people in their tracks, one that would've struck fear in the hearts of most—the Maoists were active in that region. But I wasn't going to let the disruptive Maoists interfere with the important work of Helping Hands. So, I thought, I'll deal with the insurgents if or when the time comes. We organized a medical team who traveled to Kathmandu and stayed there for a couple of days, after which our team set out for Phalebas, spending the night in a hotel along the way.

Two district officers came to our hotel that night and asked to speak with me. After we moved to a private location in the hotel, the district officer with the more commanding presence said, "We are here to advise you against opening a clinic in Phalebas. There's a big risk to you and your people. The Maoists have control of the area, and it is unstable and dangerous."

"The Maoists will seize your clinic and demand that you treat the wounded rebels," added the more reserved officer with his arms crossed over his chest.

I wasn't going to let terrorists interfere with our clinic. I knew the locals, including the Maoists themselves, wanted and needed services that the government could not provide. "Listen, the work our medical team offers in our clinic is for everyone. If anyone is wounded, we will be there to help, whether the patient is a Maoist or not. We won't discriminate. So, please don't interfere with our important work," I said, making eye contact with both officials. They wore grim expressions in response to my insistence, but that didn't stop me. Nothing was going to stop us. "We'll proceed at our own risk."

"Okay, Narayan, sir, don't come asking for help if you get into trouble," said the reserved officer.

"Fine." As far as I was concerned, our business was finished. "Have a nice evening, gentlemen." And I headed to my room, cursing the darned Maoists.

I wasn't a fan of the Communist Party. They lied so much, saying to the people, "Give us your support, and we will give you equally distributed wealth. We'll take wealthy people's properties and distribute them among you." Poor people believed their propaganda and voted for them. It was the same story all over the world. Communists promised everything to poor people, who put their faith in them, and the communists never delivered on their promises.

Communism is falling apart all over the world; it fell apart in Eastern Europe and Russia and is falling apart in South and Central America. It is not a good system for the people or the countries. Communist leaders subvert democracies. They turn their countries into dictatorships. Once they're in power, they become power-hungry and blind to the needs of the people.

The next day, a busload carrying our Helping Hands medical team set out for Phalebas. When our bus got stuck a few times on the rough and rocky road, we had to get out and push. Some people were alarmed by this, whereas others thought it was a great adventure. We were just anxious to get to the village before anyone else tried to interfere with our operations.

When we arrived, we received a huge, warm welcome from the village people, which was amazing amidst the Maoist problem. Interestingly, later I learned that the many Maoist insurgents were in the welcoming crowd.

Thousands of people lined up to welcome us with flowers and garlands. Red Maoist flags flew all over the village. People stood alongside the road and urged the bus to stop. I emerged from the bus and strolled between two lines of people offering blankets, scarves, and red garlands.

I was amazed that they had erected many gates for our welcome and built a big stage in the middle of nowhere. We inaugurated the clinic from that stage. Bhola Sharma made it all possible; with his initiation, the Phalebas clinic was born.

In the spring of 2005, we opened a permanent clinic in Phalebas with 14 staff members, an X-ray machine, ultrasound equipment, a laboratory, and a pharmacy. That any clinic in the village would have such modern medical equipment and services was a huge deal. The government had not been able to provide those things, which is why the locals were so happy with Helping Hands. We spent a good chunk of money just to open the clinic, and for years we paid the salaries of the 14 staff members. Our investment improved thousands of people's lives, who were now hopeful that their conditions and illnesses would be treated, and they would live healthier lives.

A Nepali television crew shot footage of our welcome, my speech, and Helping Hands' work in Phalebas. It made headline news. According to the government television station, it was a five-minute broadcast that the army, initially, did not allow to air. A newscaster at the station went to bat for us. She told the army that we weren't doing anything wrong; in fact, we offered free medical services to the people of Phalebas. Finally, the segment was aired, and the government officials who saw it were shocked that we received a bigger welcome than the King! So, they allowed the segment to be aired only once—that was enough for them.

While the Maoists were still underground, the army constantly attacked and wounded the insurgents. At night, the insurgents would come to our clinic for treatment. They let our doctors know when they were coming, and the doctors had to ensure that no one, other than the doctors, would interact with them. If the doctors didn't guarantee confidentiality for the Maoists, the doctors' lives could have been threatened. Sometimes, they would take doctors from our clinic to Maoist strongholds and return them in the morning.

Although the Maoists destroyed many organizations through ransacking, extortion, or killing, they never hurt our personnel and never destroyed or permanently closed our clinics. The Maoists recognized the benefit of our services. They knew that, although I was living in America, I was from Nepal, bringing help to Nepal's people; so, they believed in me and the work of Helping Hands. Their only condition was that we provide them with free medical care and medicine.

However, one time the Maoists seized the Phalebas clinic by holding the doctors at gunpoint, tried to steal the ultrasound machine, and demanded that the clinic close. But the doctor said the machine was his personal laptop, put it in his suitcase, and carried it to safety in Kathmandu. Talk about thinking on his feet!

They sent the doctors home to their villages. It was a power play to demonstrate their sway in Nepal. Another time, the Maoists forced the clinic to close because they came looking for medical help, and a doctor did not cooperate. The clinic was closed for a time, and the only way the Maoists would consider reopening it was if our team and I humbly requested that they authorize the reopening. I dictated a message taped by a reporter, and the tape with my humble request was sent to the Maoists. With that, they reopened the clinic.

Maoists in Bandipur

During a Maoist uprising in the fall of 2000, Helping Hands had 12 American plus eight Nepali doctors and nurses working in a camp in Bandipur. It was 10:00 at night, and the medical team was asleep in their tents when, suddenly, gunshots rang out. The team was terrified and didn't know what to do. The Maoists grabbed our doctors and demanded medicine to heal the wounded Maoists.

Our American doctors were very frightened by the insurgency because they had to operate on wounded Maoists at gunpoint. Though no harm came to the Helping Hands team, we halted operations. Later, I received a letter from the Maoists expressing their immense appreciation, stating that we wouldn't have any more problems with them. When I read the letter to my medical team, they agreed to start working again. We moved them from tents to homes so they would feel more secure.

I told our doctors always to wear Helping Hands T-shirts when they walked in the mountains, and the Maoists would leave them alone. That was my understanding with the Maoist rebels—you keep your hands off our people, and we treat you for free. And, sure enough, they didn't bother the Helping Hands medical team members anymore. They didn't ask them for money as they did with everyone else. I developed a modicum of respect for the Maoists because they kept their word and never hurt us. The only time they really impacted me was after they emerged as a bona fide political party and needed money. When the fighting stopped, the extortion began.

From Maoism to Communism

The Maoists caused me trouble from 2000 to 2013. Through stealing and extortion, they took around $400,000 worth of my property. Even though the Maoists were formidable enemies, I wasn't concerned that they would kill me—I never hesitated to confront them. Their top-level people knew me, and I knew them. The Maoist organization wasn't all bad, but some bad people were enriching themselves through extortion.

In late 2016, the Communist Party and the Maoists merged. The Nepal Communist Party is now the ruling political party and is the largest communist party in South Asia. Even though Nepal is officially a communist country, it is nothing like Nicaragua, Honduras, or Venezuela, which are more totalitarian. The Communists and Maoists in Nepal are collaborating and no longer behave like terrorists. For a time, under their rule, Nepal became a democratic and peaceful country.

However, since 2017, the collaboration between the Communists and Maoists has been deteriorating. They're attempting to separate into two political parties again. They make unrealistic demands of each other and jockey for position to seize the highest posts—trying to grab wealth and power. Corruption is rampant in Nepal, starting with the country's leaders. For example, in November 2017, 33.5 kilos of gold disappeared from the Kathmandu airport, smuggled somewhere inside the country. It remains an unsolved mystery, but there was likely government involvement.

Millions of dollars go missing every year in Nepal, and the government doesn't attempt to address the corruption. And it is widely believed that there was government involvement in the case of a 13-year-old girl who was raped and murdered in 2018. Thus, the government covered up the case, which remains unsolved. More recently, during the coronavirus pandemic, lots of medical supplies have gone missing. The losers in the equation are the Nepali people looted by officials drunk with power. Thankfully, the Nepali people are protesting and rioting—fighting the corruption in their country.

Photo Gallery II

Nepal is home to some of the most majestic mountains, the Himalayas, and some of the most beautiful people in the world. I include some striking photos of Nepal, her people, and culture.

A small sample of my life's work is shown in the photos of Helping Hands' cataract trek to Khandbari, which included my parents and sister contributing to the effort. There were many treks to other villages, including the dental camp in Num.

Also included are several examples of flyers that announced and documented Helping Hands' medical treks. Newspapers featured numerous stories about our work.

The philosophy of Shumei, which originated in Japan, gave me a more spiritual understanding of my place in this world. My experience with Shumei, and my initial efforts to introduce Shumei to Nepal are illustrated in the photos toward the end of this gallery.

As our group hiked from Khempalung to Khandbari, we came across an 85-year-old lady adorned with precious ornaments, herding yaks in the jungle alone. I couldn't resist the urge to capture her gorgeous essence on film.

Aerial photo of the Mount Everest Range.

Arun Valley with Mount Makalu to the right, the fifth highest mountain in the world, and to the left, Mount Chamlang. This picture was taken from the Tulmingtar airport.

Fishtail Mountain in the Annapurna Range in the Himalayas.

During World War I and World War II, many Nepalis served in the British army. The so-called British Gurkha Army, known as some of the bravest soldiers in the world, received their salaries in coins. The wives, not aware of the value of the coins, preserved them by making necklaces and ornaments. That tradition continued into the 21st century. Although infrequently, you can see the necklaces in some regions of the Nepalese mountains. (1991)

This woman wears a nose ring that's customary for some tribes in the mountain region of Nepal.

In the mountains of Nepal, people age faster because they lack nutrition and quality water. This man is just 60 years old.

Many Nepalis start smoking during childhood because it's trendy and they lack the health education that would teach them about the negative health effects.

This photo of an over 200-year-old fig tree in Khandbari reminds me of my childhood. I loved climbing its branches. The roots spread over a quarter mile. Sadly, the tree was chopped down in the 90s for building construction. The Hindu community worships this type of fig tree which represents the god Vishnu. (1986)

This man spent three hours gathering food for his animals. Once they were fed, he spent the day plowing in the field. (1992)

I grew up drinking locally brewed beer that Nepalis call chyang or jand. To make the beer, fermented millet is pressed out by hand and the juice is strained. (1986)

In 1998, I rode a horse with my five-year-old daughter, Regina, in my lap as these children watched us. She said to me with teary eyes, "Dad, I want you to buy clothes for these children and help them go to school." Her words motivated me to help the people of Nepal.

This girl's parents left her at home to take care of her younger brother while they went to work. Like so many Nepali children, these two had no chance to go to school and build a better future. My wife, Sreejana, who has sacrificed in my absence, has always said, "Take care of Nepali women and children and help build their futures." That's why I am committed to investing in health and education in Nepal. (1991)

As I walked through the hills and valleys of Nepal, seeing young children herding cows and goats, something struck me. I thought, why can't they have an opportunity to go to school? This inspired me to build schools and hospitals. I'm proud to say I've spent over 35 years providing education and healthcare to thousands of students and patients. (1986)

The Bhotia people, also known as Sherpas, live at high altitude in the Northern Himalayan Range. The Bhotia pictured below are from the area of Makalu, the fifth highest mountain in the world. During the snowy season, January-April, they descend to warmer areas. They walk seven to eight days on dangerous mountain trails to get to towns like Khandbari to pick up a year's worth of supplies to carry back home. In 1992, when these photos were taken, they didn't have schools and hospitals in their villages, but now the government and NGOs, like Helping Hands, have reached out to help them.

In 1992, a Bhotia woman carried her child in a basket (not from the same group as on the previous page). The Bhotia people traveled with their entire family on long and difficult journeys. The children were carried this way for many days.

A young boy from a Bhotia family travels with his mother, carrying a kid-sized basket. He's eating lunch and sharing Raksi, a tequila-like drink, with her. (1986)

The Sherpas celebrated a successful trek by picking me up. We felt sad parting ways. (1986)

Dr. Mark Frank and Karen Frank on our first trekking trip with Boulder friends in 1986. We encountered a boy whose cheek was impaled by a stick and a dead girl in a basket whose mother didn't realize she had passed.

In November 1987, I asked my friend, Amy Newfield, to drop off a letter for my wife from Num, Nepal. Three weeks after I arrived home in the US, the letter finally reached me, and I handed it to her.

Our first Khandbari medical camp in 1988 organized by me. Approximately 10,000 people came for treatment. We saw as many patients as we could—3,000 people in ten days. But close to 7,000 patients left without being seen. This prompted me to bring more medical camps to the area. The legacy continues.

In 1990, I took my third medical group to Khandbari. Our living arrangements included a tent for the kitchen, Sherpa guides, volunteers, and me.

I brought American medical volunteers in 1991 to my village to perform cataract operations. It was the first time such an operation was launched in Khandbari. My parents welcomed the group at their home.

Screening cataract candidates in Khandbari in 1991. Out of 1,000 people, we selected only 120.

A Helping Hands volunteer with our kitchen crew in Khandbari in 1991.

Surgeons preparing to perform cataract operations in Khandbari in 1991. 120 patients received new lenses from American and Nepali surgeons. At one point, the electricity was cut off by the Communists, forcing us to temporarily halt operations.

A 55-year-old cataract patient expressed his extreme gratitude for his life-changing operation. He said, "Narayan Babu, thanks to you, I can now see the tika (red dot) on your forehead. Because of my blindness, my family kept me in the corner with the goats and cows. Now I don't need anyone's help to function."

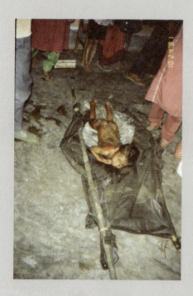

This boy was brought to our Khandbari medical camp on a stretcher in October 1991 after his siblings pushed him into boiling water unknowingly, while playing. He was lucky to be treated that day by Western medical doctors.

During the cataract operation, the hospital was full, so we housed 80 patients in another building and some in a makeshift shelter outside.

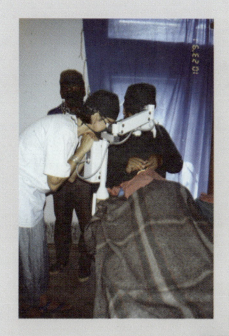

Dr. Sanduk Ruit, surgeon, operating on his first cataract patient on October 23, 1991. Although Dr. Ruit wasn't well-known back then, he is now the most renowned ophthalmologist in Asia. Dr. Chris King, an ophthalmologist from the US, said if he ever needed a cataract operation, he would fly to Nepal so that Dr. Ruit could perform the procedure.

Dr. Chris King, ophthalmologist, videotaping riots while Dr. Sanduk Ruit looks on. The doctors were unable to work because the Communists cut off the electricity to our camp. When the patients, their families, and the people of the town found out what had happened, they rioted against the Communists.

The cataract clinic in Khandbari completely full with patients. (1991)

The first day of distributing food to the cataract patients in 1991. I bought all the fruit in town to ensure our patients were sufficiently nourished. My father, Surya Bahadur Shrestha, is on the far right. My uncle, Tej Bahadur Shrestha, is in the middle, and my younger brother, Dharma Raj Shrestha, is on the left. The girls I sponsored to go to school, including Niru (Tamang) Basnyat, are also pictured.

My parents distributed fruit from the market to cataract patients.

My sister Shanti Shrestha and my father Surya Bahadur Shrestha celebrating the last of seven days of food distribution to the cataract patients and their families.

After we completed our work in the Khandbari medical camp, our team hiked up to the Arun Valley. I wanted to take a picture of these women we encountered on the way. We had to wait an hour so they could dress up for the photo. (1991)

The Khandbari volunteers and school children waiting with garlands to welcome the medical volunteers and me at the Tumlingtar airport in 1991.

This photo was taken in 1992 at a village near Khandbari. There was chaos in the crowd because people were arguing and cutting in line for medical services. I persuaded them that the proper way to receive free medical services was to wait patiently in line.

Volunteers enjoying themselves by participating in a volleyball tournament during their break. (1992)

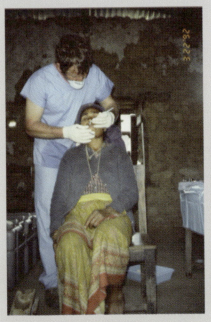

Our temporary dental clinic in the village of Num, Nepal, in 1992.

Kerry Sambling and I in 1992, standing in front of the medical volunteers' tents. When Helping Hands goes to Nepali villages, this is the best way to camp without disturbing the people of the village.

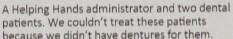

We passed through Chichila during our two-day walk from Khandbari to Num. Today, it is a two-hour drive on paved roads.

A Helping Hands administrator and two dental patients. We couldn't treat these patients because we didn't have dentures for them.

Dental supplies at the temporary Num village clinic.

Sherpa cooks in Num at the Helping Hands camp.

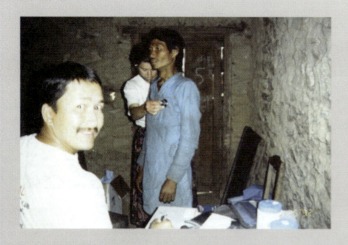

Dr. Raj Bandhu Maskay (my brother-in-law) volunteered with our Num dental clinic in 1992. I invited him to visit the US that fall, and he went on to earn a master's degree from University of Northern Colorado-Greeley. He landed his first American job with the US government in Alaska. He is happily living with his family in Delaware.

Our dental camp in Num didn't having proper chairs or tools for treatments other than extractions. We helped hundreds of people with toothaches. We pulled out over 1,700 teeth in eight days! (1992)

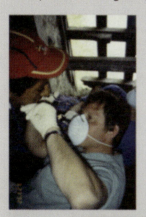

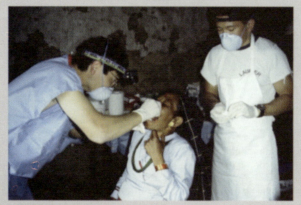

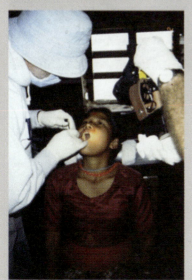

This woman walked from the Northern border of Nepal and Tibet, China to our dental camp in Num. It took her two days because she was in excruciating pain. Once we extracted her teeth, she said she could get home in a day because she was pain-free.

Shambhu Neupane assisted the dentist by shining a flashlight in the patient's mouth. This was our only lighting in the dental camp.

These ladies were some of the porters in Walung Village in the Arun Valley in 1986. Pasang Sherpa (on the left wearing a baseball cap) was the head guide, caretaker, and organizer. He later became a member of the Nepali parliament and a philanthropist, having become wealthy through land ownership and doing business with Belgium.

The lowland porters can only go up to 6,000-8,000 feet altitude carrying big loads on their backs. After that, either the Sherpas or yaks, the high-altitude porters, carry the loads. (1986)

After providing healthcare to Nepali patients in the Khandbari medical camp, the American medical volunteers hiked for two weeks to the Annapurna Range in the Himalayas. I captured this stunning photo of Fishtail Mountain in 1988 while we hiked.

The American medical volunteers canoed Phewa Lake, in Pokhara, Nepal. The Anapurna Range is in the background with Fishtail Mountain towering above the other peaks. (1988)

To get to Khandbari, sometimes we had to charter three airplanes and a helicopter. In 1997, one of the planes was forced to land at a different airport because of bad weather. We weren't notified of the rerouting and worried all night long. The next morning, we were so relieved when the plane arrived at the Tumlingtar airport.

I call these Nepali ambulances. Patients are often carried this way to Helping Hands clinics.

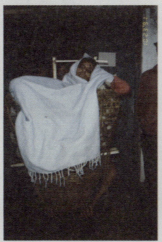

In 1999, I brought 26 medical and dental volunteers from the US and Canada. They slept in tents on the Surya Boarding School grounds.

In 1989, I established a Lions Club in Khandbari. I was the third vice president of the Boulder Lions Club, and I delivered the Lions Club jackets donated by our club to the Khandbari Lions Club. These men later became Helping Hands volunteers. (1991)

Mr. Bholaman Shrestha giving me my daily shower at the Bandipur camp in 1994. He was once a member of the British Gurkha Army. He was one of my best friends and assistants. He served me for ten years, traveling all over Nepal to help me with my endeavors. I rewarded him by bringing him twice to the US. Now he resides with his family in London.

In 1997, two medical students from Kirksville, Kansas, went to Wana, Nepal, where Dr. Gupta was born. The people of Wana had never seen white people before.

These four girls, Niro, Sushila, Gyanu, and Shita, (left to right) are the first students that I sponsored through Health Trek. (1991)

In 1999, I presented the Semester in Nepal Program proposal to the Tokyo Asia University and the study abroad director of Western Washington University.

Construction of the Helping Hands clinic in Dharmasthali began in 1999. The completed building.

In 1999, some of the medical and dental volunteers and Dr. Gupta Bahadur Shrestha (standing in the back), the CEO of the Helping Hands Community Hospital in Kathmandu, Nepal.

Helping Hands volunteers and I walking through Khandbari in 2000.

HELPING HANDS in NEPAL

DHARMASTHALI CLINIC INAUGURATION

Sreejana Shrestha inaugurating the clinic

Sreejana Shrestha chatting with local women

Dispensary at clinic

Dispensary at clinic

Patient check-up at clinic

HELPING HANDS in VIETNAM

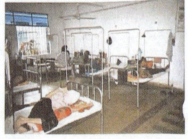

HELPING HANDS HEALTH EDUCATION

HELPING HANDS
HEALTH EDUCATION

*Providing Medical Relief Services
And Education Help
to the People of
Nepal, Vietnam & Nicaragua*

NEPAL   **VIETNAM**

NICARAGUA

HELPING HANDS HEALTH EDUCATION

- Helping Hands Health Education is a non-profit organization registered under 501(C)(3) in 1992 though it was established in 1988

- The main objective is to provide low cost quality medical services through the help of western medical and non-medical volunteers

- It has organized more than 100 village camps in remote areas of Nepal providing medical services to over 300,000 poor and needy people

- Over 1,000 medical professional, medical student and non-medical volunteers have provided their service in Nepal

- It has established five permanent clinics in Nepal to provide sustained health services to people in need

- It has extended its medical services in Vietnam (from 2005) and Nicaragua (from 2006)

948 Pearl Street, Boulder, Colorado 80302
Phone: 303-448-1811; Fax: 303-440-7328
Email: helpinghands@saanr.com; Web: www.helpinghandsusa.org

HELPING
HANDS
IN NEPAL

— Daily Camera photos by David Gilkey

CAIRRYING PATIENT:

HELPING HANDS IN NEPAL

By CHRIS ROBERTS
Camera Staff Writer

ORGANIZER: Narayan Shrestha, Boulder businessman and organizer of the trip, takes narritives to organize people waiting for treatment after the clinic was first set up. The man to the right of Shrestha had to carry the woman who was unable to walk to the clinic.

PEOPLE FLOOD CLINIC: By the third day, people were crowding the clinic, some with minor ailments and simply wanted to be touched by a Western doctor. The flood of people made it necessary to set up a triage to determine who had the greatest need.

DOCTOR'S QUARTERS: Emergency room Dr. Charlee Banquin walks past the doctors' quarters at the clinic near Bandipur, Nepal, which can be seen in the background. The team used outhouses and ate dinner cooked on portable stoves.

EYE EXAMINATION: Dr. Kimberly Johnson does an eye exam on a patient at the Bandipur clinic in central Nepal, west of Kathmandu.

DENTISTRY: Chuck Hazen, team dentist, works on a patient.

I gave the welcoming team instructions for taking care of our Japanese guests. They were to take them to the Surya Boarding School.

Five welcoming girls, traditionally called pancha kanya (unmarried girls), welcoming our guests, Alan Sensei and Masahide San, with a dance in January 2010. This highest level of welcome was organized by the Surya Boarding School.

At my birth house in Khandbari in January 2010 with Alan Imai Sensei to my left and Masahide Koyama to my right. My cousin and his wife are also pictured.

To honor our Japanese guests, Surya Boarding School students lined up in two rows from the school boundary's gate to the classroom.

Alan Sensei beaming after having a wonderful time that morning.

Alan Sensei requested this picture with my portrait displayed on the wall behind us.

Kunihiko Wakamatsu Sensei, the head of the center, (seated to my right) and I at the Shumei Gifu Center in November 2019.

A young Shumei member and I at the Shumei Gifu Center.

Shumei members including Yumie Sakai, my interpreter and speech translator, and I visiting the Utsunomiya Center at the Nikko Toshogu, Tochigi prefecture, a world cultural heritage site.

In August of 2010, Sreejana and I were invited to visit the Shumei International Institute in Crestone, Colorado.

A Hoshi-sha (a person learning to provide selfless service to others) gave us a walking tour of the building, grounds, and the Natural Agriculture field where potatoes, corn, and daikon radishes grew. When we pulled these radishes from the ground, we couldn't believe how robust they were.

CHAPTER 13

The Nursing College and Community Hospital

I'm just a small human being that tried to do something good—that's my area and knowledge. The thing that I've learned is that compassion is such a powerful force in my life.

I GOT THE GREATEST INSPIRATION from my number one human being, Mahatma Gandhi. He set out to free India from Britain with a philosophy of peace—with a non-violent revolution. Dr. Martin Luther King Jr. , who said Mahatma Gandhi was his guru, also inspired me very much. Another hero was Nelson Mandela, who sacrificed so much for his people. Ordinary people cannot be like them, but they can inspire us to emulate them. I am not Mahatma Gandhi. I'm not Martin Luther King. I'm not Nelson Mandela. I'm just a small human being that tried to do something good and, along the way, I've learned that compassion is such a powerful force in my life.

A Nursing College Born in Nepal

In 2001, the International Health Program at Yale University invited me to speak to residents and medical students about Helping Hands. While there, I saw a story in *USA Today* about a shortage of 500,000 nurses in the US. The same evening, I turned on the TV in my hotel room, and CNN had a ten-minute story about the nursing shortage causing some hospitals to close. Other stories featured nurses coming to work in the US from countries such as the Philippines and South Korea. But because many had difficulties with English, there were problems such as frequent miscommunication with doctors about prescribed medications.

In Nepal, many nurses had a strong command of English. Perhaps they could have helped, but they didn't have the nursing education required in the US. I wanted to explore this situation, so I investigated the state of nursing education in Kathmandu. Up until 2001, I discovered that no campus offered a bachelor's degree in nursing in all of Nepal. Nurses had only a 10th-grade education followed by three years of nursing courses. They had a lot of work experience but not enough education. They needed to obtain an Associate Degree in Nursing (ADN) to prepare them to take the National Council Licensure Examination (NCLEX) to get licensed in the US.

I wanted to open a nursing college in Kathmandu with the goal to admit many students, but I ended up getting only 20. The Nepali government did not understand the idea, so they didn't cooperate. I met with the president and secretary of the recently formed Nepali Nursing Council. They didn't know who had the authority to grant the opening of a college, so they didn't approve a license.

To find a solution, I visited many universities in the US, including Eastern Kentucky University (EKU), recommended by a professor from the University of Kentucky (UK), a dentist friend. A Nepali man, living in Colorado, visiting Eastern Kentucky—who would have thought? On my second visit, I met with the chairman, Peggy Truder, and dean, Dr. David Gail, of the Nursing College. The dean said, "If the chair says yes, then we can do it, but we need to figure out how."

So, I came up with a proposal. If Nepal wasn't going to approve a full ADN program in Nepal, then why not have just a year and a half or one year of basic courses over there, get some practical experience in a US hospital, and then become an Eastern Kentucky student?

I really liked Peggy Truder and found her to be very friendly and helpful. I asked her, "How many can you admit?"

"100."

"What? Okay, I'm in! Can you do one year there and the rest here?"

"That's the best way to do it. We will have space for them."

"Wow! Okay, let's sign an agreement," I said. We drafted and signed an agreement right then between EKU and Helping Hands. I flew back to Nepal to show the Nursing Council the agreement.

But the Nursing Council representative said, "Even though you're teaching one year here, you need to introduce the students to a hospital—right?"

"Well, not necessarily," I said.

"No, you have to introduce them to a hospital here. You must affiliate with a hospital. But you don't have to do that for a year."

We opened a college called SANN Institute of Nursing (SION) integrated with EKU, born in Nepal. I could not manage SION alone, so I advertised for a partner. I got four partners to run the program for a year.

A group of doctors, the dean, the chair, and faculty members of the nursing department of EKU wanted to visit our facility in Kathmandu. It was a palatial building with a university sign. They loved it and took loads of pictures.

I made a request of King Gyanendra, "I have a group of American friends from Kentucky, and they would like to see Your Majesty. Is there any way you can give them an audience?"

When we went to the palace, the Kentucky educators wore jeans because the King insisted on casual dress. We greeted him with gifts of Kentucky bourbon and Kentucky candies. He gave a very relaxed and friendly audience to my friends. I found him to be very down to earth.

I encountered many obstacles, mainly from the US Embassy, with the first 20 students at the nursing college. After the audience with the King, the group came back to the US. Then, the principal of our college and a partner went to see the consul of the US Embassy in Kathmandu. The principal of SION, Dr. Tara Uprety, was a Nepali scholar from Northern Texas University with a doctorate in nursing. She was not supposed to go to the embassy and reveal my goal for the program. She said to the consul, "Narayan hired me to take care of the nursing students and train them. Our goal is to bring the nurses to the US and employ them there."

Even though it was the truth, I didn't want it conveyed to the consul that early. Indeed, my goal was to help the nursing students find jobs in the US after they got their degrees in the US, so they could send money back to their families in Nepal and thus help Nepal.

The consul was alarmed at my game plan to employ all 20 students in the US, so he rejected all the visas. I was devastated. A year of their education was lost, as were the costs of the teachers and housing. I had invested around $200,000 of my own money. I invited a few partners to join me later—Ang Tshiring Sherpa, Pemba Sherpa, and Kanchha Gurung.

One of the nursing students was the daughter of one of my partners. He didn't have any worries about my long game, even though his daughter didn't get a visa. Like most of my partners, he trusted that I could make it happen—that the students would eventually get visas.

I was back in the US when I got a phone call from Shyam Piya, Administrator (who died in 2006), notifying me that all 20 students were denied visas. He shared the news that some of the students who did not get visas went berserk, destroying computers and tables at SION and shattering windows with rocks. This further added to my stress in having to replace the equipment and repair all the damage.

It became my enormous task to approach the US Embassy and request visas for my students to study in the United States.

I called the dean and the chair of EKU and conveyed the news about the visas. They were also devastated. I planned to meet with them at EKU since they were the ones who were tasked with issuing invitations to readmit the students to the university.

Upon my arrival, we convened the International Office Director, the chair of the Nursing College, the dean of the Nursing College, and myself. We decided it was best to send an official letter to the US Embassy in Kathmandu. The chair and I went to Senator Mitch McConnell's office and requested that he send a letter to the embassy on behalf of the university.

Two days later, when I was in a meeting with the dean, the chair's office notified him that we had received an answer from the embassy. The letter said that since the embassy was aware that the students hoped to continue working in the US after earning their degrees, they did not qualify for the F-1 student visas. With the F1, one can stay in the US for an unlimited amount of time if one is a student. The letter recommended that the students be sent on J-1 visas instead. With the J-1, one can only stay in the US for a set amount of time, without the option of renewing the visa, and then one must leave when the visa expires.

With the ability to issue J-1 visa requests, the university decided to create J-1 visa forms in each student's name. I returned to Nepal and gave the forms to the students to complete. When the students and parents saw me return with a second batch of visa forms, more than half of the students and parents believed in me, but the others were filled with doubt.

Out of 20 students, 11 eventually got visas. Two of the 11 needed help to secure their visas. One didn't have enough money, so I gave her parents a loan. When their daughter secured a visa, they repaid me. The second one obtained a student loan.

Unfortunately, nine students did not get visas, and I heard secondhand that those students and their parents were very upset. I had meeting after meeting with them, but no one raised their voice or confronted me. I thought, *What's going on?*

A parent stood up and said, "I think you should know we constantly talk behind your back. We feel so angry we could strangle you, but the minute we see you in person, we can't say anything bad about you. You have that kind of power and energy. We have an enormous amount of respect for you. Make us an offer, and we will respect your wishes."

I said, "Whatever money you have paid me, I will double what you spent for the year. I will also compensate you for your lost time." The students had paid 2.7 million rupees. I repaid them 5.4 million rupees from my own pocket.

With my offer, their animosity dissipated, and they were finally happy. But the loss of money and damage to my reputation taught me the huge lesson that I should be very careful before I admit a second batch of students.

I invited each student and his or her parents to my office and warned them. "If you want to drop out of this program, please do. I'll refund your money. If you want to continue, I cannot guarantee a visa for you, but one thing I'm working toward is establishing a bachelor's degree in nursing at my college. If you can't get a visa to go to the US, we can just educate you here."

The parents said they were willing to take a chance. The parents and students each signed a document stating that they wouldn't give me trouble if the students didn't get visas.

To establish a bachelor's degree in nursing, I needed university approval. So, I went to Purbanchal University to speak with my friend, Mr. Thoren Kharkee, the vice-chancellor. I said, "Come to the US with me to learn about bachelor's degree programs in nursing. Let's open one in Nepal. Then you can permit my organization to award bachelor's degrees." I told him about Kentucky and the great universities there.

"Great, let's do it!" said the vice-chancellor.

By the time we visited Kentucky, I had exchange students from the SANN Research Institute in Nepal attending two-year colleges all over Kentucky. A powerful Kentucky state senator told the governor about my students in Kentucky. The governor gave me the Kentucky Cardinal Award, declaration, and plaque.

The vice-chancellor was impressed and approved the bachelor's degree of nursing for my college, SION. I could now call it a college because it was university-approved and affiliated with Purbanchal University. We had 20 students as second-year bachelor's degree nurses. And in the second batch, we had 15 students.

I managed to send close to 40 nursing students to Kentucky, and for those who couldn't get a visa, I offered a bachelor's degree at my college. But even though I had an affiliation with a university, the Nursing Council did not approve my program because I didn't have a hospital in which to educate students in a practicum. I went everywhere in Kathmandu looking for a hospital, but none agreed to an affiliation. When a college is affiliated with a hospital, the hospital must get paid. No one asked me for money, so I didn't realize that was part of the deal.

The parents and students went berserk and came after me, looking like they wanted to kill me. "You risked our children's future and wasted their time. Who's going to pay for those two years and the money lost? You must pay us! Now!"

"Wait, wait! I'm going to find a hospital," I said. I truly believed I would find one. I was their one big hope. When I reassured them, they put trust in me once again. I promised myself and them, "No matter what it takes, I'll go the extra mile to make this happen."

I felt so much pressure; I stayed in Nepal for seven months straight, trying to make my vision and the nursing students' dreams happen. Fortunately, I had a clinic in Kathmandu with an outstanding reputation staffed with 18 doctors, surgeons, nurses, and staff. I thought, *Maybe it's time to upgrade my Helping Hands clinic.*

Opening the Helping Hands Community Hospital

Never having found a hospital to affiliate with, I came up with the idea to open my own hospital. Crazy? Possibly. But it seemed like the only path forward. Even crazier, I had just two weeks in which to do it!

I'll never forget that year of my life. Not only did the Maoists harass me, but the Nursing Council did not approve my program, and the parents and students were on my case. I concluded that the Nursing Council was the entity I needed to please to make this work. I figured once I got the hospital, they would approve my program.

"Give me two weeks," I said to the parents. "In that time, I'll open a hospital and get a license. Then we'll sign an agreement for ten years between my hospital and my college."

They left me alone for two weeks. To demonstrate my commitment, I chose to give my passport to the immigration office. I went the extra mile to show them the sincerity of my devotion. Without my passport, they knew I wouldn't flee the country; to think that I would was a crazy notion because I had so much invested in helping the people of Nepal. Plus, I'm not that kind of guy. Over the years of my service to Nepal, living in Colorado, my heart and mind were always devoted to the Nepali people. They believed in my work. They knew I wouldn't abandon them. My goal was to give Nepal and her people the best education and healthcare services.

A young devotee of Sai Baba, Mr. Lok Darshan Shrestha, invited me for dinner. I had known him as a child before I left for the US. His family and mine were friendly. And my brothers and his brothers were friends. He knew me very well. I told him that I wanted to open a hospital during our dinner, and I was looking for a house to rent or buy. He was keen to help me and told me there was a suitable house for sale in Kathmandu.

I went to see the owner, who said it was for sale for $500,000. I would have to rent two more houses to have enough for a 100-bed hospital. I offered $450,000 plus a $10,000 down payment to get it done. My idea was to get a $300,000 bank loan against the house, and I would still owe the owner $160,000. In a week, I secured the building, and, at the same time, I applied for a license for a hospital at that address.

I contacted four doctors who were employees of the nearby Helping Hands clinic opened in 1995, asking them if they would work at the hospital. The group included Dr. Udaya Man Dangol, urologist, and Dr. Hem Limbu, orthopedist. (Helping Hands sponsored their education to make them surgeons.) Also, part of the group were Dr. Sam Gautam, cardiologist, Dr. Sam Shrestha, general practitioner, and Dr. Gupta Bahadur Shrestha, known as "Dr. Gupta" in Nepal, who was in charge of the Helping Hands clinic at the time. I gave them the authority to run it and promised not to intervene.

I told them to move and renovate the clinic, and I would cover the expenses. I spent $100,000 on renovations alone. I also supplied beds and equipment for around $300,000. There was no fundraising. I sold land in my village to finance this venture, borrowed money, and used money from my personal business account.

I approached the Health Minister, Mr. Lilamani Pokharel, whom I didn't know well. A friend of mine had introduced me to him. He gave me his word that he would help me out, and I couldn't have been happier. But as it turned out, it wasn't so easy to get the license.

For seven days, I went to his office and sat there from morning to night, waiting for him to approve a license. I needed a quick turnaround time, but he was busy with other priorities. I spent so much time and effort to get the minister's sign-off. Finally, on the seventh day, he signed the license. If I hadn't been so persuasive and doggedly determined, it wouldn't have happened that quickly.

After I finally secured a license, I gave it to Dr. Gupta, and we celebrated. I appointed him to run the hospital. The hospital and the nursing campus signed an agreement. Helping Hands Community Hospital was born in 2007, which saved SION, the nursing campus. The 100-bed hospital is a nonprofit established for the people of Nepal and to help nurses gain work experience.

I had three partners in SION. When I had to refund the students, the three partners asked to be bought out. I had to come up with $100,000 right away, or they would lock the college's doors, and the parents would go berserk again. In the nick of time, I found another partner; actually, a group of eight, who wrote me a check for $65,000. I distributed the money, and everyone was happy.

The nursing campus was doing well, but the Maoists gave us trouble because it was making money. Also, the Nepali Nursing Council was becoming increasingly demanding. My principal told me that she was required to hand over money whenever a Nursing Council representative came to inspect. It didn't matter whether the Nursing Council approved our operations or not; we had to pay them. And that money came out of my wallet, every time.

After Kalpana Nepali received her master's degree in nursing, I brought her in as the college administrator. The principal was a doctor with a Ph.D. in nursing, an elderly lady, a beautiful person. Kalpana started working under her and did a good job. But the principal and the accountant didn't like Kalpana because I trusted Kalpana more than them. Kalpana had earned my lifelong trust by running my business in Boulder while I went to find a wife in Nepal.

The principal wasn't cooperating, and Kalpana was frustrated. Then we had to move from the beautiful building to a lousy one because somebody purchased it. Kalpana moved the nursing campus very efficiently, like she had moved my shop in Boulder.

One day, six Maoists came to me and demanded $20,000 at a closed-door lunch meeting. They said, "You were approved for 15 students, but you have 20. We'll get you 30. Give us $20,000, and we'll get approval from the Nursing Council."

"That's impossible. I can't admit 30 students. The university won't allow it. Once I get the documents approving the increase, I'll pay you," I said.

But they wanted the money right then and there.

"No way," I said.

Later, while working in my hotel room, a group of Maoist rebels went to the nursing school, attacked my teachers, destroyed the computers, demolished the desks, and ransacked everything inside. The students were chased out and went to the police to report the violence. But who could identify the perpetrators since they came disguised? Furthermore, the police force's hands were tied. There was no law and order in the country. Even if they could have identified the perpetrators, what could they do? The Maoists had so much power. If you didn't do as they said, you could be punished or killed.

I spent a lot of money repairing and restoring the nursing college. I didn't share this incident or the expense with my board members or family. I didn't want to alarm them or to have them try to persuade me to stop my work in Nepal.

I was so fed up with the Maoist problem, I sometimes felt like quitting. But I could not. The hospital had just opened, and I wanted to introduce a nursing program to the country. I was the first one to introduce a bachelor's degree in nursing. Leading by example and giving a country know-how is important. My program spurred many others. There are now 40 bachelor's degree nursing programs as well as many master's degree programs.

After I secured a license for the hospital, I retrieved my passport from the immigration office. I threw a dinner party with the parents and students to celebrate. One parent was a Maoist who stood up and badmouthed me and my programs, condemning my work. He accused me of pretending to do good things for the Nepali people but only serving myself. He said he didn't trust me. The Maoists never had positive feelings about people doing good works in Nepal. Thankfully, the other parents defended me and my work, saying I was trustworthy and very dedicated to Nepal and her people. They told the Maoist fellow that he could withdraw his child from my program, but that they were going to stick with me. The fellow sat down and was silenced.

Not only did the problems with the Maoists persist, but trouble was also brewing on the nursing campus. Despite Kalpana being an excellent administrator with an impressive background, she frequently fought with the teachers. She always maintained a positive attitude and did her best to deal

with the faculty members. They simply weren't of her caliber and didn't value
her expertise. Sadly, the nursing college wasn't a good fit for her. Kalpana
notified me of her resignation and left. It was our great loss that it didn't work
out with her. After she left, we were forced to move yet again, several times.

Selling the Hospital and SANN International College

Each time we moved, we lost furniture, computers, and other equipment.
A couple of bad employees stole much of it. After the fourth move, to regain
control, I set up an office in the hospital. Then the group of eight investors
wanted to pull out and recoup their $100,000. I signed a document that
allowed me to postpone the payment and gave me the authority to run the
company but not the ownership. The problems mounted, as did the losses.
The hospital was supposed to make payments to the bank in lieu of rent, but
the hospital did not pay the bank anything. I had to make the monthly
payment from the US. I decided I would sell the building and pay everyone
off.

I found a buyer for $800,000. We signed an agreement that he would buy
the building in six or seven months, and I received a $30,000 retainer. I trusted
him, but he played games with me. It turned out he was a Maoist who hated
me and only paid me $60,000 toward a payment of my loan. I fought him for
two years, then decided that I would also sell SANN International College.

SANN International College was a liberal arts and science college I ran
alongside Semester in Nepal, both under the umbrella of SANN Research
Institute. It was solely mine, but I was harassed by so many parties—students,
parents, the government, and Maoists—I was getting frustrated doing
anything in Nepal. I thought I should have a partner in this, too. In 2011, I
found a company that wanted to invest in my institute to which I sold 20
percent. But the hospital building wasn't in my name when I bought it. The
bank wanted to put the building in a company name, so I purchased it in the
name of SANN International College. The people in the company said they

weren't going to claim the 20 percent from the hospital building. But Mr. Jagat Shrestha and Mr. Mahendra Joshi, representatives of the bank, who became my partners, claimed they owned part of the hospital building. This was legally valid. I made the mistake of putting it in their names. I trusted them, and they betrayed me. Later, when I wanted to sell the building, they demanded their share. They took $200,000 from the sale of the building.

Dr. Subash Ghimire, the buyer of the hospital building, was a dentist and a Maoist. He was a very nice fellow, or so I thought. He quickly became antagonistic and fought with me at every turn. He offered to buy SANN International College and the hospital building for $1.1 million. I agreed because I didn't want to fight. We drew up an agreement using his attorney. I trusted him, and he betrayed my trust. He didn't give me $1.1 million. I ended up getting only $700,000, which paid the bank, the owner of the house, and everyone else. He shafted me for $400,000. Then he wanted $6,000 in rent per month from the hospital. If the doctors of my hospital could have paid that rent to me, I would not have had to sell the building.

In hindsight, I had made another mistake. When a group of doctors from our hospital offered to buy it, I did not believe they had the money. Instead of believing my people, I believed Ghimire.

I forgave all the bad actors because my concern was the Nepali people. And when they benefited, I was happy. My wife always says, "Don't be bothered by what you lost. We had it, and we lost it. But we didn't really lose. We gave." If all humans could forgive, then the world would be a better place, without any animosity. But, of course, forgiving isn't always as easy as we'd like it to be.

Eventually, another group of doctors from our hospital, 50 of them, including Ghimire, got together and bought a huge new building. They asked me if I would support moving to the new building. At first, I was against it, but then I decided if they were growing and helping the people of Nepal, I would support them. It was a beautiful building. To help them, I asked two friends, Jon Kaufman, the Director of H2OpenDoors, and Jack Barker, the Founder and President of Innovative Water Technologies, to donate drinking water filters. Their companies collaborated with the Boulder Rotary Club to donate three filters costing $25,000 apiece, one to the hospital and two to my villages in Eastern Nepal. This was the first hospital that provided filtered, clean drinking water in the country.

Having overcome so many obstacles, I finally crossed the finish line with a beautiful hospital and a nursing campus. At times, I jumped sky-high and crashed to the ground. I was bruised but not broken. My heart was determined, and my mind set. I vowed to keep fighting and spending my time and money to help the Nepali people. Although these projects took more time than anticipated, I understood that was the nature of life.

The Helping Hands Community Hospital is prospering, and the nursing campus with 30 students is running very well. Although I don't own the hospital building, the hospital continues to provide top-notch medical services to the Nepali people. I also don't own the nursing campus anymore, but the organization continues to educate and train nurses who provide the community with high-quality health care. In the end, I am very happy that I enriched many people, lifted them up, and brought them greater health and happiness.

But my job is never done. At home in Boulder, I constantly think about Nepal. When my wife and I go to the grocery store to pick up food for the week, I look for products like flashlights that would be useful in Nepal. I fill my cart with things to take back to Nepal, saying to my wife, "This is for Nepal."

"I'm sick and tired of hearing about Nepal as if she's your second wife," she says, seemingly serious, but she can't keep a straight face for long. She laughs and says, "I'm not really jealous. You are doing great things for the Nepali people. Your face brightens up when you do, and that is what I like to see."

CHAPTER 14

Sewing Nepali Seeds in America

By planting seeds with enough sunlight, water, and care, Nepalese Americans blossomed, providing unique offerings through their thriving businesses in the vast ecosystem of American commerce.

IT WASN'T ENOUGH TO BRING MY FAMILY MEMBERS to the United States. I also wanted to help them get a foothold in this country and thrive. When they arrived from Nepal, Sreejana and I typically gave them housing and a job or a business to run. Most took the opportunities and ran with them, building on the foundations we had set up for them. Everyone we brought over to the US, with a couple of exceptions, is very successful. There are too many to name, so I've chosen to highlight five—my nieces, Sarita Shrestha, Mina Shrestha Maskey; my two youngest brothers, Surendra and Jiban; and a painter named Padma Lama. Their stories show that with support, startup capital, hard work, business savvy, and innate talent, anyone can prosper in this great country.

There are hundreds of other Nepalis who have come to the US with our assistance. Except for a few bad apples, everyone's story is one of success and prosperity.

Surendra Shrestha

My brother Surendra is the second from the youngest, number eight in our family of nine children. He's a go-getter, clever, charming, smart, and kind. When I brought Surendra over in 1982, while he was still in high school, he learned a lot about life in America, and life in general by watching me as I navigated life in Dallas and Boulder. He was the first person I brought to the US.

He earned a degree in civil engineering from Metropolitan (Metro) State University in Denver, and he had many opportunities, but he wanted to be his own boss. I had opened a store in Steamboat Springs, Colorado, also called Old Tibet, and we had been in operation for a year or two. A Nepali and an American were running the store for me. It wasn't all that profitable, but we weren't losing money, so I kept it going in hopes that sales might pick up.

I thought I could offer Surendra the Steamboat store—the opportunity to take over the business. I said, "If you want the Steamboat store, it's yours if you'd like to own it." He took over in 1999.

Surendra has been very successful in his ventures. When he was single, he took in my mother and father. Later, he launched a wholesale business called Serenity Tibet with his wife and daughter. They do an excellent job.

He always says to me, "Brother, I really respect what you've done in your life, and I've learned so much from you. You've guided me, showed me the world, and brought me to the US when I was just 16 years old. I feel more American than Nepali, although I love Nepal just as much. You were always there when I needed you. You are always with me, and I will respect and love you forever."

I'm happy and proud that my legacy of giving inspired him and helped seed his success.

Sarita Shrestha

My niece Sarita is the second of six girls in my older brother's family. In Nepal, in their early days, her father, Bashu Dev Shrestha, and his wife, Ratna, were struggling rice and vegetable farmers. The girls helped their parents farm tomatoes, rice, and corn. Bashu Dai constantly worried because he had so many daughters to feed, and they barely made ends meet. In fact, they frequently didn't have enough. In Nepal, boys are often valued more than girls. Back then, girls were more of a liability than an asset to a family.

In 1988, on my fifth trip to Nepal, I saw Bashu Dai's 16-year-old daughter, Sarita, standing in an open field, looking skinny and weak. It pulled on my heartstrings to see her so fragile. A massive earthquake struck Nepal that year, and many people were in desperate circumstances recovering from the devastation. This earthquake was smaller than the one in 2015 but was devastating for the Eastern part of Nepal. I felt very strongly that Nepal was a dead end for her—that she would languish and lead a life of desperation.

Thinking of ways to help my brother, I decided to plant a seed for him and bring my niece to the US. I requested that Connie and Nelson Louderbach, preparing to go trekking in Nepal, visit his family with the goal of sponsoring Sarita.

They happily agreed to sponsor her and went to Khandbari to visit Bashu Dai's family and meet Sarita. The Louderbachs fell in love with Sarita, so they were delighted to sponsor her. When Sarita came to America, the couple housed her, and she went to school in Conifer, Colorado. However, she grew homesick for Nepali food and culture, so she came to live with us.

She lived with us throughout high school. Sreejana and I were like parents to her, helping her through the rough and rocky teenage years. With her family struggling back in Nepal, she was always worried. The fact that we were helping them brought her some comfort.

In addition to her studies, Sarita worked as a cook at our restaurant at 921 Pearl Street. She excelled in this role, and we trusted her with any job we gave her. She went straight from school to the restaurant and worked until 10:00 pm, arriving home at 11:00 pm. She had to get up early at 7:00 am to catch the school bus. It was a very demanding life, but she rose to the occasion.

A year later, the Louderbachs went back to Khandbari and brought her sister Kabita to the US. Both girls sent some of their earnings to their family back in Nepal while working for us. With the three of us helping, Bashu Dai was able to build a house in Kathmandu. His family's future was looking much brighter.

Sadly, Connie passed away many years ago, and Nelson left us in July of 2020. The Louderbachs were a kind and compassionate couple who remained close friends until they died. I will be forever grateful for their bringing my nieces from Nepal when they desperately needed help. If not for them, my nieces might not have had the opportunity to come to the US so early in their lives. May they rest in peace.

At Metro State University, Sarita majored in civil engineering, and she married in 1999. Instead of pursuing engineering after graduation, she told me she had dreams of running her own business. Ask, and you shall receive! I gave her a Nepali restaurant to run in Avon, Colorado, which she ran for eight months. Then I opened a Thai restaurant in Boulder called the Buddha Cafe. She told me she preferred to run that one. She and her sister Babita, who came to the US in 1999, ran it for a year with moderate success. Sarita transferred sole ownership of the restaurant to Babita in 2008. The Buddha Cafe continues to prosper under the care of Babita and her husband.

After she left the restaurant, Sarita opened an import shop in Denver called Mountain Imports that later became Tibet Imports. Her first location on Colfax wasn't optimal, so she moved to 6th Avenue which proved to be a much more profitable location. Tibet Imports specializes in imported goods and handmade malas made of wood, seeds, beads, and more.

Sarita's husband, Naresh, and their son, Sean, manage the store with a little help from her niece. Sarita's special touch is her handcrafted mala beads. Mala beads are Hindu and Buddhist cultures' equivalent of Catholic rosary beads, comprised of 108 beads. "Ma" means unconditional love. "La" means garland. "Mala" means garland of love. Malas are used for keeping count while reciting, chanting, or mentally repeating a mantra or the names of deities. This practice is known in Sanskrit as "japa."

Sarita teaches people how to make mala beads and how to use the malas. She also shows people how to customize and repair malas and how to charge the stone beads with different spiritual mantras.

Sarita offers Vedic astrology readings out of her store, which are in great demand. Vedic astrology is an ancient science based on the Vedic scriptures of India. Astrology charts are based on the date, time, and place of birth. A horoscope is like a snapshot of the cosmos at the time of your birth. Sarita teaches the wisdom of the planets, stones, and Vedic astrology. She shows people how to make customized prayer beads connected to their Vedic astrology.

People seek advice from Sarita. For example, a pregnant woman who needed to go into labor consulted with her. Sarita opened her crystal bible book and said to the pregnant woman, "You need Unikite beads." Sarita gave her a card explaining what Unikite does, the stones, and advised her to wear them to facilitate labor.

One day, a woman came into Sarita's shop when she was making malas at the counter. She said, "I'm a buyer at Core Power Yoga. We would like to sell your mala beads. Is that something you could provide?" Core Power Yoga is the largest yoga studio chain in the country, with over 200 studios.

Thinking she meant two or three, Sarita said, "Sure. No problem."

"Great. We'd like to start with 300," said the buyer.

"How many?" Sarita asked, thinking she had heard wrong.

"300."

Sarita had to think quickly and came up with a price on the spot. When she did, the buyer said, "Great! You've got a deal!"

The orders started in the hundreds but eventually grew to 1,000 per month. She enlisted the help of her sister and her mom to keep up with the demand. The mala beads are handmade—the women put plenty of love and good intentions into each knot they tie. Core Power distributes Sarita's mala beads throughout the country, including Boston, New York, and California, but primarily in Orange County, California, because there's a huge demand there, including from celebrities.

To imagine Sarita that day so long ago in the fields of Nepal, with an uncertain future, and to contrast her with the woman she has become, offering her gifts and treasures to the world, I feel so very fortunate that I had the wherewithal to help and guide her to a much more fulfilling path and one on which she touches and enriches so many lives. She's a true jewel like the stones she uses to create malas.

My niece has achieved the American Dream, running a thriving business, making a good living. She's happily married with a son in college. She is one of the success stories, demonstrating that one can achieve great things in the United States through hard work and an enterprising spirit.

Padma Lama

One day in 1989, I was visiting a Thangka seller in Kathmandu. He was a very shrewd businessman with an inventory of thousands of Thangka paintings of ornate Buddhist figures. When I was choosing pieces to buy, one painting caught my eye. I thought, *I must have that painting regardless of the price.* As it turned out, the price wasn't very high.

"Can you give me the name and address of the painter?" I asked. "If you connect me with the painter, I promise to buy 150 Thangkas from you." I later sold all the paintings at our store.

The buyer told me the painter's name was Padma Lama and gave me the location of his place in Kathmandu. The next day, my brother DN and the then-mayor of my village, Shambhu Neupane, and I visited the painter. I couldn't believe my eyes. Padma was dirt poor, living in a dark, smelly shack. He was painting Thangkas using a small foot stool as a table and a brick covered with cloth as a chair. His mattress was made of hay, and he used the same brick he sat on as a pillow.

The minute I walked in, I cried, "Why does a human have to live this way?" After I composed myself, we chatted about his life. I discovered he had a wife and children back home in a village in the Kabre District. I showed him the painting I had bought from the seller. "Did you paint this?"

He nodded. "Yes, sir."

"Will you sign it, please?"

He smiled and did as I asked. I had bought the painting for a friend in Oregon, and I later hand-delivered it to her.

I later found out that Padma Lama sold his paintings for 400 rupees or $8. And the Thangka seller sold the painting to me for 1600 rupees. So, basically, the painter was getting little value. The businessman made a lot more as a middleman.

"I would like to meet you again. I'm going to take you to America."

"Please, sir, if you could make that happen, I would owe you my life," he said with his hands joined in prayer. His face was gaunt, but it didn't stop him from having a hopeful smile.

I suspected I was his only prospect for a better life. I made it happen by arranging for him to come to the US on a visitor's visa. It took a lot of behind-the-scenes work, but I was so motivated to help lift him out of poverty. The effort was well worth it.

In the late 1980s and the 1990s, I had an extremely close connection with the US Embassy. Whenever I requested to sponsor and bring people to the US, everyone was granted visas. I had complete confidence that they would work with me in 1989 when I approached the embassy about Padma Lama. I asked Padma to dress in a robe like a holy lama to get the visa. In their passports, Nepali people typically list their profession as a farmer. Padma had done the same, thinking that was the right thing to do. Unfortunately, his visa was denied because he had listed his profession as a painter in the visa application, which contradicted his passport. I immediately called the embassy to speak with the consul. I explained the mix-up and confirmed that Padma was indeed a painter. With that phone call, I secured him a visa.

When Padma came to Boulder on a visitor's visa, he handcrafted his lovely paintings out of Old Tibet. I bought his paintings for $250 apiece and sold them in our store. Initially, he was thrilled with the opportunity to make a decent living as a painter. But as Padma saw the new world of opportunities in the United States, he became more ambitious. One day, without warning, Padma vanished from the apartment I had given him. I was concerned that he was missing because I could get in trouble having sponsored him as a visitor. When I checked with the Nepali community, I learned that, despite not having a work permit, he had landed a job as a cook in a Boulder restaurant where he could earn more money. In 1992, while working as a cook, he applied for asylum, and with that asylum application granted, he could officially work with a work permit. He eventually obtained a green card and citizenship.

I lost track of Padma for ten years. Then, in early 2000, I traveled throughout the state of Kentucky, looking to establish relationships with universities there. At Bowling Green in Western Kentucky, an international office director took me to a Nepali restaurant for lunch, and, lo and behold, I discovered Padma was the restaurant owner! I couldn't believe my eyes! Over delicious Nepalese food, I learned he brought his family members to the US. He bought a couple of homes and sent his children to college and graduate school to become an attorney and a doctor.

Padma calls me at least six times a year and says, "Thank you, thank you, thank you, sir. Because of you, I am here in this great country, and my children are flourishing in a way they could never have back in Nepal. I owe it all to you."

I'm delighted that he was lifted up from a life of extreme poverty and brought to a place where he and his family could thrive.

Mina Shrestha Maskey

In 1989, I traveled to Nepal with Sreejana and our son, Anu, just six months old. We were there with many American students, running Semester in Nepal for the first time. We traveled with the group to celebrate the first semester, and I hosted my son's sixth-month rice feeding ceremony to celebrate the time babies transition from their mother's milk to rice. At the time, we were also demonstrating the Gamow Bag. I combined the three events and invited 300 people.

When I left Nepal for the United States in 1977, Mina was just one year old. She is the fourth child of my second oldest brother, the late Ram Bahadur Shrestha, who had six children. When I returned in 1989, Mina was 13. During that time, Mina was always traveling with us. She was cute, always laughing and smiling. Her attitude brought Sreejana and me so much joy. We talked to Mina's parents and asked if they would let us take Mina to the US to educate her. They agreed, and we brought her to America right away. Securing a visa for Mina wasn't a problem. Her level of education was very low, so we enrolled her into the 7th grade as soon as we could.

Mina was a fantastic cook, friendly, and very upbeat. She made friends quickly; everyone loved her. Mina, Sarita, and Kabita were helpers in the kitchen at Narayan's Nepal Restaurant and lived with us. They were the workforce of our restaurant and one of the main reasons we were so successful.

At the same time, Sreejana's brother, Pranesh Maskey, was also living with us. He managed The Climber's Bar in the basement of our restaurant. Eventually, Pranesh had to move out of our place because the house was getting too crowded. He rented an apartment in Boulder.

One day, we heard that Pranesh and Mina were in love. I asked Mina if it were true, and she said yes. We arranged for them to get married in 1993. They moved to Fort Collins. Pranesh is such a hard-working, good-looking, and kind man. He was so pleased that he found Mina because her way of doing things is gracious, professional, and honest. Their partnership is so successful. They have no competition in the Fort Collins market. Mina and Pranesh own two stores, a beautiful home, and have two intelligent children, Pramit and Smriti.

In America, people shouldn't sit around dreaming about success. They must emerge from their homes and open their eyes. They will see dollars flying everywhere they turn. People who immigrate from other countries can be successful in just a few years with friendly and hard-working attitudes. When Nepalis come to America, they see nothing but opportunities because they have gone through the pain and sadness of hardship in Nepal. They believe in earning from their sweat instead of extending their hands for a handout. The US has countless opportunities for opening stores, restaurants, and other businesses. Most Nepalis had nothing in their country of origin and have plenty in their new home.

Jiban Shrestha

Jiban, my youngest brother, gained early experience running a business when Sreejana and I gave him a mountain bike shop in Kathmandu to run, which he did for two years. Despite having a successful bike shop, he dreamt of coming to America. He obtained his green card through my mother when he was just 20. He only had a 10th-grade education but wasn't interested in any more schooling. Despite not being academic, I knew he was enterprising from watching him run the mountain bike shop. When he arrived in America, I made him the front desk manager of our first Boulder restaurant, Narayan's Nepal Restaurant. A few of my family members worked there.

Later, when I opened an Indian grocery store in Fort Collins, I sent Jiban and his wife, Renu, to run the business. Unfortunately, the timing was all wrong. In 1992, there wasn't much of an Indian or Nepali crowd in Fort Collins. After six months, Jiban and Renu complained to me that it wasn't a viable business. I closed the grocery and moved them to one of our recently opened restaurants a few blocks away, Narayan's Nepal Restaurant, which was run by a relative on my wife's side. I sent another brother's family to work with Jiban and Renu. Things didn't work out, so I decided to sell the restaurant.

We needed to find a better opportunity for Jiban, so I suggested that he go to Colorado Springs, a thriving and affluent city south of Denver, without an East Asian import store at the time. The market seemed rife with opportunity, and since our Boulder and Denver stores were thriving, I guessed a store would do well there. Jiban acquired inventory and made connections with wholesalers in preparation to launch a store. He found a space in Manitou Springs, a small, touristy mountain town close to Colorado Springs. In 1994, he opened a small store, Everest Tibet Imports. Within a year, Jiban realized his location wasn't good for business, so he closed his store in 1995 and moved it to Bijou Street in Colorado Springs, where he thrived.

Six years later, when visiting my brother's store, I noticed a restaurant across from his store that was clearly struggling. I strolled in, chatted with the owner, and made an offer on the spot. In 2000, we opened Narayan's Nepal Restaurant in Colorado Springs. I asked Jiban if he was interested in running it, and he said, "No, thanks."

But later, when he saw customers consistently flocking to the restaurant, he approached me. "Would you sell me your restaurant, brother?"

I thought, *My youngest brother's store is right across from the restaurant. I have to drive two hours every week to manage and run our restaurant. To keep it in the family, it is best to sell it to my brother.* A year and a half later, I agreed, and he paid me. Later, he changed the name to Everest Nepal Restaurant, and it is still thriving. It was a smart move to have Jiban become the owner of the restaurant.

Jiban opened two more stores in Colorado Springs, the second in Old Colorado City in 2001, and the third in the Chapel Hills Mall in the summer of 2003. He sells merchandise very much like that of Old Tibet. His three locations are doing well, and he also owns a couple of buildings in downtown Colorado Springs.

Despite Jiban and Renu having only high school degrees, they have been very successful in the United States. In addition to their business success, they have two beautiful children, daughter Rabina and son Rishab. Renu is one of the keys to my brother's success. Not only is she a hard worker, but she's also a competent buyer, a saleswoman, a renovator, and a cook. Together, they are a successful team. In the US, you don't need to be highly educated to be successful. You don't even need to be proficient in English to prosper. You just have to be enterprising and a hard worker.

Renu's hard work and love for her husband have made all the difference in Jiban's life and are the primary reasons for his success.

My Other Siblings

When my sister, Shanti, came to the US with her family in 1992, her fortunes changed. We helped her gain a foothold by giving her a restaurant in Denver. She soon opened another eatery and a gift shop called Mount Everest on the 16th Street Mall. If that's not enough, she also works as an interpreter at a hospital in Denver. She and her husband, Shyam, blossomed in their new life, raising three successful daughters. The eldest, Salina, earned a nursing degree and married her childhood sweetheart, Anurag Amatya. He earned his master's in business administration from Yale. Her second daughter, Manisha, has a master's degree in international affairs from the University of Denver and is married to Athul Shrestha, a computer engineer. Her third daughter, Marina, is living with her parents and working hard to launch her career. With her family flourishing and her grandchildren born in America, Shanti has never looked back to the years of toil and trouble in Nepal.

We brought my brother Dharma to the US and later brought his wife, sons, and daughter. When he first arrived, we gave him a restaurant to run as a partnership. After he cultivated the skills and knowledge required to become an independent restaurateur, he moved to Nebraska and opened five restaurants in one building! Dharma prospered and returned to Boulder to launch Little Buddha, an imports store. His three children opened businesses in partnership with their father. He owns homes in Colorado and Kathmandu. Dharma and his wife, Chandra Kumari, live happily in Colorado. I blazed the trail and pointed them in the right direction. They paved the way to reach the promised land. Chandra always says that they appreciate my work in their life. Dharma says, "If you had not been born in our family, we would still be struggling in Nepal. We are blessed because of your kindness in bringing all the siblings to this promised land. Now we are thriving and living happily."

My brother Ram Dai and his wife, Mana Maya, had five other children besides Mina. All his children have found success beyond their wildest dreams. Susan and Suman founded and run a thriving dog food company in Seattle. The dog food, made from Nepali cow's milk, is one-of-a-kind and supports farmers in Nepal. Later, Susan married Aliza and Suman married Kritika.

Ram Dai's oldest daughter, Dina, and her husband, Nawaraj, have a Nepali giftshop on Colfax Avenue in Denver. Nawaraj is also a Nepali actor. Ram Dai's son Joshan and his wife, Anju, have two children, and own a gas station with a convenience store. They are doing excellent work and living in Longmont. And finally, Ram Dai's son Roshan, and his wife, Bina, are living in Longmont, Colorado, with two sons, doing very well, and working for a successful company.

Ram Dai became the renowned governor of the Lions Club in Nepal. While he was succeeding economically, he found out he had double kidney failure. Ram Dai visited me in Colorado, for the last time, in the spring of 2015. Jared Polis, then US Congressman of Colorado District 2 and now the Governor of Colorado, came to my home since Ram Dai wanted a picture with the congressman. A few months later, my brother died. We attended his funeral in Nepal, where thousands of people came to say farewell.

By planting the seeds with enough sunlight, water, nourishment, and care, each one of these Nepalis-turned-Americans blossomed, providing unique offerings through their thriving businesses in the ecosystem of American commerce. They've enriched Americans' lives with treasures from another world that pique Americans' curiosity about Nepali culture, customs, and way of life. Nepalese Americans are conduits between two cultures, helping to build a more peaceful and prosperous world.

CHAPTER 15

Success Begins at Home

When a person is happy inside the home, happiness outside the home follows.

IN MY TRAVELS TO EAST ASIA, Southeast Asia, Central America, and beyond, people often ask me about my secrets to success. When I reflect on it, I believe luck and timing played a big part. It also required planting myself in the right soil, dreaming big, never giving up, sharing my wealth wisely, and being surrounded by the right people who make all the difference. I'm fortunate to have a wife who consistently provides support, inspiration, and encouragement. Sreejana never hesitates to give me feedback on my ideas, which are sometimes admittedly wild-eyed. When you dream big, not all your dreams are worth pursuing. It's important to identify the worthy ideas and the ones that are best left on the cutting room floor. I've always found Sreejana's input and judgment to be spot-on. I'm blessed to have a wise, sensible, smart advisor who also happens to be my wife.

A Foundation for Success

When I came to the US in the 1970s, discrimination was prevalent in the South, especially in Texas. But I didn't let the prevailing attitudes toward black and brown people stop me from pursuing my educational and professional aspirations. My dream was to make money and support my family and community in Nepal. Texas proved to be a difficult place to make friends and build a community, so I relocated to a place with more promise. I was one of five Nepalis in the entire state of Texas and the only one in Dallas. By 2015, that number had expanded to 9,000 Nepalis in Dallas alone!

Once I moved to Boulder, Colorado, and planted myself in the right environment, my life blossomed in ways I never thought possible.

Back in the early days when I was still a bachelor, I left no opportunity unturned in the United States and Nepal, especially at the intersection of the two countries and cultures. I saw dollar signs everywhere, and with every step, with each new venture, I grabbed more dollars. The abundance of opportunities provided me with the time, connections, and friendships necessary to succeed. I don't consider myself an exceedingly clever guy, but I've been lucky and knew how to recognize and seize these opportunities. Sometimes inspiration just strikes; creativity, confidence, and courage give me the ability to make dreams become a reality. Always having a positive can-do attitude is also essential to this.

In the village I grew up in, there was nothing. Even so, I dreamt I could become someone. Sure enough, by 20, my dream came true. I created an incredible opportunity for myself managing the Tumlingtar Airport without my father's help by making connections with friends and their parents and relatives. From the very beginning of my life, I always wanted to pursue my dreams. That attitude helped me make things happen. I not only made my dreams come true, but I discovered ones I didn't even know I had.

I was always motivated by the giving theme. I began to view the human heart as God and the human body as a temple. Embracing this perspective, I wanted to help people in the name of God. Doing so gave me even more opportunities, success, and passion. Giving to others filled me with the energy and inspiration to grow my businesses more quickly. I made the human God happier and, as a result, prospered in Colorado.

Dare to Dream

This is the only life you're given, so dare to dream big. You may not always make your dream a reality, but you must try. If you don't, your dream will remain a notion or a fantasy. If you try and succeed, you will be happier, having designed a life just for you. Keep in mind that anyone can succeed. Success isn't limited by country of origin, race, culture, or class. If you weren't born into the right station in life, don't see yourself as nobody. Don't see yourself as incapable of becoming what you dream to be. Everyone has unlimited potential if harnessed correctly.

I tell people all the time: it doesn't matter how old you are. You must open your mind, listen, and absorb information. Don't waste your time with a closed mind. Take in the good things and throw out the bad things.

One can conceive of anything. As humans, we all have power. We all have wishes. We all have dreams. But know this: if you want to see things happen, you must create them yourself. If you want to do something good, you must come up with something—a clever idea, a novel business approach, a new nonprofit that meets unmet needs. For some lucky people, the destination is already mapped out; they don't have to go searching. All they must do is carry out their destiny.

Never give up on pursuing your dreams. My attitude for making things happen is this: I may think a door has slammed shut. Perhaps I tried something, and it didn't work out. But I never thought, *I'm such a failure.* Instead, I thought, *What the heck? One door closed. Nine other doors are waiting to be opened.* I choose a door to see if it opens. Once I have opened it, I may only see darkness. But I've always believed I could turn the light on, go inside, and make my dreams happen. Once you've brightened the room, you'll see the world is beautiful and filled with opportunities. Don't ever think you can't do it. Because you can! You can make a difference, not only in your life but in others' as well. When you make a difference in another's life, you may believe they're the happy one. The truth is you will be ten times happier than the person you helped. Why? Because you lifted them up.

It's important to remain humble about your work. If you boast, it detracts from your mission and purpose. There's no need to promote yourself when you're making a difference. Making a difference is all that matters. Let others sing your praises if they feel compelled.

I have always been persistent and determined; it's part of my DNA. I don't worry about what's next. I feel confident in the future because I believe in myself and my ability to make things happen. When I look toward the future, I don't see darkness; I always see brightness. Instead of fixating on the worst outcome, I focus on the best outcome. My attitude is: if the worst thing happens, it happens. So what? But if you want the best thing, you must make it happen.

Share Your Wealth Wisely

If you prosper, it's important to share your wealth wisely. If you share your wealth and make other people happy, you will feel richer. Sharing your wealth wisely means that you must be able to cover your expenses into and through your old age. If you spend injudiciously, then you cannot help others. If you have enough until you die, you can share your excess with other people. For example, when you're onboard a flight and the oxygen mask drops, you must put your mask on first before you help others. You must ensure you are strong and self-sufficient before helping others.

It's important to help others in a way that empowers them. This means you're not just providing temporary, stopgap measures, like housing or feeding them. You must seek solutions that allow them to stand on their own two feet, so they aren't forever dependent on your charity.

For example, when I visit my village, I see poor kids running around. I find their parents and promise to send their children to school. When they graduate from 10th grade or 11th grade, I say I can bring them to the US on a student visa to finish high school and begin college. And once they come here, I might put them in my house and send them to college. Once they graduate and land a job here, they stand on their own two feet, and they also start sending money to their family.

And in the village, if I spot young people with incredible work ethics but no opportunities, except working in the field, I act. I give them a business, like a shop, or seed money—a few thousand dollars—to start a business. They may open stores, restaurants, or bars to make a living. I might also call a friend with connections and say, "Hey, this man or woman is really good. Will you please help them get started?"

Blend Three Essential Ingredients

The three essential ingredients for leading a life of giving include having support from your family at home, leading with heart, and having enough money to help. If any ingredient is missing, the equation will be thrown off balance, making it more difficult for you to help others in need.

I've always had excellent support at home and didn't have to worry about my children because my wife had that covered. She was managing our businesses, balancing budgets, and taking care of the children, all at the same time. Sreejana's refrain for decades has been, "Let me work here in Boulder to support you. I'll take care of our businesses and children so that you can keep helping others." Her competence and encouragement greatly bolstered me.

Of course, obstacles always arose. Sometimes we didn't have enough money, or health issues slowed my momentum, or governments and people in need in the target country hindered my work. Despite encountering one or more obstacles, and sometimes all at once, I never stopped helping. Helping can take many forms, like building a school, building a hospital, and donating money for a child's education. At times, my businesses at home faltered, but then I borrowed and sent money to people in need. I did whatever it took. What mattered wasn't debt or borrowing. What mattered was helping people.

I'm very soft-hearted, and when I see someone in trouble, for example, if they have no support from their family, are struggling financially, or suffering from a health problem, it melts my heart, and I want to jump to their rescue.

Whatever I have, I want to share it right then and there to ease their hardship. And if I cannot, I feel so helpless; it is agonizing for me, for my heart.

But there is a cautionary tale for soft-hearted types. Sometimes when people see that I'm kind, instead of accepting the gift of my kindness, they find ways to take advantage of me. They think, *How can I shaft him, take money from him, and enrich myself?* So, while helping people, I sometimes was looted— got really taken advantage of.

A Happy Home

When a person is happy inside the home, happiness outside follows. Similarly, when a person is happy in their mind and body, they are happy on the outside. If someone is frustrated and unhappy, they frown, and the world frowns with them. My wife and children make me happy, allowing me to be happy out in the world. They give me the power and strength to help others.

Without Sreejana, I wouldn't be where I am today. She's the source of my success. She is the reason for my wealth. She has been my everything from the very first day we met. I've never had to worry about her and her capacity, wisdom, friendship, kindness, and tolerance.

Sreejana would say to me, "We can work harder and make money and spend it here in the US, or we can spend it in Nepal, where it goes much further. We can make a difference in the lives of people in the villages, and that's what you're good at."

I am on center stage performing the hands-on work, but backstage someone is directing me, working harder, supporting me.

She'd say, "I've got our children, the store, and our businesses covered. You keep helping the people of Nepal and elsewhere." My wife always reminded me that hundreds of thousands of children out in the world needed my help. I derived energy from helping. She'd say, "If you see the poor and the hungry, feed them. If you see the sick, take them to the hospital. Take care of them." That's the kind of woman she is.

My wife is a very strong but kindhearted woman. She holds the financial reins in the family and makes sure to balance our budget. She loves Old Tibet and wants to run the store as long as she can. She works tirelessly, hand-crafting bracelets, earrings, and many other treasures out of stone beads and beautiful gemstones.

At the end of each week, she deposits Old Tibet's earnings into our business account. Sometimes, when I'm overseas, and we chat on the phone, she says, "Guess what happened?"

"What happened?"

"You don't know?"

"No, I don't."

"A little mouse came into my account and took some money!"

That little mouse is me.

God blessed me with wonderful children and a lovely wife. Because of their support and happiness, I've had the opportunity to continue to help others. My work has made me a successful and happy person.

My children, Anu and Regina, gave me strength, even though I wasn't always around. They are the most peaceful, understanding, kind, and tolerant children that one could ever ask for. My children understood I was giving so much to the people of the world. From two weeks old until he was off to college, Anu grew up at Old Tibet attached at the hip to Sreejana. Anu was always smart, tolerant, humble, and very understanding from an early age. He never said bad things to me or my wife. He never used four-letter words at all.

My daughter, Regina, is four years younger than Anu and liked to play with him, although they fought at times, as siblings do. She has always been very independent and bold, even as a toddler. She never wanted help with things, always insisting upon doing everything herself.

One time, when she was three, we were in a jammed elevator in a Manhattan hotel. She said to a tall man in front of her, "Mister, you'd better watch out. There's a little girl behind you."

And the man looked back, "Oh, excuse me, ma'am. I'm so sorry."

"You are excused."

I couldn't believe it—her self-confidence and boldness! She was not afraid. She has never been afraid. As an adult, she loves yoga, meditation, the outdoors, and friendships. She wants to have a nice job and a family, but first, she wants to have adventures and travel solo, making friends along the way.

As my children grew up and I was overseas, we kept in touch by talking, emailing, and FaceTiming. Even though I was away, we were close. Both are superbly good kids. We never had to say, "Hey, do you have homework? Go sit down and do your homework." Of course, all the credit goes to my wife.

Without such an incredible wife providing ongoing support, most men couldn't be successful, no matter what they say. Sreejana not only managed Old Tibet but also our restaurants and other stores and our many employees while raising babies. And she's still working.

At times, we've struggled financially, which prompted me to question what I was doing. I thought maybe I should quit my philanthropic efforts and focus on creating a thriving business. But then I realized God helped me to help others. God made me strong enough so I could help other people.

In my household, my wife is the boss, but we share a mutual respect. Early on, I made many mistakes by not asking for her advice or not listening to her if she offered it. All that has changed. I listen when she tells me in her gentle way about the right things to do.

In 1997, I planned to buy three buildings in downtown Boulder on 19th Street between Pearl and Walnut. At the time, the buildings, housing seven units, cost between $300,000 and $400,000. In total, I was planning to buy buildings worth one million dollars. When I put down a $100,000 deposit, Sreejana approached me and said, "Do we really need this? Our family members back in Nepal need so much help. We can save hundreds of people from hunger. Let's help them instead."

And my experience was such that $1 went a long way in countries like Nepal, India, and Nicaragua.

I agreed because I wanted to alleviate our family members' pain and sorrow, which, in turn, would lighten our psychic load. We would not have to carry that pain and sorrow with us to bed every night.

Buying land and houses in Boulder cannot fill empty stomachs in Nepal, and I had seen so many hungry people there. By not purchasing those buildings, thousands upon thousands of people would be helped— educationally, physically, and mentally. I could use the money to open businesses and create jobs for them so they could become self-sufficient. Pouring money, time, and effort into others is much riskier than buying those apartment buildings would've been. But the high risk of giving often results in the high reward of watching others prosper.

Inspiring Others to Dream

When I was leading a group in Nepal fall of 1989, I went on a hike with a 72-year-old botany professor, the late Dr. William Weber from CU-Boulder, his daughter, Heather Weber, and a few other trekkers. After we had gone a couple of miles, he and I sat down on a makeshift bench, and he said, "I saw the school you opened in your village. What are you trying to accomplish with that little school, Narayan?" He said it as though he didn't think it was a worthy pursuit.

"I'm planting a seed for the community. This little school will educate not only the children who attend my school but also the parents and the community."

"In what way?"

"Well, the parents, whose children are not in school, will change their perspectives when they see others' children speaking English and improving in the areas of math, reading, and writing. Then they will start bringing their children to my school."

"Oh," he said, "that is good. You know what you're doing, Narayan?"

"No, I don't."

"What you're doing is helping someone, somewhere, somehow, seed their dream. Then it will grow. You're bringing your earnings from the United States right here to your village. In not forgetting your roots, you're setting a good example."

I thought, *Wow! He's quite right.*

With my time and attention from 2014 until now, that little school has become the largest of its kind in the region. In the entire district, there are currently 200 schools, 36 of which are high schools.

Someone must be the first person to take a risk turning their dream into a reality and, if it's a worthy dream, others will follow. Dream-making is a leap of faith and an act of courage.

We come into this world empty-handed, and we leave the same way. Hopefully, we will leave behind a legacy of good work, kindness, goodness, tolerance, and compassion. No matter where you were born, your dreams will likely come true if you heed my advice.

CHAPTER 16

My Introduction to Shumei

The human heart is God, and the human body is a temple.

WHEN I WAS YOUNG, Nepal prided itself on being the only Hindu kingdom in the world. People believed that the King of Nepal was an incarnation of the Hindu God, Vishnu. And because of that, he was the ultimate ruler of the country. Therefore, Nepal did not allow other religions except for Buddhism.

A Reluctant Hindu

Despite being born into a Hindu family, Hinduism wasn't a perfect fit for me. Even as a child, I resisted the religion's rituals. When the brahmin or holy man came and gave us blessings, you were supposed to bow and place your forehead on his feet. One time as a child, I sobbed when I was forced to bow at a brahmin's feet. I wondered, *Why? Why do I have to touch my head to his dirty feet?*

Later, in 10th grade, I began to question the segregation and caste-based discrimination in Nepali society. People were labeled "untouchables" as a basis for discrimination. There were societal rules for untouchables, such as whose homes they could enter and whom they could eat with. Only select people were permitted to go to the pond to scoop water for drinking, while others were forbidden. If the untouchables tried to get water, they would be kicked out or even beaten to death in some rare cases. Many in Nepali society accepted this inequality, but I found it difficult to understand and accept. I wondered, *Why aren't all humans the same?*

I also questioned the rituals around mourning after a death in the family. If a parent died, the sons were expected to shave their heads, eyebrows, mustaches, and could not be touched by other people. They had to cook their meals in a very small, secluded area for 13 days, wearing nothing except clothing covering their private parts.

The point was to show how much you were suffering. But I thought, *The person is dead. They can't see their family suffering. The anguish is pointless. What kind of belief is mourning through suffering?* The brahmins enforced these rituals because they were written in the holy book. But the book was written by humans, not by God, to perpetuate a system where holy men retained power, were respected, and provided them the means to earn a living.

I thought, *When my parents die, I will not mourn like this.*

Although I have always respected the Hindu religious tradition I grew up with, it frustrated me at times. I thought Christianity might suit me better. But at the time, you weren't allowed to talk about it. You couldn't even own a Bible in Nepal.

On Christmas morning, at the age of 15, I listened to an educational broadcast on the radio. The presenter was sharing stories about Jesus Christ and the meaning of Christmas. I was fascinated with the details of Jesus' birth and his life story. His message of devoting his life to the poor resonated with me. I wanted to learn more. I was unlike most people in my community, whose world was confined to the surrounding valleys and hills. I was always curious about the world beyond.

I learned that there was no caste system in Christianity; that all humans were the same. I was very drawn to Christianity because of this. I believed if countries wanted to develop, they needed to root out the notion that some groups are superior to others, like in a caste-based system. Also, I thought people must not judge others by their looks, clothing, or speech. Anyone could become anything they wanted. It was a mistake to underestimate the capacity of others.

Once I learned about Christianity, I wondered, *How can I get a copy of the Bible?* I asked a friend who was traveling to India, where they had freedom of religion, if he could get me a Bible. He said he was nervous about bringing the religious contraband in his backpack across the border into Nepal. Nevertheless, he somehow managed to do it without getting caught and secretly slipped me the illegal holy book. I quickly stashed it under my bed mat. I couldn't wait to break it open and read the forbidden pages.

Every morning for three hours, my father meditated, chanted, and read the Bhagavad Gita, the Hindu holy book. He was a very devoted Hindu. Meanwhile, I had smuggled in a Bible, which I kept tucked under my bed mat and read clandestinely by the light of a small lamp while the rest of my family slept.

One time my father found me awake late at night. "What are you doing, not sleeping?" he asked.

"Oh, Dad, I'm studying for tomorrow," I lied.

"Oh, okay, okay." And he left.

Heaven and Hell

As an adult, having read the Bhagavad Gita, the Hindu scriptures; the Ramayana, an ancient Sanskrit epic; and the Bible, the gospels of Jesus; and being familiar with Buddha's teachings, I knew that so many of the religious themes and goals were the same. If you did good things in your life, you went to heaven when you died. If you did bad things, you went to hell. I thought, *How in the world could people know there is a heaven and hell?* No one had traveled to either place, snapped photos, returned to the land of the living, and published them in magazines or newspapers, with the headline, "Proof of Heaven and Hell." They seemed like made-up stories to shape human behavior for the better.

I believe in heaven and hell, but here on Earth. If you do good when you're alive, you create heaven in your part of the world. If you harm others, you create hell. Growing up with Hinduism and Buddhism, I never had the opportunity to go to a Christian church. I vowed that someday I would. So, when I moved to Texas, I embraced Christianity by being baptized and regularly attending Bible study and prayer service. Initially, I thought Christianity might be a good fit for me, but I soon noticed the hypocrisy of Christians.

You were expected to give ten percent of your income to the church in the name of God, or else you weren't a good Christian. Not only was the church taking your money in the form of tithing, but also the government charged taxes. This made it difficult to give more of one's paycheck to the church.

Meanwhile, who was getting richer? The church and the government, of course. And, still, some people didn't have enough to eat. Those who could afford to would give, and those who couldn't afford to were still expected to give. What kind of charity was that?

The other thing I noticed was that Christians, like my ex-in-laws, Albert and Dorothy Hooker, preached a message of inclusion, but the minute they left the church, they would discriminate, like not letting people of color into their homes. In the name of Jesus, they said good things but did bad things. And they called themselves Christians? If they had been real Christians, they wouldn't have discriminated. Again, the question arose for me. *Where do I belong?*

In my hometown of Boulder, you didn't have to go to church, temple, or gumba. There was no pressure to pick one religion over another. Boulder was an eclectic mix—Buddhists, Hindus, Christians, Muslims, and Jews living together in harmony. Its openness allowed people to explore and practice whatever religion worked for them. Or even no religion. Many atheists call Boulder home.

After visiting the mountain villages of Nepal, when our Boulder trekking group ran into the child we saved and the one who was tragically dead, I learned I must not waste my time looking for God in a temple, masjid, church, or gumba. Why? Because the human heart is God, and the human body is a temple. The heart is God in that it feels, speaks, hurts, and loves. Lifting each other up happens through the human heart. Happiness on Earth happens by making your heart clear and pure. We make Heaven on Earth by loving, caring, respecting, and tolerating others, so we can live in harmony.

I wanted to please as many hearts as possible. To that end, I decided to open hospitals and schools instead of temples and churches.

My Introduction to Shumei

One afternoon in March 2009, my wife called me from Old Tibet and said, "Hey, a couple came in looking for you. They wanted to talk to you about spirituality."

"Really? Why?" I asked, thinking they were probably Jehovah's Witnesses or Hare Krishnas.

"I don't know."

"Well, where are they from?"

"They looked Japanese to me. They said they'd come back in a few days."

A few days later, I was in my office in the back of the store. My wife strolled up to my desk and said, "They're here. Do you want me to send them to your office?"

"Yes, please."

They introduced themselves as Yoshiyuki and Kaori Tominaga and said they wanted to share the Shumei philosophy with me.

They seemed like nice people, but what was Shumei? I had never heard of it. I hoped it wasn't a strange cult and that I wouldn't have to make up an excuse to end the conversation and hurry them out.

They explained that Shumei is a spiritual organization that fosters health, happiness, and harmony by applying the wisdom and insights of the spiritual leader, Mokichi Okada, to whom its members refer to as Meishusama. He taught that a world free from sickness, poverty, and discord could be realized through the three Shumei principles of the Jyorei, Natural Agriculture, and the appreciation of art and beauty. They explained that the Shumei philosophy believes we need to grow our food naturally in a process they call Natural Agriculture, which is like growing organically but without manure.

I learned more about the teachings of the Japanese philosopher Mokichi Okada, Meishusama, "enlightened spiritual teacher," as the couple referred to him. My understanding was that the Shumei philosophy maintained that the Divine Light was power; God's power is solar energy. This made so much sense to me. In my view, all life on the planet is dependent upon the sun. Energy which comes from the sun is Divine Light. Therefore, the sun is the true God. The sun existed long before any human and their religious idols. Shiva, Ganesh, Buddha, and Jesus Christ are all human made.

I was immediately drawn to it.

The couple explained that Shumei philosophy teaches tolerance, understanding, and compassion. It promotes first helping yourself by cultivating a pure mind and heart with positive thinking. The philosophy recommends that you practice Natural Agriculture in your backyard or on your land. Clean mind, clean heart, clean body.

The couple asked if we could provide them space—a corner of our shop every Saturday for five hours—for Jyorei. At the time, we had three stores in Boulder under the same company name—Old Tibet—in the following locations: 948 Pearl Street, 1136 Pearl Street, and 15th and Pearl.

"What's Jyorei?" I asked.

They explained that Jyorei is a healing practice that means "purification of the spirit." Jyorei uses Divine Light to dissolve the spiritual impurities that are the source of all physical, emotional, and personal problems. It involves two people, one who gives and one who receives. The person receiving Jyorei often experiences feelings of tranquility and well-being. The giver benefits by gaining a larger capacity for compassion and love for others. They further explained that you sit with your eyes closed, and a Shumei member gives you Jyorei from a distance. In Shumei, the Divine Light is God. The belief is that the members carry the divine within, as if they were holy amulets, and by sharing the divine with others, they share its healing energy. Later, I experienced the healing power of Jyorei for the first time.

I said, "Yes," to their request to offer Jyorei in our store even though I wasn't sure what I had agreed to. Little did I know it would be life-changing for me.

Shumei in Crestone, Colorado

For about one and a half years, Yoshiyuki and Kaori Tominaga offered Jyorei in our shop. In August of 2010, they invited my wife and me to Crestone, Colorado. Sreejana's sister-in-law, Srija Maskey, joined us. The couple was there to welcome us to the beautiful Shumei International Institute (SII), one of the best spiritual establishments in Crestone out of many, including Buddhist, Christian, Hindu, and Muslim.

We first viewed a video presentation on Shumei, and then we went to the sanctuary to chant and receive Jyorei, followed by coffee, tea, and snacks in their dining room. A Hoshi-sha (a person learning to provide selfless service to others) gave us a walking tour of the building, grounds, and the Natural Agriculture field where potatoes, corn, and daikon radishes grew. Yoshiyuki and Kaori Tominaga joined us as well. They explained that Crestone is not fertile land; it's sandy and rocky.

I was impressed by the well-disciplined staff who spotlessly cleaned every square inch of the facility and grounds. They were so humble, kind, and compassionate toward their guests.

Then a Natural Agriculture staff member gave us a tour of the Shumei Natural Agriculture garden. He said to us, "Would you please pull a daikon radish from the ground?"

"Really? Okay." I bent down and tugged a radish from the ground. I kept pulling and pulling and pulling. The radish was almost a foot long! We were astonished.

"All you need for healthy plants are water, sun, and soil, and the fourth ingredient is human love," the agriculturalist explained, smiling. "Chemical fertilizers are slowly poisoning the soil, our food, and living creatures. To establish Natural Agriculture, it can take three to four years to clean the soil because the effects of the chemical fertilizers persist, poisoning the insects that are good for the soil and the plants."

I loved the idea of growing food in soil that was free from chemicals. "Oh my gosh, this is great!" I said, clutching the gigantic radish. "I want to introduce this agriculture to my village in Nepal, where I have a school, and I own land. Would it be possible to talk to your leader?"

"Unfortunately, it's not possible. It's difficult to set up an appointment. He travels a lot," said Yoshiyuki.

"If there is any way we can arrange for a meeting, please help me. I don't care how long it takes," I said.

"It's difficult, but I'll try. Now, I'd like to take you to see the sand dunes and a waterfall. Does that sound good?"

"Yes, we would love that," I said.

Yoshiyuki and Kaori took us to see the shifting sand dunes and a lovely waterfall. We removed our shoes and socks and waded across a stream to see the waterfall. The water was chilly at first but so refreshing. As we emerged from the stream, the couple sat on the banks with clean white towels ready to dry our feet before we put our shoes and socks back on. That meant so much to me. I couldn't believe how much the Shumei members bent over backward to please their guests. After I wiped my feet, they took the wet towel, folded it properly, and put it back into their bag.

I had a headache and was sneezing and complained to my wife. I thought maybe my allergies were acting up.

Yoshiyuki overheard and said, "May I give you Jyorei?"

I sat, and he gave me Jyorei. Amazingly, five minutes later, my headache was gone. I was astonished because usually my headaches lingered. Since that day, I've never had a headache again. Pretty miraculous! And during Jyorei, I felt the Divine Light come into me and penetrate my body from head to toe. This was my first, greatest experience of Jyorei.

Around two weeks later, Yoshiyuki called, saying Alan Imai Sensei, the director of Shumei International Institute, Crestone, wanted to meet me.

On December 27, 2010, we hosted a dinner for Alan Sensei and Masahide Koyama, the nephew of the organization's current president, Kaicho Sensei. Yoshiyuki and Kaori Tominaga also joined us. During our lovely dinner, we invited Alan Sensei and Masahide to go to Nepal, and they accepted.

In January of 2011, I took Alan Sensei and Masahide Koyama to Nepal. Our flight from Kathmandu to Tumlingtar was canceled because of bad weather. We flew to Biratnagar Airport and took a Land Rover to my village. I took my guests on a rough and rocky eight-hour drive, during which we crossed rivers and drove next to cliffs. I tried to hide my fear that our journey was too strenuous. We finally arrived in Khandbari at 8:00 pm, hungry and tired. This was the first time I had brought esteemed people from the Shumei organization to Nepal. They were from a developed country, and I was so worried they were not accustomed to the rigors of travel in Nepal. The next morning, after putting them up in a hotel, I asked, "How was your ride? I hope I did not ruin your tour."

"Oh, this is the most interesting and enjoyable trip we've ever had," said Masahide Koyama.

Alan Sensei agreed.

I breathed a huge sigh of relief.

Our goal was to bring two teachers from my school to train in Natural Agriculture and living a clean life to create Heaven on Earth. We interviewed

13 people and chose two young men to bring over to the US in a year. Unfortunately, we ran into a visa snag, so it took us almost two years to bring the trainees to the US.

Masahide worked very hard to get the right kind of visa, so the US Embassy would allow us to bring the teachers to train at Crestone. The appropriate visa was a J-1, which required the teachers to go back to Nepal a year after their Natural Agriculture training.

CHAPTER 17

Making Heaven on Earth

Mysteriously, the ages advance towards the long-awaited Heaven on Earth.
After thousands of years of waiting, God's plan is now being fulfilled.
The healing of the world is too vast to be seen by our small eyes.
Even the saints cannot fathom God's great designs. Open your eyes.
Look at my work. Much surpasses understanding.
Now, the old era comes to its end as heaven emerges on earth.

—Meishusama, *A Collection of Light*

IN JULY OF 2012, AFTER THREE MONTHS of their Hoshi program in Crestone, we invited Mr. Nawaraj Rai and Mr. Bhuwan Shrestha to our home. They were Nepali teachers from Surya Boarding School training at the Shumei International Institute. They were in Crestone for one year to train in the Hoshi program, spirituality, and growing vegetables naturally. They learned to live like Shumei members—clean and pure from the inside out.

My Shumei Transformation

The first night, we prepared Nepalese food for our guests. They had eaten nothing but Japanese food for three months, and they were dying to eat Nepalese food. After enjoying a hearty feast, we all went to bed.

The next day at 7:00 am, I got up to prepare breakfast for our guests. When I went downstairs, I didn't see them anywhere, but the kitchen was spotless. When we had gone to bed, the kitchen was a mess. Then I went to the bathroom, and holy cow! It was sparkling clean! How did that happen? I never heard a peep while our guests tidied up our home.

I found them outside, cleaning and shining the big pots. I said, "Come, let's eat breakfast. Just leave those pots, please."

But they didn't do as I asked. They finished cleaning the pots and pans, stacked them, brought them in, and dried them.

"What are you doing, man? You're supposed to be our guests," I said.

"No, sir. You asked us to come to the US to become someone. We're now trained teachers. By living disciplined lives wherever we go, we can teach our children back home to become good people. We are learning late in our lives but, thank God, you invited us to learn the ways of Shumei. It's just a beautiful way to live. Thank you, sir."

I was stunned. I had never heard "thank you" from their mouths before. They had changed dramatically. That's the kind of discipline this organization teaches. Pure heart, pure mind, clean body, and clean environment. Such cleanliness allows the divine to shine.

During the four-hour drive back to Crestone to drop them off, I asked them many questions about Shumei. How did they like it? Were they impressed? What was it all about? They answered all my questions, saying that the philosophy was enormously good. They believed people should learn about it—the associated behaviors, the goodness—and share it with others. They claimed this was the way to make our family, society, and village better, living together in peace and joy. They encouraged me to read Meishusama's book, *Sincerity and Truth: A Life Story of Meishusama*. Even though I owned it, I had never even cracked it open.

I dropped them off and drove home, feeling inspired to read the book. The next day I flew to Nicaragua and carried the book with me. I landed in Managua and stayed overnight. The next day I rented the car and drove six hours. I stayed at the mayor's house in Jalapa, Nicaragua.

The people in Jalapa respect me very much because I have done many things for them.

In the middle of the night, I was startled awake. I had never seen or met Meishusama in person, but he came to me in a dream. I flew from the valley way up to the mountains and crossed over the trees, hilltops, and mountain peaks. I landed inside a building with the rays of the Divine Light shining through. Meishusama was there, smiling. He looked exactly as I had seen him in pictures. He said, "You," pointing to me, "You need to start spreading the word." And he put a crown on my head and handed me a sword. I had heard that Meishusama refers to a sword to cut through the cruel act of foes in his book of poetry, *A Collection of Light*.

I couldn't go back to sleep. Why? Because of the conclusion I had reached after talking with the two teachers, after seeing Natural Agriculture and the super-sized daikon. Who planted the trees in the forest? Nature. Who put the water here? Nature. Who created the sunlight? Nature. With our care, everything can be stronger. But we must be patient, tolerant, kind, and giving—all things taught by Hindu scripture, Buddha, and Jesus Christ. We don't need to go searching for heaven. It's right here if we make it so.

After that night in Nicaragua, my path forward was crystal clear. When I returned home, I said to my wife, "I've got to go to Crestone."

On December 28, 2012, I made the journey and spent the night. I asked Yoshiyuki and Kaori to come to my room after dinner, and I shared the dream I had in Nicaragua. "I've decided to become a member of Shumei."

They were surprised because they had been planning to say to me, "You are an important person in Nepal and Colorado, and you believe in Shumei philosophy very much. We think it's excellent timing to join Shumei, and let's share Shumei philosophy in the world together."

I thought it was meant to be. Not only my visionary dream in Nicaragua, but other reasons inspired me to become a member of Shumei. Seeing the change in my teachers from Nepal, reading about Meishusama, and the robust daikon all contributed to my decision.

I told Alan Sensei I wanted to become a member. He couldn't believe it. Nobody could believe it. They thought I was too busy juggling projects. Also, they didn't view me as a spiritual man. But I was, in my own way, given the work I did to serve people all over the world. I had no time to devote to spiritual practice. I felt a certain emptiness.

On March 10, 2013, I became a Shumei member. Alan Sensei conducted the ceremony at Crestone, and I couldn't have been happier. He handed me the amulet of Divine Light and said, "You have a new birthdate: March 10, 2013, which is written in your amulet of Divine Light."

Shumei members wear the amulet of Divine Light under their shirts. Around 300,000 people throughout the world wear the pouch.

My Visit to Shumei Headquarters

Two months later, I went to the headquarters of Shumei in Japan with Yoshiyuki Tominaga. At the time, I had such excruciating knee pain I needed crutches and a wheelchair. Still, I wanted to go. I was determined to see the headquarters in the Shiga prefecture near Kyoto.

In Shiga, they've created a heavenly paradise with buildings, mountains, roads, bridges, tunnels, and a museum under the mountain. Meishusama Hall, the main sanctuary building, was designed by Minoru Yamasaki, one of the most prominent architects of the 20th century. He was a Japanese American architect, best known for designing the original World Trade Center in New York City and many other large-scale projects. It was an unbelievable place, and I felt the embodied power immediately. The Miho Museum and its approach tunnel and bridge were designed by I.M. Pei, another world-famous Asian (Chinese) American architect.

They had a beautiful school with fine dormitories. They recruited 40 students per year—children of the members. Every day, the students woke up at 5:30 am to start their routines. In the cafeteria, the students cooked, washed, and cleaned thoroughly—the chairs, the tables, under the tables, and the floor. Their work was supervised, and if the students hadn't cleaned sufficiently, the supervisor said, "It's not good enough. Wipe it again." Everything had to be cleaned after every use.

Some seeing this might think it was overbearing and perfectionistic, but I could see, if children were taught this kind of discipline, the learning would transfer, and they would become excellent guardians of the planet.

We stayed overnight in a hotel before setting out for Kishima Island in Japan's Seto Inland Sea. That evening there was a celebration of international members who were bound for the island. Masahide Koyama and I talked until 2:00 am about the future of Shumei in Nepal.

The next day, we went to Kishima Island—a property the Shumei organization had bought for Youth Education and Natural Agriculture. To get to the island, we took a 15-minute boat ride. When I stepped onto the island, I felt like I had entered paradise, with lovely modern buildings and a shrine. They raised chickens, had acres upon acres of vegetable gardens, and ran a youth training facility. Shumei grew so many crops using the Natural Agriculture method, including rice, millet, maize, grapes, olive oil, coffee beans, and tea. They gave the visiting international members a special tour and served us lunch and dinner.

Everything was spotlessly clean, even the pathways, and every corner of the island was beautifully decorated. The Shumei chanting hall sat atop the island, with a panoramic view of the ocean and mountains. Such a spiritually powerful place! I was infused with spirituality. And every place I visited, many Shumei establishments, I was drawn to, and I truly believed that if we followed the Shumei philosophy, we could make Heaven right here on Earth.

I left Kishima Island, and Toshihiko Yazaki Sensei waited for me at the boat dock to drive me to another Shumei (Yonago) Center. We drove there with Kaori, my guide and interpreter. This excursion was just for me. The other international members went their separate ways.

They arranged for me to stay in a historic house. Five women prepared an elaborate dinner just for me. They served my meal on more than 400-year-old plates and glasses. I was so pleased with their hospitality. They went the extra mile every time. They treated me like such a special human being.

Yazaki Sensei offered to give me a traditional Japanese tea ceremony. He changed into traditional Japanese clothes to perform the ceremony. I sat in a chair because I was on crutches, and he was on the floor. The care, attention, and preparation of the tea were not to be believed. It took 30 minutes to prepare one cup of green tea! It was such a humble offering. I was in tears with all the care he took.

Unfortunately, I had come down with a cold and was feeling a little under the weather. But when I saw my lovely room, with a beautiful tatami mat floor and a futon, I felt uplifted and cared for. When I went to the restroom for the first time, I couldn't believe their toilet. The lid opened just as I entered, and a fresh plastic covering wrapped around the lid. When I sat down, it was heated! When I finished my business and pressed the button, it sprayed warm water on my bum in a back-and-forth cleaning motion. Then when I pressed another button, it dried my bottom with warm air. I thought, *I must have this toilet in my house!*

After breakfast, upon my request, they took me on an excursion to a Natural Agriculture rice farm. I had lunch at the house of Mr. Yamamoto, the farm owner. Five women prepared a meal just for me. I felt like a king traveling solo. Before lunch, they served us a special green tea. As we sipped our tea, a woman performed a lovely song with a traditional Japanese musical instrument, the shamisen. Then a second person appeared with a different instrument and performed for us. Finally, the owner of the house performed a traditional Japanese dance in my honor. Lunch was served, course after course, fresh and beautifully presented as though each dish were a work of art.

After lunch, we set out for the rice fields. We drove to the top of the mountain four miles away from his home. I saw the farmhouse, the tools, and the Natural Agriculture fields surrounding the house.

As we walked around the fields, I asked, "Where does the water come from? How do you cultivate this land?"

"Two miles away, there's a pipe laid underground connected to a water tank that runs over to here," said the rice farmer.

I was astonished. I had never seen anything like it. I thought, *Oh, my goodness, I want to convert my rice fields in Nepal from conventional farming to Natural Agriculture.*

While in Japan, I received Jyorei every day. It astonished me that I didn't need to use my crutches ever again! Jyorei is truly life-changing, but you must believe in its power to see these results.

I cried when I left my Shumei friends because of their incredibly warm welcome. When I returned home, I carried in my heart the dream that someday I'd go back to my village in Nepal and introduce Natural Agriculture to the rice farmers, restoring the ancient way of growing rice. Our ancestors once grew food this way. But to grow crops bigger and faster, we lost sight of the natural ways and gave into growing methods that increased production but were toxic to the body and the earth. By introducing Natural Agriculture to Khandbari and detoxifying the land, the people and animals would heal and live longer, healthier lives.

My Shumei Initiative in Nepal

Understanding the mystery of soils through science alone is a little foolish. What a pity! Polluting the soil poisons us in body and mind, scattering seeds of anguish. To purify our land so polluted by the toxins of fertilizers is a noble endeavor.

—Meishusama, *A Collection of Light*

Natural Agriculture is a means of cultivating wholesome food with pure seeds and without the use of any fertilizers, chemicals, or additives. The approach is GMO-free, low-input, and agroecology focused. It emphasizes the use of indigenous, natural seeds, encourages seed-saving, and stresses the cultivation of the soil in its natural state—without additional elements. The goal of Natural Agriculture is to keep the soil clean. More than an approach to agriculture, it is a way of living mindfully and in harmony with nature.

In 2015, I showed my Nepali farmers a video on Natural Agriculture and asked if they would be willing to grow rice without chemical fertilizers. They were skeptical and said if they didn't use fertilizers, they'd lose their income and wouldn't have anything to eat. Over time, after using fertilizers, the soil became depleted of natural minerals and wouldn't produce much without fertilizers. For example, with fertilizers, a farmer might expect his land to yield 20 tons of rice. Without the fertilizers, the land will yield only four tons, barely enough for the farmer to feed his family. But the farmer needs excess rice to sell, so he can buy clothes, fuel, and other essentials.

I committed to the farmers on my land to supplement their income for four years if they planted without fertilizers. I told them they could compost leaves, but that was all. They agreed. I also built a small cottage for their animals so that only oxen plowed—no machines. I further convinced my farmers by pointing out that the large trees in the forest grew by themselves—no one watered or fertilized the soil.

The first year, the Natural Agriculture approach yielded one-fourth of the farmers' normal rice crop. The second year showed more promise, but I still had to pay them to supplement their income. In the third year, the yield was close to the normal yield. Finally, in the fourth year, the harvest was greater than that grown with the fertilizer. The farmers and I were overjoyed that the Natural Agriculture method was proving to be fruitful.

In the fifth year, I approached the Shumei organization in Misono, Japan, and asked them if they would help fund an irrigation project for continuous growth of rice on my land in Nepal. They supported me, and we completed the project. With my irrigation project, the naturally grown rice has been a success. Naturally grown rice is four times more satisfying than conventionally grown rice. You don't need to eat as much because it fills you up quicker. You will not get sick if you eat naturally grown products.

Nepal is a mountainous country with the rice fields in the hills. When you apply chemical fertilizers to the land on the hilltops, the water mixes with the soil and carries the chemical fertilizer down to the creeks. The polluted water is lapped up by animals, domestic and wild, which shortens their lifespans. The farmers don't understand why their animals are getting sick and dying.

Meanwhile, the chemicals kill worms beneficial to the rice-growing process. In Natural Agriculture, worms thrive. Also, if strong winds and heavy rains pummel cropland, chemically grown rice is easily destroyed, whereas naturally grown rice bounces back in a few days.

I would like to give my sincere thanks to Masahide Koyama for all he has given me. I owe him so much for continuously supporting my vision for my village of Khandbari. With his dedication, belief, and trust, my dream to bring Natural Agriculture education to Nepal's farmers has come to fruition. For five years, he traveled to Nepal with me many times. He's an extraordinary person who supports my dreams and all my requests. When I wanted to introduce my village to Shumei students and other visitors from Japan, he brought them there. Masahide walked with me every step of the way into the rice paddies of Khandbari helping farmers find water resources to irrigate the land.

When I requested that he bring a Natural Agriculturist from Japan to my village, he did. From planting to the harvest, he was there, offering his guidance and support. When I asked him to bring videos to introduce Meishusama's teachings to the people of my village, he brought a television set from Japan to Khandbari.

He never stopped thinking: how can we fulfill Narayan's vision and wishes?

He offered guidance to young Nepalis. He taught Jyorei in a tent in remote peasant villages. He stayed in tents or thatched roof houses in rough areas, night after night. Masahide has always supported me and my vision. His friendship is so strong and valuable; I will always be grateful. He's the reason

I've been successful introducing Shumei philosophy and practices to Khandbari, Kathmandu, and many other places in Nepal.

I'm indebted to two more people. Alan Sensei played an equal role, trusting and believing in my goals and dreams and offering support and guidance. Eugene Imai Sensei, the head of Shumei America, also has always believed in me and has been good to me. With their support and trust, I can continue to make a huge difference in others' lives. This kind of support and trust energizes me to do more and to dedicate my life to Shumei.

Merging Shumei Philosophy with My Life of Giving

I didn't know what I was missing in my life until I found Shumei. For 30 years, I was searching spiritually. I didn't understand who I was before I discovered Shumei. I kept traveling, helping, and doing. Shumei philosophy bolstered me. I felt good about the help I provided to people in need, but Shumei opened my eyes to what I was doing on a deeper level.

Shumei International Headquarters in Misono, Japan, invited me to speak at many Shumei centers in Japan, 33 cities (listed in the Appendix) in all, about merging Shumei with my philosophy of giving.

I'm well-known among Japanese youth within the Shumei organization because I have spoken to large audiences at all those centers. They also come to hear me speak at my home in Boulder about a brighter future for them and to seek encouragement from me. When Japanese youth listen to my talks—sometimes 20–25 at a time—we provide Kleenex because they often shed tears of joy!

One time, after speaking to 300 young people at the Shumei International Headquarters, I was escorted from the stage to a lounge before dinner. The Shumei student assigned to escort me said with tears streaming down her cheeks, "I've never heard such powerful advice. I could listen to you all day." The senseis and my friends were impressed hearing the student's words in the elevator.

Because of my talks at Shumei centers throughout Japan, in cities large and small, many Nepali expats living in Japan came to hear me speak and have become members of Shumei. I couldn't be more honored that they wanted to see me, to meet me, and to hear me. The people I met couldn't hold back their tears when they shared their life experiences. They were lost before, and they finally felt fulfilled, many for the first time in their lives. With compassion, I encouraged and lifted them up.

Because of this, Nepali membership in Shumei has increased, something that the Shumei leaders noticed. They told me I'm doing wonderful work for the Shumei organization. I talk about Meishusama's message, and I want to spread his words and work in Japan, Nepal, the US, and throughout the world. Because so few people have heard much about this philosophy, I feel it's my mission to introduce the world to this wonderful way of thinking.

I want to leave behind a legacy of Shumei in Nepal and beyond of communities that raise beautiful, disciplined, educated children committed to making our planet a better place to live. Our founder, Meishusama, first president, Kaishusama, and the current president, Kaicho Sensei, the daughter of Kaishusama, and Tamao Sensei, the grandson of Kaishusama and son of Kaicho Sensei, and the other members are dedicated to this mission.

If there is enough support from the Shumei organization, I can enlist many hundreds of members within a year. To become a member, one must either go to Japan or come to the US, which is very difficult for Nepalis because of the expense and the visa issues. Nonetheless, I have already enlisted 54 members.

I have sent my Nepali teachers to US Shumei centers, where Japanese teachers train them in Shumei principles. So far, eight of 52 teachers have been trained. My goal is also to send them to Japan for training so they can return to Nepal with a newfound spiritual inspiration. I trust that, within a few years, we will have a beautiful Shumei center at the Surya Boarding School in Khandbari to fulfill my dream of bringing Heaven on Earth to Nepal.

How Can We Make Heaven on Earth?

If we believe that Heaven on Earth is possible, we can create it by working together and being of one mind by practicing understanding, tolerance, patience, giving, kindness, and cooperation. This is why Shumei philosophy is so close to my heart and why it will forever remain a part of my life. I'm so grateful to the members, especially those who introduced me to Shumei. We're working to spread the inspirational philosophy of Shumei to Nepal and the world. Having devoted myself to a life of giving, I'm trying to create a little Heaven on Earth.

In the Shumei philosophy the hope is:

I am now working with all my strength to create Heaven on Earth.
My hope is to realize an age free of sickness, poverty, and strife.
With God's help, a small replica of Heaven on Earth will be built.

—Meishusama, *A Collection of Light*

To make Heaven on Earth, you must be filled with kindness, discipline, honesty, integrity, compassion, and, most of all, be honest with yourself and others. You must always think with unconditional love and care: *What's better for other human beings?*

Makoto

"The answer to all our problems—those of the individual, the state, and the world—can be found in one word. This word is makoto.

"Politics becomes hollow and inadequate without makoto. The world's resources are not enough when there is not enough makoto. Moral decline and social disorder come about where there is an absence of makoto. All our problems stem from a lack of makoto.

"Unless religion, scholarship, and the arts have makoto at their essential core, they are nothing more than hollow shells.

"Makoto. Ah, makoto.

"Listen, please.

"There is only one way to solve our problems, and that is the way of makoto."

—Meishusama, from *Essential Teachings of Meishusama* by Shumei America

From *Essential Teachings of Meishusama*:

"Makoto is a Japanese word that stands for the fundamental character traits that include such qualities as charity, truthfulness, altruism, reliability, and integrity. It has a broad yet profound meaning that cannot be summarized in one or two words because its meaning varies according to context. People have makoto when their actions are aligned with their words and ideals. Essential to the practice of makoto is the consideration of others and the will of God."

In Shumei philosophy, the poem of the makoto goes like this:

Flourishing each day afresh, the power of my deeds arises from makoto; the essence of fate can be described in one single word, makoto; sincere people cultivate the treasures of makoto in their hearts.

—Meishusama, *A Collection of Light*

I read this every morning, focusing on aligning with makoto.

The first time I read about makoto, I was impressed. I went to Khandbari and displayed makoto posters in each classroom of my school. I had the teachers and students read them in the morning when they arrived and, in the evening, before they left. Assimilating the philosophy is a difficult task because the teachers aren't well-trained in makoto. Therefore, it may not be successful at this time, but if I work on grade-school children, one day, we'll make the community a small Heaven on Earth. They are the ones who can change the planet if every human faithfully works toward this. We can create Heaven on Earth by preparing our students for tomorrow.

There are small things we can do to improve our lives, but they must be done early. Later in life, it is too late. People become rigid, set in their ways—resistant to change. Therefore, my focus is on introducing Shumei philosophy in my school and building a beautiful sanctuary where my young students can practice makoto, the guiding principle of Heaven on Earth. Children practicing makoto will be like pebbles tossed into a pond. The ripples will radiate and cover the whole pond.

I greatly respect the Shumei organization and its leaders, especially the current president, Kaicho Sensei, her late mother, Kaishusama, and her late brother, Mikotosama, who have worked so hard to provide wonderful opportunities for all the members and their friends and families. Their guidance and vision have meant the world to me as I follow Meishusama, the creator of Shumei philosophy, whose vision was inspired by God. Someone had to promote Meishusama's work, and Kaishusama, who became his devotee for life until her death in 2003, was the perfect person. She passed on the philosophy and way of life to her children and will continue to inspire many members from generations to come.

I'm one of the Shumei members who can spread Meishusama's words and dreams with the leadership of Kaicho Sensei and Tamao Sensei. To help me, I have received a tremendous amount of support from Masahide, Eugene Sensei, Alan Sensei, and many board members. I give credit to Masahide Koyama and Alan Sensei, who saw my worth. There are many senseis in Japan whom I've met, some of whom are board members and Shumei center heads.

We must approach Shumei as if we're digging a hole to prepare for planting. To make it easier to dig, we must first soak the soil with water. To that end, I have been watering the land of my birthplace, softening the soil so I can easily dig and plant Heaven on Earth in my village. With the help of the senseis and members, we can make it happen by teaching future generations the Shumei philosophy and making them pillars of their communities.

Why is This Philosophy so Powerful?

Shumei philosophy spans many world religions' teachings about goodness. The difference is that Shumei goes beyond words to concrete action. Here are four ways the words translate to action:

1. Natural Agriculture enables people to eat cleaner and healthier food, which in turn makes the body healthier and the Earth cleaner. The fertilizer-free soil keeps the environment unpolluted or restores it to a clean state after the use of fertilizers. Clean soil will clean the soul.

2. One must have spirituality in their life to feel fulfilled. Like the Dalai Lama said, "Without religion, life is empty." To be a better human being, one must have faith in God. All human hearts are God, and all human bodies are temples. In other words, we are each filled with spirituality. Keeping this in mind is the best way to live.

3. Walking with Divine Light gives you energy and belief in the power of your energy. Be careful not to misuse your power, strength, and energy. That way, you will create a better future for yourself and others. Shumei philosophy is very compelling and easy to understand.

4. Once you grasp the philosophy, it's up to you. All members are free to do what they want in their lives. They can keep their religion and still incorporate this philosophy into their life.

Why, at this age, did I decide to devote my life to Shumei philosophy and use it to guide the students at my school in Nepal? I've traveled the world for most of my life and have been exposed to many belief systems and religions. I was born Hindu and raised Hindu and Buddhist, and then I converted to Christianity. Later, at the age of 62, I found Shumei philosophy. I already had the belief that you must teach children discipline and integrity, so they'll be better individuals and community members. Although I opened a school in the 1980s, I never found a path that aligned with my goals. In 2013, when I became a Shumei member, I found a philosophy that would turn children into successful adults, serving the world in selfless ways.

Through makoto, disciplined education, spirituality, and Natural Agriculture, Shumei gives children the guidance they need for successful, fulfilling, and productive lives. They can change this planet for the better with the right kind of guidance, education, environment, and discipline. Along with honesty and integrity, it will help them understand the concept of Heaven on Earth.

Most countries' leaders have not been educated in these ways. Tragically for the world, many are selfish, corrupt, lying leaders. Very few are genuinely good leaders, like Mahatma Gandhi, Nelson Mandela, and Martin Luther King Jr. We need to teach people to aspire to become like these inspirational leaders, emulating their thoughts and qualities. It's possible if we create better environments for children to learn, grow, and prosper.

Our problem is that we lack the right kind of education. The primary focus in most academic settings is on getting a good degree to land the best possible job, which, of course, is essential for individuals and families. But we also need to think about others to have clean, collaborative, and peaceful communities. Every region of the world is grappling with racism and the division of its citizens. An effective leader of a country unites the people in peace. Instead of building bridges and bringing people together, many lead their nations drunk with power, misusing their positions and influence. "Me first" is often their mindset, which further divides the people. With this mindset, there will never be peace.

Shumei philosophy's "makoto" offers a guiding principle for a much brighter future. By applying makoto to every part of our lives, we can clean our politics, clean our environment, and clean our souls. Makoto. Ah, makoto. Listen, please. There is only one way to solve our problems, and that is the way of makoto.

CHAPTER 18

My Legacy of Giving

In olden days, saints wrapped themselves in sackcloth. I do not. Those with hearts that love art are blessed. They are ready for Heaven. When looking at a flower, I cannot but marvel at God's skill.

—Meishusama, *A Collection of Light*

A NEPALI POET NAMED LEKHNATH PAUDYAL once wrote that a person who offers understanding, kindness, and tolerance bows his head for others. Likewise, a fruit-bearing tree always bends toward the earth, allowing beings to pick its harvest and nourish themselves from fruit that it grew from its reserves.

A giving tree bows under the weight of its fruit. In contrast, a tree not bearing fruit stands straight and tall, reaching toward the sky, glorifying itself. The needy passing its bare branches peer toward the sky and admire its impressive stature, but they go hungry. Of what use is a tree without fruit? It is just a monument to itself. Similarly, a man with an inflated ego works to glorify himself. Instead of worshiping the man, most people will recognize that he is flawed because he has nothing to give; he's too busy erecting a monument to himself.

My Call to Action

I have sought to bow toward others with outstretched hands. If they were broken, I sought to mend. If they were sick, I sought to heal. If they were hungry, I sought to nourish. If they were homeless, I sought to provide shelter. If they were jobless, I sought to provide work. Their needs were my call to action. I've felt the weight of others' lives on my shoulders throughout my life, and I bent in humility to serve. I didn't always succeed, but I certainly have tried.

Over the decades of working in Nepal and elsewhere, I have reflected on what needs to be done to build on the foundation I have painstakingly constructed. We must not lose sight of the fact that one day we will be gone forever. Lord knows where. Before we go, we must leave something behind for our village, town, city, or even our country. When we do good works, we must give without expecting anything in return. That is the essence of unconditional giving and love. We shouldn't give to seek praise.

I don't know how long I can keep climbing, striving, and building. I may leave behind unfinished projects, handing them over to others to carry the work forward into the future. Therefore, I'm focused on making sure my legacy of giving continues. My remaining work includes building a 50-bed hospital in Chainpur, near Khandbari. It is an ideal location, centrally located right on the highway, and home to over 200,000 people.

I've sought to advance my corner of the world, lifting up many people along the way. Launching Surya Boarding School in Khandbari 30 years ago, I dreamt of inspiring others in Nepal to reach beyond the daily struggle for survival and to thrive instead. The school continues to provide a top-notch education for around 900 children. Our Montessori program spans from kindergarten to the fifth grade. We have a lovely shrine room so children can pray and receive Jyorei. They also learn Natural Agriculture gardening—planting and growing rice and corn the natural way.

We have plans to expand and enhance Surya Boarding School. We have completed the planning and design, and I have set aside the funds. Once the coronavirus pandemic, which started in 2020, winds down, I'll travel to Nepal to kick off the construction. My goal is to expand the school to 2,000 students up to the 12th grade. We will erect expansive playgrounds and state-of-the-art science labs. We will construct a swimming pool, a football (soccer) stadium, a museum with treasured artifacts, and a well-resourced library. Ancestors' statues of my parents will stand in front of the school with a protective roof overheard. The plan is to complete all the improvements within five years.

I dream that once the school is completed, people in the region will cherish and cultivate it. Surya Boarding School will be a shining example for the whole country. Students will learn to respect their forefathers and never forget their ancestors—the ones who built the world they inherited—the ones who inspired them to dream. That will foster respectful hearts and lifelong growth with discipline. When you learn to respect others, you receive respect from others.

Many people have asked me, "Narayan, why didn't you name the school after yourself?"

I say, "I didn't want to name it after myself. Instead, I've named schools after my parents and wife, keeping the focus where it should be—on the people who made it all possible."

I chose the name "Helping Hands" for my hospitals and clinics because it's not just my hands but the hands of countless others who reached out and healed those who were sick and suffering.

People wonder who will continue my legacy in Nepal. I believe it's a matter of selecting the right kind of people to sustain and enhance my vision. I've started handpicking people for work in Nepal—planning up to three generations to carry my work forward. With my board of directors, I've already established a legacy plan for Helping Hands.

Humans must strive to make Heaven on Earth within our hearts and in the hearts of others. We must pave the way with Natural Agriculture, gardening, art, and beauty so future generations can walk more easily upon the Earth, reaching for and attaining their dreams with less struggle, less hardship, and less strife. That is a legacy of giving well worth the effort.

Appendix

List of Shumei Centers in Japan at which I have spoken, sometimes twice. 2017 and later are listed on the next page.

Time	Center	Prefecture	City
May 2014	Tokyo	Tokyo	Setagaya (ward)
	Nagoya	Aichi	Nagoya
	Nishinomiya	Hyogo	Nishinomiya
	Kanzaki	Osaka	Osaka
	Kobe	Hyogo	Kobe
	Motoyama	Hyogo	Kobe
	Tamateyama	Osaka	Kashiwara
	Himeji	Hyogo	Himeji
	Hineno	Osaka	Izumisano
	Hiroshima	Hiroshima	Hiroshima
September 2014	Kumamoto	Kumamoto	Kumamoto
	Fukuoka	Fukuoka	Fukuoka
	Kokura	Fukuoka	Kitakyushu
	Nagasaki	Nagasaki	Nagasaki
	Suma	Hyogo	Kobe
	Adachi	Tokyo	Adachi (ward)
	Saitama	Saitama	Saitama
	Saporo	Hokkaido	Saporo
	Akita	Akita	Akita
	Morioka	Iwate	Morioka
	Sendai	Miyagi	Sendai
	Aomori	Aomori	Aomori
July 2015	Tamateyama	Osaka	Kashiwara

List of Shumei Centers (continued)

Time	Center	Prefecture	City
May 2017	Yamaguchi Kochi Chiba	Yamaguchi Kochi Chiba	Yamaguchi Kochi Chiba
July 2017	Oita Gifu Hitachi Shizuoka Hachioji Toyohashi	Oita Gifu Ibaraki Shizuoka Tokyo Aichi	Oita Gifu Hitachi Shizuoka Hachioji Toyohashi
May 2019	Toyonaka	Osaka	Toyonaka
December 2019	Fukuoka Toyohashi Shizuoka Kishima	Fukuoka Aichi Shizuoka Okayama	Fukuoka Toyohashi Shizuoka Setouchi

Acknowledgments

My greatest appreciation goes to Caroly Nadelhoffer and Jeff Pinkerton, who thought so highly of my life's work. Caroly said, "Your book will be so inspirational and powerful to the reader. Please write it."

Jeff and I have had lunch once a month at least for five years. During one of our lunches, he encouraged me to write my book. "Don't wait any longer," he said.

In this book, I talk countless times about my wife, Sreejana. Without her help, none of my accomplishments would have been possible. Her support, love, care, understanding, her kind and generous ways made me successful and who I am today. Her tireless work and undying trust in what I do have made a world of difference in my life. There is an old saying: "Behind every great man, there's a great woman." Indeed, it is so true. Sreejana is a clear example of this.

You can attain success only when there are good people around you. I have had so many good people in my life who are friends, family, and acquaintances. I can't name the most important person, nor can I name everyone who has supported me. So many people have been good to me in words, deeds, and support that I value, large and small. Everyone is equally important to me. And, above all, I'll never forget the trust and support of the people who helped me when I most needed it.

Mr. Douglas Brown of San Jose, California, had a massive impact on my life by bringing me to the United States of America. If Douglas Brown had not encouraged and empowered me, if he had not trusted my ability to build a successful life in the US, I would not have worked so hard. His constant support and connections bolstered and inspired me. He has had my back since the beginning.

Dr. Peter and Dr. Diane Skafte helped guide me to college in Dallas, Texas, through their inspirational words, their presence, and their support.

A few other friends came into my life who have been pivotal in assisting me in helping others. Without their continuous support, trust, and dedication to my work, I would not have been able to help the many people whose lives I've touched. Mr. John Power is one shining example. John is my idol, guide, coach, and supporter. He has always been there when I needed him. When he traveled with me to Nepal, Tibet, Bhutan, and Thailand, he observed me in action as I formed bonds with the people I served. He was so impressed; he committed to supporting me and my organization whenever I needed it. I respect his judgment and trust in me. He often invited me to his home for political campaign fundraising events, most memorably to Senator Michael Bennett's event in Denver attended by President Barack Obama.

Similarly, Mr. George Newell came into my life in the early 2000s and has been a tremendous supporter of my philanthropic work. He is the Vice President of Helping Hands and has played a critical role in my success. He is an honest man with a kind heart and a man of his word. He believes in my work and has traveled with me to Nicaragua and Nepal. He has seen the progress I've made and the work I've achieved in my life. His yearly sponsorship goes a long way in benefitting the lives of the Nepali people by bringing monthly medical camps to Nepali villages.

I must not forget to thank Nancy and Gordon Callahan and Steve Henry, owner of the Henry Waters Accounting firm, who has served on the Helping Hands board since the 1990s. I also extend my heartfelt thanks to Susan Mitchell, Dr. Herbert Rhinegruber, and Susan Rhinegruber. The Rhinegrubers have been my friends since the late 1990s and have traveled to every country in which Helping Hands does work. Dr. Rhinegruber has been a retired physician for 20 years but has kept his license current just to serve our organization. Such incredible dedication.

I'd also like to thank Dr. Igor Gamow, who's not only a scholar and a notorious person with many inventions, including the Gamow Bag but also a kindhearted man who made the Semester in Nepal project a resounding success. Unfortunately, Igor tragically passed away in April of 2021. I will greatly miss my dear friend.

There are so many other supporters I would like to thank but doing so would fill the pages of this book.

Index

About the Author

Narayan Shrestha is a philanthropist, educator, and entrepreneur from Boulder, Colorado. Born in Khandbari, Nepal, he immigrated to the United States in the mid-70s but never forgot his roots. He has dedicated his life to helping the people of his native country. Narayan has led countless medical treks to Nepal. He has opened schools, hospitals, and many health clinics. Notably, these include the Surya Boarding School in Khandbari, the Helping Hands Community Hospital and the SANN Institute of Nursing in Kathmandu.

In 1992, Narayan founded Helping Hands Health Education, a philanthropic organization devoted to helping Nepal and her people and many other countries, including Nicaragua, Vietnam, Namibia, India, Tibet, and Bhutan. He currently serves as the President. He also founded the SANN Research Institute to coordinate his many initiatives, including the Semester in Nepal Program, which he ran with the late Dr. Igor Gamow of the University of Colorado.

He kicked off his successful business ventures in 1986 when he opened Old Tibet in Boulder, a shop offering imports from India, Tibet, and Nepal. The business expanded to offer trekking expeditions to Nepal. Later, he started other enterprises in Boulder and the Front Range, including stores, travel agencies, and many restaurants. His business success enabled him to improve the lives of his siblings, relatives, and friends, bringing many to the

United States and helping them start their own businesses, both here and in Nepal.

Narayan is married to Sreejana, whom he met in Nepal. She has been his greatest pillar of support and the inspiration for devoting his life to the people of Nepal. She has also been instrumental to the success of Old Tibet, which continues to thrive. Narayan and Sreejana have two children, Anu and Regina.

Narayan has received numerous awards, including the City of Boulder Volunteer of the Year, the Rotary Club's Humanitarian of the Year, and the Rotary Club's Service Above Self Award. *The New York Times, Boulder's Daily Camera*, and *The Denver Post* have featured him. CBS, NBC, and ABC have aired stories about him. PBS produced his documentary, *All Roads Lead to Nepal.*

Narayan has found spiritual fulfillment in Shumei, a philosophy teaching health, happiness, and harmony, based on the teachings of Meishusama, centered in Japan. Narayan has promoted Shumei, speaking at many conferences throughout Japan. He introduced the philosophy to Nepal, including Natural Agriculture, growing crops without fertilizers. Following the Shumei philosophy, Narayan is doing his part to create Heaven on Earth.